LAST MAN STANDING

To Geoffrey
3 April 1920–5 November 2017

Also by Gabrielle McDonald-Rothwell:

New Zealand's Secret Heroes
Jack Hinton V.C. A Man amongst Men
*Her Finest Hour: The Heroic Life of Diana Rowden, Wartime
Secret Agent*

LAST MAN STANDING

GEOFFREY ROTHWELL, SURVIVOR OF
71 MISSIONS, POW AND THE LAST
OF THE SOE PILOTS

GABRIELLE McDONALD-ROTHWELL

AMBERLEY

First published as *The Man with Nine Lives*
by The Book Guild, 2005. Fully revised and
extended new edition 2018

Amberley Publishing
The Hill, Stroud
Gloucestershire, GL5 4EP

www.amberley-books.com

Copyright © Gabrielle McDonald-Rothwell,
2018

The right of Gabrielle McDonald-Rothwell to be
identified as the Author of this work has been
asserted in accordance with the Copyrights,
Designs and Patents Act 1988.

ISBN 978 1 4456 8131 3 (hardback)
ISBN 978 1 4456 8132 0 (ebook)

British Library Cataloguing in Publication Data.
A catalogue record for this book is available
from the British Library.

Typesetting and Origination by Amberley
Publishing.
Printed in the UK.

To the memory of Pilot Officers Freddy Harrold RAF and Joe
Ready RAF; Flight Lieutenant John Allen DFC RAF; Squadron
Leader Bill Greenslade DFC AFC RAF; Flight Sergeant Louis
Aaron VC RAFVR; Squadron Leader Mick Brogan DFC RAF;
Wing Commander Don Saville DSO DFC RAFV; Flying Officer
Bud Keller RAF
and to
Flying Officer Roger Court DFC RAFVR, Flight Lieutenant Wally
Walton DFC BEM RA and Flying Officer John Hulme RAFVR,
who lost their lives on that fateful last mission to Holland on
8 September 1944.

Everyone lives a hundred lives, but only one of them is a life
to remember.

— an old Chinese proverb

In fleeting darkened hours they met by purpose
Joined together with but word or nod – and yet
Their spirits linked forever.
Briefly their lives, the flyers and the 'Joes'
Were touched – no drums were rolled.

They have no shrine but in the hearts of those of us
Who came to stand at Tempsford, hear the start of engines
And of voices in the air.

— E.S. Burke

The anecdotes I have recorded have not dimmed with the passage
of time, probably due to their frequent repetition when I have been
in the company of friends with whom I served, enjoying what old
Omar Khayyam calls 'the Cup that clears To-day of past Regrets
and future Fears' and causes him to 'wonder what the Vintners buy
One half so precious as the Goods they sell'. Perhaps it would have
been better if the unworthy incidents had faded from my memory,
or remained unrecorded. On second thoughts, maybe not, as they
form a colourful background to the life of a wartime pilot which
has been described as 'long periods of utter boredom, punctuated
by short periods of intense fright'. I subscribe to the latter idea but
certainly not to the former as I cannot recall a dull moment in my
war service.

– Geoff Rothwell

CONTENTS

FOREWORD

By Air Commodore W. J. Burnett DSO, OBE,
DFC, AFC, RAF (Retd)

Aviation has always attracted men of character whose spirit of adventure has inspired others to follow. War gave many the opportunity to fulfil a desire to fly which would probably have been denied to them. Geoff Rothwell epitomised the type of young man who readily accepted the challenge of wartime flying and joined the Royal Air Force.

After finishing his training, he was posted to No. 99 Squadron at Newmarket, which was equipped with Wellington aircraft. Designed by Barnes Wallis, it was the second aeroplane to employ the geodetic construction system. Its ability to absorb severe battle damage and to survive endeared it to its crews, and Geoff, like many others, owed their lives to this fact. Like its contemporaries, however, it lacked the navigational and bombing aids necessary to achieve the accuracy which only became available later. Plagued by weather and equipment unserviceability, bomber crews carried the war into Germany and Occupied Europe despite these handicaps. Their perseverance and determination to reach their targets under these difficulties is a tribute to the inspirational example and leadership of men like Geoff. On completing his first tour of operations he was justly awarded the Distinguished Flying Cross.

His second tour of operations, after a 'rest tour' in the USA, began in 1943 when he initially joined No. 75 (New Zealand) Squadron (again at Newmarket) and subsequently No. 218 Squadron, both equipped with Short Stirlings. Although the Stirling was manoeuvrable and pleasant to fly, it had many drawbacks and was not popular with aircrew. Basically, it was underpowered and unable to reach the heights attained by the Lancaster and Halifax, and consequently suffered heavier losses from anti-aircraft fire and occasionally from bombs dropped by their higher-flying companions! The war had changed markedly since Geoff last operated – aids were now available which enabled crews to locate and bomb their targets with increasing accuracy. But enemy defences were more effective and deadly with the perfection of the night fighter system as Geoff was soon to experience.

Not for them the warmth and comforts of modern air travel. Most raids were long, exhausting flights into mainland Germany. Cold and chronic fatigue were high-risk factors. Many crews were lost to enemy action. And those who survived saw the disappearance of friends and acquaintances. Out of every 100 bomber aircrew arriving at an Operational Training Unit sixty would be killed, twelve became POWs. And of the remaining twenty-eight many would be wounded. The stress on crews can be imagined.

The relentless determination and courage combined with an irrepressible sense of humour, exceptional vitality and operational skill shown by Geoff during his second tour was recognised by the award of a Bar to his DFC.

I first met Geoff in 1944 when I took command of No. 138 (Special Duties Squadron) and he was one of my Flight Commanders. Geoff proved to be a born leader and one who led by example. In fact, I had to suggest on more than one occasion that he let some of his other pilots have a chance. He countered this by selecting the more difficult operations, explaining that his crew had the experience needed for a particular task. Demanding of himself and his crew, he expected others to meet the same high standards. Intolerant of weakness, he nevertheless readily assisted those who needed guidance and advice. He was held in high esteem by his men for his consideration of their welfare and the example he set.

Geoff had volunteered for a third tour of operations and was quickly able to adapt to the special operations undertaken by the squadron – dropping agents and supplies into enemy-occupied territories of Europe on their intelligence and sabotage tasks. The skills acquired by him in his previous operations suitably qualified him to undertake these different but no less dangerous and arduous operations. Nearing the end of his tour, and on his 71st operation, I was deeply distressed when he crashed in Holland on returning from a successful mission. Fortunately, he survived and was taken a POW.

After the war ended Geoff, who had been granted a Permanent Commission, soon realised that Service life in peacetime was not for him. Still seeking a challenging and interesting career he decided to accept a position on a rubber plantation in Malaya. While aware that a state of emergency existed between Malaya and Chinese Communists in that country, he was soon to realise that in addition to a challenging new life it was also a dangerous one. Never one to be deterred by danger he persevered to become manager of a rubber estate and subsequently a planting adviser. After completing twenty years in Malaya he considered it was time to retire. New Zealand had always appealed to him, having served in a New Zealand squadron, and he decided to see if that was where he wanted to live. The country lived up to his expectations and he never regretted his choice.

This is the story of a remarkable person who contributed the maximum to the important and demanding tasks placed on him. It is an absorbing story which captures the spirit of the times and sets down for posterity the atmosphere, excitement and the dangers of those days.

W. J. Burnett
Haslemere, Surrey, April 2004

ACKNOWLEDGEMENTS

Many people have helped me to get this book to print. I wish to thank particularly Air Commodore Wilf Burnett in England for reading the manuscript, for all his advice, and for writing the Foreword, Bob Molloy in Kerikeri, New Zealand, my English teacher Sister Mary Imelda from my old school St Benedict's Convent in Auckland, and Clive and Fleur McDonald, all of whom read, corrected and edited much of the work in its early stages and who gave so generously of their time.

In Holland my grateful thanks go to Dr Theo Boiten for his invaluable advice, and to Piet de Vos and Bram van Dijk who have been such a help in the writing of several of the chapters. To Dick Broadbent, the late Fray Ormerod, and Janey Sinclair in New Zealand, Pat Trevaldwyn, Stan Hurd, Jerry Jarvis, Ian Ryall, Lucien Ercolani in England, and Norah Harriss in America, many thanks for your much-needed help and advice. To Pat Burns in Western Australia – our talks over many months so inspired me and helped to fill in much needed background information – thank you for your love and support. To Zelie Hilton and Simon Rothwell in England for your invaluable assistance, to my dear friends in New Zealand, Annette Cowley, Adrienne Perkins, and Jill Bell, who, as always, gave me their support and love through the difficult times. Thanks to Pen & Sword for permission to quote from *From St Vith to Victory* by Stephen C. Smith.

Lastly to my family – Paul, Laurence, Fleur and Luke and my sisters Helen Hinton and Sue Richardson – my love and appreciation and to Geoffrey, for your unerring faith in me and your love and support. Without your help this book could not have been written.

In the 1939-45 war, the Royal Air Force lost 55,500 officers, NCOs and airmen killed or missing on operations; 9,838 personnel were recorded as being prisoners-of-war. This was the price of victory and by far the largest share, 47,268, fell to Bomber Command between September 1939 and May 1945. A further 8,403 Bomber Command aircrew were wounded on operations and from other causes during that period, making a total of 73,741.

PROLOGUE

Strength now my fainting soul and play the man and though
such waning span of life is still to be trod prepare to meet
thy God.

– Author unknown

8 September 1944

On a bright moonlit night, a lone Stirling bomber was crossing
the North Sea. It was three months since D-Day, the invasion of
Normandy, and the end of the war in Europe was at last in sight.
The Short Stirling, one of the biggest four-engined bombers in
World War II, with a wingspan just short of 100 feet, had a huge
fuselage which could accommodate dozens of men. However, on that
September night there were only nine men on board – the crew of
seven and two secret agents codenamed Draughts and Backgammon.

The pilot, a tall, ginger-haired squadron leader, sat at the
controls of the Stirling. The bright moon kept darting behind
the clouds and he thought the dark sea, hundreds of feet below
him, looked like swirls of ink. He was dressed snugly in a blue
battledress top and blue trousers. At the last moment he had
decided to wear an officer's raincoat over the top of his battledress.
Two pairs of gloves, silk and chamois, were worn under leather
gauntlets. Lastly, instead of the customary flying boots lined with
sheepskin, he wore his uniform black shoes. A leather flying helmet
completed the outfit.

The two secret agents sitting in the back of the aircraft, Tobias
Biallosterski and Pieter de Vos, were dressed in civilian clothes.

They were returning to Holland to join the Dutch resistance movement in the field.

The moon shone brightly in the cockpit of the Stirling, lighting it up as if it were day, but it was bitterly cold inside the bomber and the squadron leader shivered in spite of his warm clothing. The lights from the instrument panel glowed in front of him. This was going to be his last sortie before taking over the squadron. He had gone over the whole operation in his mind. He had always done this – it was inherent in him. He left nothing to chance and by doing so he was prepared for every eventuality. And that was why on his return he was going to be promoted to the rank of wing commander.

The awards of the DFC in 1940 and Bar in 1943 had come as no surprise to his crew and his family and friends. He was a born leader who commanded respect, with a strong personality, meticulous in his work, and with a particular eye for detail. He was on his third tour of operations and had completed seventy sorties with little rest in between the tours. Now he let his mind wander to what he would be doing in a few days' time. He would probably go on leave down to Essex to visit his parents; he knew they would be pleased to see him. And then there was Sweet Pea. Perhaps they would go down to the sea where they would stroll together, he would smoke his pipe and they would stand on the cliff overlooking the sea, relax.

The voice of the navigator cut into his thoughts. 'Five minutes to go to the Dutch coast, Skip.'

'Roger, Mac, but we've got a problem ahead,' he replied.

Their take-off had been late and it was now around 1.30 a.m. They were half-way towards their ETA and as the squadron leader looked in the direction of the Dutch coast a giant cumulonimbus cloud towered directly in the path of the bomber. He cursed Taffy, the met officer, who had assured him there would be no weather problems to worry about that night. He knew that the giant cloud was too massive to fly around. His first thought was to try to climb over it. However, he realised the Stirling was incapable of achieving the necessary altitude. He decided instead to fly straight through it, climbing from the present 500 feet and levelling out at 6,000 feet.

It was rough going, so rough that the flight engineer, Derek Shaw, called out, 'Airframe's taking a beating, Skip.'

'Roger, Derek, we may have to abort,' he said into the intercom.

The pilot repeated to himself, 'straight and level, straight and level' but it was difficult to do this, it was contrary to his instinct and all he had learned in his five years of flying when survival depended on continual changes of course and altitude to throw the enemy radar off the scent. The needles on the altimeter and air speed indicator flickered dangerously, the artificial horizon showing the turbulence tipped the huge aircraft from one wingtip to the other as it plunged up and down. Fearing structural damage, the squadron leader knew that the only course of action now was to drop down to sea level and try to fly beneath the storm. At 150 feet, with rain pelting against the windscreen, he switched on the landing light and saw a turbulent sea beneath them. Then without any warning they were in brilliant moonlight. The storm had disappeared as suddenly as it had arrived and they were in clear skies.

In the back of the Stirling the agents breathed sighs of relief. They had sat nervously through the storm, wondering if this was to be yet another abortive attempt to reach their homeland. Their previous scheduled flight the night before had been cancelled because of bad weather. Now that the storm was behind them their spirits rose. The captain of the Stirling resumed course for Spanbroek and 'Mandrill', the codename for the reception for the agents.

The moonlight was now strong and white and clear and the squadron leader started to relax now that the immediate danger was over. He thought of his crew. This was their fifteenth operational sortie on Special Duties. In the time they had flown together he had got to know them well and he knew they had confidence in him. He had learned very quickly from his earliest flying days to fly relaxed, never to anticipate the flak, the night fighters, the searchlights, the terror of the target. There was always a sense of pent-up excitement of not knowing what was in store for them, and after a job was done, and done well, he could sit back and congratulate himself and the rest of the crew. It was always a combined effort.

They had been flying north to avoid another storm over the Friesian Islands and had now turned south and were going to make landfall over a horseshoe-shaped bay on Vlieland, a small island with scrub, tussock grass and sand dunes. They looked low and flat in the moonlight. They set course across the Waddenzee for Mandrill.

When it was time to drop the two agents, Bob Wilmott, the dispatcher, opened the Joe hole and the agents sat with their feet dangling in the slipstream.

Far below him in the moonlight the squadron leader could see a light flashing the Morse code letter 'N'. This was the signal to drop the agents. He turned on his microphone: 'OK, Roger,' he told the map reader in the nose of the aircraft. 'I've got visual contact. Get the Joes out first, dispatcher. We'll drop the containers on the way back.'

'Roger, Skipper. All set to go,' said Wilmott.

The bomb aimer pressed the light switch. 'Let 'em go, Bob,' he said. And after pushing them through the hole with his boot, Bob closed the hatch cover.

The aircraft flew on for a while and circled once over open country to confuse the Germans in the event of their radar having successfully picked up the Stirling. Returning to the reception, containers of arms were dropped and carrier pigeons in small cardboard cylinders were thrown out over villages. They then set course for their pinpoint on the causeway and the horseshoe-shaped bay on Vlieland again.

They were flying at a height of about 300 feet when Roger Court came on the intercom to tell the navigator he could see the bay on Vlieland ahead and that they were a little to port of track. Mac, always meticulous, came up to the cockpit to see for himself. As he looked through the windscreen the Stirling suddenly dropped as though it had hit some very solid object.

'Jesus! What was that?' said Mac to the squadron leader.

The squadron leader did not answer. His mind was in a whirl. His hands started to sweat. The airspeed was increasing rapidly and the instrument panel veered crazily. Instinctively he hauled back on the control column.

'Mac! Give me an emergency course to base,' he yelled.

'Steer two-seven-oh to start with,' was the immediate reply.

He realised the air speed indicator was inoperable. The needle had dropped to the bottom of the scale. It was registering 250 knots, which made him think the plane was in a dive. Then the starboard inner propeller flew off and fire broke out in the engine. He knew they were going to stall and pushed the control column forward. There was no fuel pressure now on any of the engines except the port inner. He gripped the wheel, fighting to keep the Stirling on a straight course. As he did so, he knew they were going to crash because they were losing height rapidly, and that there was nothing he could do to prevent that happening. He rejected quite calmly any idea of returning to base, and then right after that, the thought of baling out. In those few seconds making those decisions made him feel entirely alone. He realised he was totally responsible for the safety of his crew and for the aircraft.

'Ditching stations, everybody,' he shouted to the crew, thinking they were going to crash in the Waddenzee.

The fire in the engine had now spread into the wing and, as they lost altitude, he could see they were flying over sand dunes. And then, dead ahead, a hillock, which came up to him abruptly. He pulled with every ounce of strength on the control column, at the same time hearing Mac call out: 'The starboard wing's stalling.'

He had forgotten about everything now – his promotion, his family, Sweet Pea – all was forgotten, as the wing hit the ground at a speed of 120 knots and slewed the huge aircraft around to starboard.

As the Stirling hit the ground, the land came up to him at a furious slant and the moon, still shining brightly, danced crazily before his eyes. The squadron leader was aware of being thrown violently against the control column and of the sickness rising in his stomach. As the moon hurtled towards him he felt himself being lifted and thrown through the air by a force which was unrelenting, all around him the noise of splintering metal.

I

THE BAY OF ISLANDS

My soul, there is a country
Far beyond the stars.
— Henry Vaughan, *Peace*

January 2000
The green and white cottage is set far back from the road and up
a long driveway shaded on each side by a profusion of native trees
and blue and white agapanthus. I park my car and walk up a short
path to the front door. As I knock, the sweet and heady scents of
manuka and honeysuckle drift up from the garden below.

A short pause and he opens the door.

'Gabrielle! Come in. You found the house OK?'

My hand is firmly shaken and I am taken into a room leading out
on to a balcony where I have my first view of the Bay of Islands.
It is breathtaking. A turquoise-coloured sea stretches limitlessly,
mirrored by lazy puffs of clouds moving in an azure sky. A yacht
race is in progress and we stand there for a few minutes watching
the tiny white shapes gliding out of the marina below.

The house is surrounded by green hills and a cottage garden
leads to a bush, thickly-planted with punga, manuka, rata, totara,
kowhai and other native New Zealand trees. The air is warm and
sweet and clean and in the distance I hear a tui singing its strange
and exquisite song.

Maybe this is heaven.

I mention this and he laughs. It is a rich laugh, full of humour and charm, lighting up his face.

'That's why I live here,' he says. He has a deep, beautifully modulated voice, a voice that commands, without seeming to.

Reluctantly I step back into the lounge and sit down. It is an interesting and somewhat unusual room, liberally sprinkled with paintings and artefacts from the Far East in between a profusion of books and photographs in silver frames. He has obviously travelled a good deal.

Without appearing to do so, I study him. Despite his age he is a good-looking man, tall with very blue eyes, straight-backed with wavy grey hair nearly white now with the odd sprinkle of red. It is a face full of strength. Rothwell's a strong personality, I had been told, a leader of men, a remarkable man with an even more remarkable story, a war hero who was decorated with the DFC and Bar, the *Croix de Guerre & Palme* and the Order of Leopold II & Palme – the last one an unusual decoration. He was a man who had had nine lives and who had well and truly lived them.

Yes, already I could see that.

Aloud I say, 'You know why I'm here? I want to write a book on your life, if you'll let me.'

'Can't think why,' he says. 'I haven't done anything that interesting.'

'I'm sure that's not the case,' I say, 'but would you mind telling me your story?'

He agrees and I settle back in a comfortable chair, feeling the warmth of the summer's gentle breeze drifting in through the open door.

I have no idea how long we stay there talking. All I know is that the early afternoon drifts quickly into evening. Every so often I interrupt him with a question or two and he answers unhesitatingly. His memory is good, remarkably good after a gap of over fifty years, and I can see why he was decorated in the war. There is an intractable strength, an energy and an air of responsibility which is still tangible. We walk out on to the balcony again, the air heavy with the early evening scent of jasmine and roses.

'I love this time of the evening,' he says. 'The birds preparing for bed and the sounds of the night animals.'

As if in answer a lone morepork, the New Zealand owl, calls out plaintively to its mate far in the distance. *Morepork, morepork* – a strange, but oddly calming sound. Down below in the garden a young thrush scratches around in the earth for one last worm. The movements of the thrush in the soil send a light scattering of dust on to some withered asters. It has not rained for some time.

It is starting to grow a little cold and we walk back inside. He closes the door to the balcony, shutting out the sounds of the night. There is still much to talk about, so much I want to ask him. How did he survive all those years flying on dangerous operations and then afterwards living through the Emergency in Malaya, three assassination attempts and bouts of malaria which nearly cost him his life? And why had he settled in a little country like New Zealand, thousands of miles away from his country of birth? A million questions.

Then there is the girl, Sweet Pea.

I look over at the photographs on a small antique table. Yes, there he is in RAF uniform, with the three stripes of a squadron leader on his arm, leaning against the side of a Stirling aircraft, a tall handsome figure standing out against the figures of his crew.

'You look very young in that photo.'

'I was nineteen.'

Nineteen.

There is another photo of him, smaller and in sepia, partially hidden amongst a collection of books and ornaments. He has his arm around a girl – a young, good-looking woman with dark, curly hair. She is dressed in the uniform of the ATS (Auxiliary Territorial Service).

'Is that a photo of her?' I ask. 'Is that Sweet Pea?'

'Yes, that's her. It was taken when we were both on leave in 1943.'

There is a pause and then I ask him about his decorations. I know that he had got his DFC and Bar for three tours of duty with Bomber Command. That was extraordinary in itself – to have survived three tours when a pilot's chances were one in three and one in two towards the end of the war. But the others – the *Croix de Guerre* and the Order of Leopold II – they don't give those gongs for nothing.

'Have you heard of SOE?' he asks me.

'Yes, of course. The Special Operations Executive, set up by Winston Churchill in 1940, I think, to co-ordinate resistance activities in occupied countries, to "set Europe ablaze" as Churchill said.'

'Well, I was part of that organisation,' he says.

I feel the familiar sense of excitement, the feeling I get when I smell a good story.

'Were you in SOE when you crashed? And were you shot down?'

'Ah! That's the odd thing. After all these years I still don't really know what happened. Sometimes I think it could have been sabotage, as there were other inexplicable incidents at Special Duties and I've always had a feeling the Germans knew we were coming.'

This story is beginning to sound better and better. But I want to get back to the girl, Sweet Pea.

'What happened between you two? Why, if you loved her so much, didn't you get married? Did you ever meet her again?'

He is silent for a moment, stretching his long legs. Then he goes over to a mahogany desk and hands me a leather folder. In it are several documents, photographs and letters.

'You'll find in there just about all you need to know.'

In the distance I hear the shrill, piercing noises of crickets and the screech of a possum. I know we are going to be in for a long night.

2

EARLY DAYS – ENGLAND
1920–1935

Happy those early days!
When I shin'd in my angel-infancy,
Before I understood this place
Appointed for my second race,
Or taught my soul to fancy aught
But a white celestial thought.
 – Henry Vaughan, *The Retreat*

This story begins in 1920 when on 3 April a strong, healthy male child was born in Didsbury, then a country town near Manchester in the north of England, to Maurice and Ethel Rothwell. They named the boy Geoffrey Maurice. Geoffrey was a big baby with a shock of bright red hair and huge blue eyes. His early childhood was happy and secure. Maurice and Ethel were happily married and he was surrounded with laughter and love. But it was his mother, Ethel with the laughing blue eyes, to whom he was closest. She was invariably understanding, even when he got into childhood scrapes, which was often, and he always knew that somehow she would make everything all right.

Maurice differed from Ethel in that he was a somewhat stern and strict man who found it difficult to show emotion, especially love. But there was no doubt he loved his family. He had a sense of humour and enjoyed life with his family. He was a buyer in the textile business and his tall figure was always recognisable by his pince-nez and the vast array of pens in the breast pocket of his suit. He was a self-educated man who, despite having left school at fourteen, was well-informed, capable and ambitious. Widely read, he had taught himself elementary French and Pitman's shorthand, was a devotee of classical music and played an excellent game of chess.

Ethel Rothwell was essentially a homemaker and her family and home were her life. Born in Handforth in rural Cheshire, where her parents had an orchard, she had the skills of a countrywoman – she knew instinctively what food was good and how to cook it to keep it so. Her pies were renowned and sought after.

When Geoff was four the family moved to a terrace house which overlooked the Manchester Grammar School playing fields. An incident from those days stands out vividly in his memory. Sir Alan Cobham, the celebrated aviator, had force-landed his aircraft, which was part of Cobham's Flying Circus, not far from where they lived. They raced up the road to see it in a small field bathed in early morning sunshine. Surrounded by people talking and pointing animatedly, Geoff clutched his mother's hand in excitement, looking at the huge aircraft, its wings glistening in the summer sun.

His first school was a private kindergarten and it was a miserable time for him as he was painfully shy and sensitive. Tall – head and shoulders above the other children – and gangly, with red hair, he was constantly teased. One day he was so distressed that he peed his pants. This distress was compounded by the teacher making him stand in a corner. The shame of this embarrassing incident has always remained with him. He fared no better at the elementary school at Platt Lane. The teasing carried on and the teachers either did not know, or did not care.

'This will pass, Geoffrey,' said his father, 'and you will overcome this. Hitch your wagon to a star.'

In July 1930 Geoff's sister, Patricia Mary, was born. Right from the start Geoff adored her. The little girl had beautiful red-gold hair and Geoff, being ten years older, was fiercely protective of her. By now the family had moved to Urmston near the Cheshire border and life started to look up. Maurice Rothwell was earning a healthy salary as a buyer and was able to afford the services of a nanny. They owned a car and also a lingerie shop, expertly looked after by Ethel. It was a good middle-class life with a three-week holiday each year with friends in North Wales.

Sometimes Ethel would take Geoff to stay with his cousins, the Hodgkinson boys, in Disley on the Lancashire/Cheshire border, where his maternal grandparents lived. Days would be spent running wild in the country, fishing, swimming in the river, making huts in the woods and playing at soldiers. When the afternoons were too hot they would lie on the grass, trying to identify the many birds. It was a wonderful life, which instilled in him a love of nature which he still has to this day.

Not long after Pat was born the family moved to Chapel Allerton in Leeds, where Geoff was able to walk to Roundhay, his new school, the first school where he was truly happy. Roundhay, established in 1903, was an all-boys grammar school. It was here that he became friendly with Louis Aaron, who eight years later would be in his flight in 218 Squadron and who would win the Victoria Cross posthumously. At Roundhay the emphasis was on sport, and Geoff, who was physically strong, discovered he was good at all sport, especially rugger, which he loved.

However, unknown to Geoff, the good fortunes of the Rothwell family were coming to an end. The Depression of the early 1930s hit the family hard when he was eleven or twelve. Maurice, who was possibly one of the more highly paid employees, was one of the first to lose his job. Typically, he and Ethel never mentioned these worries to Geoff. Maurice finally found a job but this necessitated another move – this time to Mill Hill, in North London. Unfortunately for Geoff, this meant moving to another school – Christ's College in Finchley. Set in an urban environment with no emphasis on sport, it was vastly different from Roundhay. Soccer, not rugby, was played and again he was ribbed by the boys for his red hair and height, but worst of all, for his northern accent. He was desperately unhappy and for the first time in his life became aware of the class-structured society in Britain. This led him to develop an intense dislike of such things which would last throughout his life.

The early 1930s was a fascinating time in which to live. There was always a chance of seeing not only small flying machines but huge airships such as the German *Graf Zeppelin* or the British R101, the world's biggest airship, which was to crash a few months after its trial flight, killing everybody on board. The flying machines could often be seen looming out of the mist unexpectedly and landing on some remote field.

Geoff could be a real handful. He would continually get into mischief, usually with a friend also named Geoffrey. With their boisterous personalities the two Geoffs were the terrors of the local neighbourhood, especially when they reached their teens. Their pranks knew no bounds. Pat Rothwell, five or six at the time, remembers screaming in terror as the two boys – one at the top, one at the bottom of the stairs – threatened to throw her to each other.

'I am sure my poor mother must have nearly had a heart attack every day at this stage of her life,' she says.

As well as the continual pranks, Geoff would tease his maternal grandfather, Grandpa Wildman, who would usually take the teasing but would complain to his daughter. 'You mark my words, Ethel,' he would say, 'that lad will come to a bad end one day!'

There were indeed times when Ethel Rothwell would throw up her hands in horror; what would become of this boy? Perhaps Grandpa was right, he would come to a bad end.

Despite his unhappiness at Christ's College he excelled at sport, earning praise from his teachers and a grudging respect from his classmates. He took part in school plays and discovered he had another talent – acting – which helped to boost his ego. But he was still restless and often miserable because he was, essentially, a dud at lessons, possibly because of his unhappiness at school. It certainly wasn't through a lack of intelligence. Despite having an ability in English, geography and chemistry, he never passed a single exam except the Royal Society of Arts in French, so he decided that school was a waste of time. There was an exciting world out there and he couldn't wait to get to it. When he was fifteen his father gave him an ultimatum – either he came in the first ten in his form in the end-of-term exams or he would have to leave.

He came twenty-second out of twenty-five. And that was that. Geoff left school and was launched into the labour market of 1935.

3

STORM CLOUDS OVER EUROPE

When the sun sets, shadows, that showed at noon
But small, appear most long and terrible.
— Nathanial Lee, *Oedipus*

Last months of 1935
The world of 1935 was very different from that of the early 1930s.
Great Britain had recovered economically from the Depression
and accordingly there were many more jobs available in England.
Meanwhile, tensions had been building up in Germany with
reports in newspapers almost on a daily basis of the growth of
the National Socialist Party (the Nazi Party) under the leadership
of Adolf Hitler who was steadily gaining in popularity. Unknown
to the rest of the world Germany had been rearming for some
time. Also the thuggery of the Stormtroopers, or 'Brownshirts' as
they were known, towards the Jews had been slowly but surely
indoctrinating the public into accepting or at least tolerating a
dangerous attitude of racial hatred.

The British, with the exception of Winston Churchill, First
Lord of the Admiralty, were slow to realise just how far-reaching
Hitler's ambitions actually were. Churchill expressed his feelings:

When we watch with distress the tumultuous insurgence of
ferocity and war spirit, the pitiless ill-treatment of minorities,

the denial of the normal protections of civilised society, the persecution of large numbers of individuals solely on the ground of race ... one cannot help feeling glad that the fierce passions that are raging in Germany have not yet found any other outlet but upon themselves.

However, very few people took any notice of these chilling words and as the 1930s progressed the dark shadows spreading across Europe finally turned into rumblings of war. In 1936 civil war broke out in Spain. This conflict was to rage throughout the country for almost three years, Francisco Franco later becoming Fascist dictator in 1939. In the same year, 1936, Hitler and Benito Mussolini, dictator of Italy, became military and political allies when they signed a 'Pact of Steel' – an alliance which committed one partner to help the other should his country be involved in a war. France, bitterly divided and fragmented since the end of World War I, was a country which had, according to historian Denis Brogan, 'the psychology of a defeated nation'.

In 1938, as the world looked on helplessly Hitler marched into Austria in just a few days. Part of Czechoslovakia, the Sudetenland, was to follow.

At this point Neville Chamberlain, Prime Minister of Great Britain, flew to Germany, arriving on 15 September. On 30 September Chamberlain, the French Premier Edouard Daladier, Hitler and Mussolini signed the Munich Agreement, which allowed Nazi Germany's annexation of Czechoslovakia. Tension and fear now reached fever pitch.

Having failed every exam at school except French, Geoff felt his employment prospects were not that good. He didn't have a clue in the world what he wanted to do, other than a vague feeling of wanting to fly aeroplanes. He was good at only two things, sport and acting, and those seemed dead ends. Eventually, through his father, who was now employed as Manager of the London Co-operative Society's largest store in Romford, Essex, Geoff applied for and succeeded in obtaining a job as an apprentice carpenter with the building firm John Laing & Sons.

In 1937 the Royal Air Force was rapidly expanding and Laings were contracted to build a number of airfields. Geoff, now living in digs, was sent to work on the new airfield at Benson near Oxford.

Working at RAF Station Benson were two Fairey Battle squadrons. The Fairey Battle, which had been developed in the mid-1930s for the RAF, was a single-engine light bomber designed and manufactured by the Fairey Aviation Company. It had a wingspan of 15 metres with a top speed of 414km an hour. Geoff's proximity to the aircraft was fuelling a growing ambition to fly aeroplanes and he spent much of time watching the aircraft taking off and landing. In his room was a photograph of a Spitfire in a vertical turn over the Great West Road in the vicinity of what is now Heathrow Airport. He would imagine what it would be like to fly such an aircraft. Magazines such as *Flight* and *Aeroplane,* which taught him how to identify an aircraft from its silhouette or from its parts, became compulsive reading. The late 1930s was an age of discovery, of challenge and ambitions, of hopes and dreams. Aviation flourished in this decade and aviators such as Charles Kingsford-Smith, Amy Johnson and Jean Batten, who dressed in white overalls with matching helmet, were the heroes of the day and it was no wonder Geoff was caught up in the excitement of it all.

RAF Station Benson in Oxfordshire was soon to become the main operational station for the Photographic Reconnaisance Squadrons. Construction of the airfield had begun in 1937 as part of the expansion of the RAF and in response to the threat of war from Nazi Germany.

But the world of 1938 as Geoff knew it would soon be changed for ever. Britain was on the point of war with Germany. After the perceptibly aged Neville Chamberlain had returned to England from his trip to Berchtesgaden in the Bavarian Alps, waving a piece of paper signed by Hitler proclaiming the so-called Peace Agreeement – 'Peace in our time' – two-and-a-half million British men under sixty were mobilised. War was inevitable.

One of Geoff's closest friends, John Allen, had joined the Air Force on a Short Service Commission and was stationed at RAF

Station Hornchurch. His enthusiastic descriptions of life in the service and the joy of flying Spitfires were all Geoff needed to decide that he, too, had to become a pilot. In 1938 the Air Force was accepting pupil aircrew at the age of eighteen and he did not have long to wait. But it would be difficult to get out of his apprenticeship and he worried over his parents' reaction. The weeks passed slowly and on his eighteenth birthday he applied for a Short Service Commission in the General Duties Branch in which aircrew were commissioned.

That was when he hit his first obstacle. As he was under twenty-one, the application had to be countersigned by a parent or guardian. This posed a dilemma as he had good prospects with Laings and he doubted whether his father would agree to him throwing away the opportunity of a career for a ten-year commission. There was only one thing to do – forge his father's signature. But having inherited much of Maurice's deep sense of integrity he felt like a criminal and agonised for weeks over what he had done.

Finally, he was called up for an interview at the Air Ministry in London. This was where he ran into the second problem. His interview was for the following morning and as he lived some distance away in Oxfordshire, it was necessary for him to stay at his parents' home in Essex overnight. There was nothing for it but to take his mother into his confidence. She was surprised to see him and thrilled at the unexpected visit...

She sat quietly listening to her son as he told her of his plans, her brain trying to take in what he was saying. The spring day which had been warm had now grown cold, and outside a strong wind was sweeping the leaves into great piles in the garden. She looked at her son as he talked to her, all the while noting the strong profile, the clear blue of his eyes, and his large, capable hands.

Yes, he would make a good pilot, her son. But he was her only son, and that was the trouble. He would be flying an aircraft and they were dangerous machines. He might go far away ... and if war came ...

Outside, rain started to fall and she sat there, listening to the steady patter on the window.

She smiled brightly and hugged him. 'My son, my son in the Air Force,' she said. 'I'm so proud of you.'

Now all that remained was for his father to be told. Once again his fears proved groundless. When Maurice heard Geoff's plans and realised that flying was his heart's desire, he wished him the best of luck. Geoff knew he was fortunate to have such understanding parents.

The following day he arrived at Adastral House in a state of nervous excitement and was directed to a waiting room where he found himself to be one of many young men, all looking as nervous as he. In true British fashion no one spoke to anyone else. He remembers little of the interview except there were five men sitting behind a long table, one of them in a group captain's uniform.

There was a chair for the applicant, placed with precision so that he was facing the interrogator in the middle, with two members to the right and two to the left. His father had told him to fix his eyes on the gentleman in the middle, so he gave him what he hoped was a pleasant smile but was probably a nervous smirk, and said, 'Good morning, sir.'

'Now don't be nervous,' his father had told him. 'Look at the interviewers and try and imagine what they would look like in bathing costumes!'

He was told to sit down and the questions began:

Do you play rugger?

Do you drive a car?

Have you ever flown in an aeroplane?

He was able to answer all three questions with a clear conscience, if he stretched a point or two. He had played rugby at his school in Leeds but at his London school had played only soccer. He was also able to rustle up a few makes of cars when they asked him what types he had driven. The list sounded quite impressive for those days – Austin (the family car), a Morris, Ford (he had hired one to go to a rally once), Lanchester (this was the most sensational as it had a fluid fly-wheel – whatever that meant). As for the flight, he was on less safe ground as it had been a joyride from a field in a de Havilland Fox Moth.

The questions went on:

Have you ever been air-sick?

Have you any fear of heights or been sick on a roundabout?

Happily, he was able to answer truthfully in the negative and was at this stage becoming quite elated with his progress. Quite unexpectedly, he was brought back to earth with a bump with a question on trigonometry which he was unable to answer. Maths had been one of his worst subjects and he had never even heard of trigonometry.

Despite that, at the conclusion of the interview he was told he had passed. As he explained:

> The relief we all felt at having come through the interview successfully broke down the British reserve and the room was a hubbub of noise as we compared notes. The medical was noteworthy for a loss of independence by having to produce a specimen of urine. A young lady issued me with a flask, indicated a screen, and told me to provide a sample. I wondered what she told her friends she did for a living! And so ended the '*per ardua*' on the way to the '*ad astra*' – 'By steep and toilsome ways to the stars,' as the RAF motto went. Spitfire! Here I come. Time will show how wrong I was.

The next few weeks were spent anxiously waiting for the post for the call to arms. Finally the letter from Air Ministry arrived and nervously he tore open the buff envelope.

> You have been accepted for a Short Service Commission in the General Duties Branch of the Royal Air Force as a pilot subject to the satisfactory completion of Ab Initio (from the beginning) flying training at an Elementary & Reserve Flying Training School.

But wait:

> With the proviso that you provide Air Ministry with a certificate to the effect that you have reached School Certificate standard in the subject of Trigonometry.

His heart sank. There was just no way he could join the RAF now as the necessary certificate was not in his possession, nor was he ever likely to acquire one.

However, luck was with him. Shortly after this shock he was putting up a shelf in the office of the Commanding Officer of 150 Squadron at the recently opened RAF Station Benson. Geoff looked at him working at his desk. He might be able to help. What did he have to lose?

Plucking up courage he said: 'I hope you'll forgive me, sir, but I've just got to join the RAF.'

Bill Hesketh was a charming, rugged wing commander and he knew that the tall, earnest young boy standing in front of him was enthusiastic and eager.

Just the type of bloke we want, he thought.

'But you must join,' he told Geoff, and then read the letter. He looked up. 'How are you going to go about getting this certificate?'

'I've no idea, sir.'

Hesketh thought for a minute and then telephoned the Station Education Officer, Bill Fallowfield, and told him the story. 'We must help this young chap to get into the Service,' said Hesketh.

After putting down the telephone Hesketh said to Geoff. 'Go over to Station Headquarters and have a chat with Bill. We think the obvious answer is for him to coach you in trig. It shouldn't take long to achieve the desired result.'

Geoff had fallen on his feet *again*. When the coaching was completed Fallowfield sent off a certificate to the Air Ministry to the effect that Geoff had reached the required standard. Predictably, he has never had any occasion to use this form of mathematics in his life.

When the acceptance letter arrived from the Air Ministry it instructed him to report on 24 July 1939 to No. 7 Elementary & Reserve Flying Training School at Desford, Leicestershire, for ab initio training. On satisfactory completion of the course he would then be posted to No. 4 Flying Training School at Abu Sueir, Egypt for Intermediate and Advanced training. He would be known as a Pupil Pilot or a P/P. This was a surprise to Geoff. The reason became clear when the Air Ministry letter of appointment was read carefully. It stated that he had been granted a commission of four years on the Active List followed by six years on the Reserve, or six years on the Active and four years on the Reserve in the General Duties Branch subject to successful completion of the ab initio course.

'It looked as though my feet were now firmly placed on the first rung of the ladder which I hoped would lead me "ad astra".' He gave notice to Laing's who were sorry to see him go, returned home in early July and prepared for his new life. 'I did a crash course in how to tie a double-ended bow tie, and bought a dinner jacket, trousers and boiled shirts for dining-in nights. I was to wear this outfit once only before the outbreak of war six weeks after the course commenced, which brought an end to such formal occasions.'

Little did Geoff realise in his excitement to join up that Britain was on the brink of war. With Austria and Czechoslovakia swallowed up by the German war machine it was only a matter of time before other countries fell. But to him and hundreds of other young men at that time, the political situation in Europe was less important than the prospect of starting an adventurous new life in the services.

24 July 1939 was a warm, cloudless summer's day and all thoughts of impending war were far from Geoff's mind as, dressed in sports jacket and flannels, he arrived at Desford.

I had been lucky to get a lift with my aunt and uncle who were returning to Sheffield after visiting my family. When we arrived the reception office was full of young men filling in registration forms. I joined in and after booking in at the Mess, being allotted quarters, and drawing flying kit, we all flocked to the aerodrome (a word which would soon be replaced in our vocabulary by 'airfield', as we became conversant with aeronautical terms) to look over the D.H.82 Tiger Moths which were lined up in neat rows on the grass.

The de Havilland Tiger Moth was a two-seater biplane designed by Geoffrey de Havilland and built by the de Havilland Aircraft Company. Characterised by its distinctive yellow colour and with a wingspan of 8.94 metres it had first flown on 26 October 1931. It was produced in large numbers for WWII service as a basic pilot trainer.

The following day they were divided into two sections, one attending lectures whilst the other was flying. They were shown how to operate their equipment, put on parachutes and introduced to their instructors.

My instructor was a Mr Wardell, an Irishman. We were given instructions by the Chief Ground Instructor as to the procedure for the course and informed that the officers were known as 'Flights'. On no account was the Royal Air Force to be referred to as 'Raff' but always by the full title or by its initials. The new language also termed 'aeroplane' as 'aircraft'.

Eventually Mr Wardell entered the crew room where the pupils were gathered and called some names amongst which was Geoffrey's. He took them out to the airfield and they were instructed on how to swing a propeller and how to start the engine. Then followed a short talk on what they would be doing in each lesson in the air.

Impatient, Geoff couldn't wait for his first flying lesson. But first there were certain formalities to complete – signing in at the mess, registering at the flying school run by Reid & Sigrist, drawing flying kit, and learning how to fit Gosport tubes and foam rubber pads in the helmet ear-pieces.

In his book *Bomber Command*, Max Hastings wrote:

Those who came to the RAF did so because they passionately, single-mindedly, unashamedly wanted to fly. The Hendon Air Displays, the hugely publicised exploits of Lindberg, Hinckler, Amy Johnson, all these had seized the imagination of their generation. Above all, perhaps, it had captured that of young grammar-school boys of modest, conventional lower middle-class backgrounds from which they yearned to escape.

Real friendships were made that first day at Desford. Geoff chummed up with Freddy Harrold and Joe Ready and the three soon became known as 'The Three Musketeers'. Fair-haired Freddy Harrold with a First from Cambridge, whose sole ambition was to fly, looked as if he would be more at home on a Hollywood film set. His distinctive walk with its long stride set him apart from the other entrants. Wild and courageous Joe Ready from Prince Edward Island in Canada had been rejected by the Canadian Air Force; being just under five feet three, he failed to meet the height requirement – five feet four inches. Always worried about his thinning hair, he would rub liniment into his scalp in the hope it would make his hair grow. Then there was good-looking Richard Kay-Shuttleworth who, during the course, would inherit a peerage and sign his name with a single S. The thirty-odd spirited young men who registered for training in Desford that July were typical of the young pilots who would become the mainstay of the Royal Air Force. As Max Hastings put it:

These young men were the innocents. They were young men who cut their hair and cultivated rakish little moustaches, precursors of the later handlebars.

Geoff's obsession to fly Spitfires led him to talk non-stop about the subject, with the result that his fellow pupils nicknamed him Spitfire, soon shortened to Spit. This stuck with him all the way through training until he was posted on to heavy bombers. He soon settled into the routine of flying training, which consisted of ground lectures on elementary theory of flight, engines, signals and meteorology, and a few sessions on the Link Trainer, a flight simulator. The actual flying was limited to two flights a day of approximately forty minutes each.

On 25 July, Geoff flew for the first time in a de Havilland 82 Tiger Moth N6477, a flight he will never forget. He sat in the back seat watching the mechanic swinging the propeller and listening to the engine fire. And then excitement such as he had never felt before built unbearably as the Tiger Moth bumped across the grass. It lifted seemingly effortlessly into the air, and finally he relaxed into calmness as it became airborne.

The aircraft gained height and then levelled off. He felt like pinching himself to make sure this was real. Maybe he was dreaming? But it was exactly as he had imagined it would be. The day was perfect, warm, with only a slight breeze. He gazed down on the country spread out far below them. It looked like a patchwork quilt. He wanted to shout out loud: 'Look at me, I'm flying like a bird.' He was surprised that there was so little sensation of speed until they lost height near the ground as they came in to land. All too soon they touched down.

Now he was convinced more than ever he had chosen the right career. He was born to fly. Full of enthusiasm, he tried to remember everything the instructor had told him and resolved to read even more about flying.

The course progressed and pupils began making their first solo flights – a milestone of course in any pilot's history. On 2 August Geoff flew in DH82 N6477 with a new instructor, Moxham. 'I'd like to see you do a spin, my boy,' he said. 'Now do one more.'

Geoff did one more and then Moxham told him to take him back and land. After landing, he said: 'Now taxi back for another take-off.'

At the end of the airfield they turned into the wind and Moxham undid his straps, hauling himself out of the cockpit. He pulled Geoff's helmet away from his ear and said, 'Right, you young bugger, away you go, and don't forget to come back here to pick me up! Good luck.'

Filled with a mixture of elation and excitement, Geoff taxied to the take-off point, the little Tiger Moth bouncing across the field. Remember what you've been taught, he told himself. Turning the aircraft into the wind, he checked he had a clear take-off run, then opened the throttle. Using the rudder to keep the aircraft straight, he eased the stick forward and the tail lifted. Check speed – 50 knots – now ease the stick back ... gently ... lift off ... He was airborne! He had done it! He throttled back and continued to climb to 500 feet, the land slipping away beneath him, then turned 90 degrees to port. He throttled back to cruising power and levelled off at 1,000 feet. So far so good. The magic of those moments would never be repeated! The sensation of being alone above the earth produced a feeling of euphoria. What more could anybody wish for? As he flew he sang, looking down at the earth far below blending into mottled hues of blue and green, 'I'm flying, I'm flying! It's me, Geoff Rothwell! Look up.'

The airfield disappeared behind the port wing and he did a 90-degree turn to port to bring the aircraft on to the downwind leg of the circuit. He passed the end of the airfield and made another 90-degree turn to port. Now for the final approach.

Suddenly he realised he was too high and sideslipped to lose surplus height. He levelled off, finding the aircraft floating a little due to the lack of the instructor's weight in the front cockpit. Now down, and the aircraft landed with a soft *bump. bump, bump* on the grass. A good landing.

He remembered to pick up Moxham, who was waiting with a friendly grin and a pat of congratulations as he climbed into the front cockpit. 'Well done, lad.'

It had taken Geoff nine hours and twenty minutes' dual instruction to go solo. If this was flying, surely it was a piece of cake.

Although there had been an uneasy quiet in Britain since the signing of the so-called Peace Agreement by Chamberlain, many people in the midst of the glorious summer of 1939 were lulled into believing Hitler could not possibly wage war at such a time. Surely Germany had learnt lessons from the Great War and would think twice before entering another world war? And was Nazism really as evil and monstrous as many thought? Each night they listened to the news in the vain hope it could be an appalling dream, but as the weeks passed there was talk only of war.

In those darkening months the new Royal Air Force recruits gradually increased their skills as they were introduced to the more interesting exercises such as aerobatics, forced landings, air navigation and instrument flying. They discovered the loop, the slow roll, the roll-off-the-top and the stall turn, and improved their handling ability. Aerobatics, a new skill, held no attraction for Geoff. He found gentler flying to be more attractive, preferring to hang on to his breakfast.

After he had clocked up twenty-five hours he was assessed as to his capability as a service pilot. He passed the test without any trouble, but although he was progressing well in practical flying, there was one area which was a concern. He was not at all mechanically minded, he failed to understand how an engine worked, and at one of the lectures asked a question which was so elementary the instructor asked, 'Are you taking the mickey out of me?'

It was obvious that unless he received tuition he would fail the Engines examination at the end of the course. But once again luck was on his side. His good friend Joe Ready, who was something of a mechanical genius, instructed him each evening in the mysteries of the workings of the internal combustion engine. So successful was his tuition, and Geoff's capacity to regurgitate information, that he not only passed the Engines paper with a mark of 96 per cent, but beat Joe, who managed only 94 per cent.

On 1 September 1939 the British Government advised the German Government that unless it could give satisfactory assurances that Germany had suspended all aggressive action against Poland, Britain would, without hesitation, fulfil its obligations towards Poland. No such assurances were received and the world waited.

Sunday, 3 September dawned warm and sunny, and all pupil pilots were ordered to assemble in the mess at 11 a.m. to hear a broadcast by Neville Chamberlain. Hitler had invaded Poland. France and Britain were now at war with Germany.

Geoff felt stunned. *War?* What would the implications be for him, for his family? For a moment the world stood still as he tried to take it all in. And then he was overcome by a strange mixture of apprehension and excitement. He would be on active service, fighting for his country. But what if the war were to finish before his training was completed? His training must be finished before that happened.

When the broadcast ended they were addressed by an executive of Reid & Sigrist who had been a pilot in the Great War. 'Give 'em hell,' he exhorted them. 'Never had any time for the Hun meself.'

For Geoff, and thousands like him, life was never to be quite the same again.

4

BACK TO THE CLASSROOM

In doing we learn.
– George Herbert, *Outlandish Proverbs*

For the second time in twenty-five years Europe was at war. Immediately after Chamberlain's announcement sirens sounded, sending people hurrying to the shelters, but it was a false alarm. Terror bombing and gas were the greatest fears. In the days following, a blackout was enforced, and people with cars had to learn to drive with dim, hooded lights at night. Everybody had a gas-mask, carried in a neat cardboard case which was also used as a general handbag for ration books, identity cards and cigarettes. Over one million children with their names written on labels were evacuated from major cities. Housewives made curtains from heavy, dark material for the 'blackout' and covered windows with sticky tape to avoid flying glass. Wardens patrolled the streets, banging on doors and shouting 'Put that light out', and everybody sang 'Run, Rabbit, Run'.

The British armed forces mobilised for war and members of the reserve forces received call-up notices. The Soviet Union, in alliance with Germany, seized part of Poland and marched into Finland. A British Expeditionary Force and some squadrons of the Royal Air Force were sent to France, and on 19 September 1939 Hitler swore that 'Germany will fight to the bitter end.'

For Desford's pupil pilots, one of the immediate effects of the outbreak of the war was that each night they had to patrol the airfield with batons to keep would-be German saboteurs at bay. This seemed rather melodramatic as one could hardly imagine the German number one target would be Desford and its couple of dozen de Havilland 82s, but it did bring home the seriousness of the war.

Geoff's posting to No. 4 Flying Training School in Egypt was cancelled. His new posting after his course finished at Desford would be to No. 12 Flying Training School at RAF Station Grantham for intermediate and advanced training, a disappointment as Lincolnshire did not sound nearly as exotic as Egypt.

Geoff completed the course with 56 hours 25 minutes and an '*Average*' assessment as a pilot. He was now an acting pilot officer, the lowest of all ranks of those holding the King's Commission. That night there was considerable hilarity in the mess. Their ab initio training was over and they could celebrate.

Before the outbreak of war pupil pilots on completion of their ab initio course were sent to a training depot at Uxbridge, but this had changed with the call-up of the Reservists and now they were sent to a newly opened unit at Hastings on the south coast. Owing to the large number of personnel requiring accommodation, feeding, etc., conditions were chaotic when the Desford contingent arrived on the scene. However, blocks of flats, hotels and seaside were requisitioned and they were billeted in one or the other.

They were lectured on a variety of subjects, including RAF ranks, saluting, how to avoid VD, etiquette and how officers were expected to behave (as gentlemen at all times!). An apocryphal story was related by one of the lecturers concerning an airman who reported sick. When the sick bay NCO asked him what was wrong with him he said, 'I've gotta pain in me testykles, Sarge'.

'In your wot?'

'In me testykles, sarge.'

'Ow long 'ave you been in the Service, lad?'

'Six months, sarge'

Well, listen to me, boy. Officers 'as testykles, warrant officers and sergeants have balls, and you, you 'orrible little AC2, you 'as bollicks. Now, you got a pain in your wot?'

'In me bollicks, sarge.'

'That's better lad. Fall into line and the MO will see you in ten minutes.'

The new acting pilot officers were taught how to march with the emphasis on physical fitness, and these activities were performed on the sea-front.

'Swing your bloody arms! Shoulders back,' shouted the tough little NCO instructor. 'That's not the way I taught you, Mr Rothwell. If you can't do it properly I'll have to stop your weekend leave – sir.'

At Hastings they received their new uniforms and now they could pack away their civilian clothes. It was to be five and a half years before they wore them again, and for some of them, never. But such thoughts were far from their minds in the exhilarating atmosphere of the early days of Britain at war. At the end of the course they were given a short leave and told to report to Grantham. As proud as they were to be wearing their new uniforms, they were conscious of the empty space above the breast pocket on the left side – where their wings would eventually be sewn.

Grantham was a peace-time station. The camp was situated at the top of Spittlegate Hill above the town and the officers' mess, which was still on a pre-war footing, the messing being let out to contractors, was old and comfortable, with ivy-covered walls. Geoff came down to breakfast to a table laden with cereal, milk and cream, eggs cooked in a variety of ways, bacon, kippers, kedgeree and various types of fruit. Not only had he never seen anything like it but he did not realise the men had to pay for all that wonderful food. As an acting pilot officer he was paid 11s 10d a day, a fortune to him, until he received the Mess bill. Deductions for food and various funds and subscriptions pruned the gross sum so severely that at the end of the month there was little left over.

The men were interviewed by the Commanding Officer, Group Captain Robinson, an aged bachelor on the point of retirement, and asked to state their preference on posting after completing training.

'I'd like to go to a fighter squadron, sir, preferably one equipped with Spitfires,' said Geoff.

Robinson looked up from his desk and said, 'You'd never get into a fighter with those long legs, my boy. It's bombers for you. I'm posting you to the Anson flight.'

It was a huge disappointment but eventually Geoff realised it would be safer flying a bomber with extra engines. The disappointment was mitigated slightly with the news that Freddy and Joe were also posted to the same flight. The three friends were to stick together right throughout their training.

Pupils earmarked for fighters were trained on single-engined Hawker Hart, Hind and Audax aircraft, whilst the remainder flew twin-engined Avro Ansons. The 'Annie', as it was affectionately known, was a docile aircraft whose only vice was a mechanically operated retracting undercarriage requiring a phenomenal number of turns on a handle. 'We were spared this irksome task in the Initial Training Flight as the undercarriage was retracted for local flying,' recalled Geoff.

'Taking off from Grantham airfield was adventurous,' recalled Geoff, 'owing to it being dome-shaped, making it impossible to see what was in your path on the take-off run on the other side of the dome. It was amazing we had no accidents through this topographical feature. It is a testimony to the high standard of instruction that our course was free from accidents all the time we were at Grantham.'

The winter of 1939 was one of the coldest experienced for some time and the country was covered by a blanket of deep snow. RAF Grantham was short of rations, so all pupils were sent off on leave.

Geoff and Freddy went to London and while there decided to see the revue at the Prince of Wales theatre. There they met two attractive singer-dancers, Joan Terry and Beth White, with whom they became friendly. Geoff was to see much of Joan in the next few months but although he liked her and enjoyed spending time with her, he knew the romance was not going to lead to anything more serious.

Flying was paramount at this stage in his life. It gave him intense pleasure such as he had never experienced. It was always a delight taking off from Grantham on clear, crisp, frosty mornings, and gazing down on the countryside far below he could see the tips of church spires showing just above the early morning mist which covered the low-lying villages. Romantic and picturesque sights such as this enhanced the pleasure of flying, especially as the intense cold of the unheated Anson caused acute physical discomfort.

The Avro Anson with a wingspan of 17 metres was a British twin-engined aircraft. Developed in the mid-1930s from the earlier Avro 652 it was commissioned by the RAF and initially used in maritime reconnaissance alongside the larger flying boats. The Anson flew first on 24 March 1935 but by the outbreak of World War Two it had become obsolete in front-line combat. Its first flight was March 24 1935 and it was used primarily as a trainer for the RAF, also the Fleet Air Arm, and the Royal Canadian and Royal Australian Air Forces.

Pilots under training were equipped with a Sidcot flying suit, the warmer sheepskin Irvine jacket being reserved for crews on operational squadrons. Although the Sidcot had a 'teddy bear' lining, it was always a relief to return to the crewroom stove to thaw out after hours spent in a draughty aircraft.

It could be difficult and dangerous flying in such conditions, and on a solo navigational cross-country exercise to South Cerney in Wiltshire on 21 November 1939 in Anson 4978 Geoff was unable to see anything on reaching his ETA as the airfield was shrouded in mist. Just as he was wondering what to do, he saw an airfield on a hill clear of the low-lying mist. This, he discovered, was Kemble. He had no choice but to land. He taxied up to a hangar, surprised by the absence of any ground staff. As he was switching off the engines a broad Australian accent greeted him with, 'And where the bloody hell are you from?'

The voice belonged to a diminutive flight lieutenant with a pencil moustache.

'I'm from Grantham, sir,' Geoff replied. 'I was looking for South Cerney.'

'Well, this is Kemble, a Care and Maintenance Unit,' said the pencil moustache. 'Come into the office. Want a cup of coffee?'

'Thank you, sir,' said Geoff.

'Geez mate, don't keep calling me sir. My name's Don Saville.'

The two men immediately struck up a rapport and Saville, whom Geoff describes as 'a great bloke and one in a million', told him about himself. On completing a Short Service Commission in the RAF he had become an Imperial Airways pilot. When war commenced he rejoined the RAF and now flew all types of aircraft on delivery flights. While Geoff and Saville were talking, another Grantham Anson landed.

'Geez, I've got to do something about this,' said Saville. 'What's the name of your Flight Commander, Geoff?'

He immediately telephoned through to Grantham, lambasting one of the instructors who just happened to answer the telephone for sending pupils off without checking weather conditions at their destination.

'It was refreshing,' remembered Geoff, 'to meet an officer senior in rank with such a friendly and informal manner, particularly to a pupil such as I was at the time.'

Training at Grantham was carried out at the time of 'the phoney war', when there was little enemy aerial activity. The acting pilot officers were therefore able to complete the course without any interruption, including night flying when they were most vulnerable to surprise attack from enemy intruders. Shortly after, the conflict would burst westward with the German *blitzkrieg*, or lightning war, overwhelming Denmark, Norway, Holland, Belgium and Luxembourg.

'We are fighting for a moral issue,' declared a *Daily Mail* editorial in January 1940 denouncing proposals for bombing Germany. 'We should do nothing unworthy of our cause.'

After approximately fifty hours' flying in the Initial Training Flight and passing an examination in certain subjects, Geoff was awarded his 'wings'. With his log book endorsed 'Average proficiency as pilot on type', he now moved over to the Advanced Training Flight, where he learned to drop practice bombs on a range, find wind speed and direction at 6,000 feet, camera gun firing, formation and instrument flying and cross-country navigation. Finally the course was completed and he passed out as a qualified service pilot shortly after his twentieth birthday in April 1940. Once again he was given an 'Average' assessment as a pilot, but with an added note that 'he has a tendency to carelessness but should be very reliable with more experience – Squadron Leader (Lord) MA. Douglas-Hamilton'.

Geoff was unaware he had demonstrated any carelessness but was quite satisfied with the rest of the assessment. And so, with 156 hours 35 minutes' total flying time under his belt and a few hours short of 100 on twin-engined aircraft, he approached the next step towards becoming an operational pilot with a posting to a Wellington Operational Training Unit at Harwell.

On the last evening at Grantham a mess party was held amidst great hilarity, developing into a 'rag' against the junior course. Geoff was one of the first to become involved in this, having one of his arms held by the opposition whilst his supporters hung on to his waist and pulled in the opposite direction. Suddenly there was a tearing noise and the sleeve of his tunic was completely ripped out at the shoulder.

All his kit had been sent on in advance to his next station and he was left only with overnight luggage which did not include a spare tunic. On arrival in London he headed straight for the Piccadilly branch of Hector Powe, his tailors, for an urgent repair. The elderly salesman never turned a hair when Geoff took off his greatcoat and pulled the severed sleeve from his pocket. 'These things do happen, sir,' he said, disappearing behind the scenes with sleeve in hand and uniform jacket over his arm. Ten minutes later he returned with sleeve and jacket mended.

'The tailor has used some reinforcing thread, sir,' he said, 'but it would be advisable to use more care at future mess parties. There will be no charge this time but it won't apply to any future repairs!'

Geoff later remembered: 'There was a touch of sadness about the breaking up of our course as we all went our different ways. We had been together for almost nine months and now had to make new friends and tackle fresh problems on our own. We were rapidly growing up as the day when we would become fully-fledged operational pilots drew closer.'

5

BOMBED ON A RACECOURSE

You ask what is our aim? I can answer in one word: victory – victory at all costs, victory in spite of all terrors; victory, however hard and long the road may be; for without victory there is no survival.

– Churchill

10 May 1940
Winston Churchill, the First Lord of the Admiralty, was now the new leader of the British people. He faced a huge challenge. With the Great War still in the minds of the British people, 'the war to end all wars', he was asking them to fight again, twenty-one years later. His primary aim was to spread confidence throughout the British nation but he knew it wouldn't be easy. Privately, he was deeply worried. Three days after taking office he addressed the House of Commons for the first time as Prime Minister, giving his well-known speech in a grave and trembling voice.

I have nothing to offer but blood, toil, tears and sweat. We have before us an ordeal of the most grievous kind. We have before us many, many long months of struggle and of suffering.

On completion of the FTS course at Grantham the new Pilot Officer Rothwell was posted to 15 OTU (Operational Training Unit) at RAF Harwell, which was a more relaxed station than those to which he had been accustomed. The station in Berkshire, 17 miles north of Reading, had been a grass airfield and at the outbreak of World War II became part of No. 38 Group Bomber Command.

Instructors treated new pilot officers as equals rather than pupils and the pleasant atmosphere made the course interesting and enjoyable. They were formed into crews once they had finished with circuits and bumps (as landings were usually called), and it is indicative of the high standard of RAF training that it required only two hours twenty-five minutes' dual instruction before Geoff went solo on Wellingtons.

The Vickers Wellington, widely used as a night bomber by Bomber Command and designed in the mid-1930s by Barnes Wallis of Dambuster fame was a British twin-engined long-range bomber with a top speed of 378 kms and a wingspan of 26 metres. Used at the start of World War Two up to late 1943, it was then relegated to a secondary role. A Wellington crew consisted of pilot, navigator, wireless operator and front and rear gunners.

Geoff found flying the twin-engined bomber enjoyable and stimulating, finally curing him of his burning desire to be a Spitfire pilot. He was ideally suited to this as flying heavy bombers demanded a good measure of sheer physical strength and Geoff had this in abundance. He would later find out that even after two or more years of training and operating bombers, most wartime pilots found it a strain coping with technical problems such as taking off and flying and landing the heavy aircraft in one piece, let alone coming to terms with fighting the enemy.

Airmen say that contrary to popular mystique, there was no special temperament that equipped one man to fly a Spitfire and another a Lancaster, the job made the man. Only a handful of men in Bomber Command could throw a four-engined bomber through the sky with absolute assurance, or indeed wished to.

– Max Hastings, *Bomber Command*

Training on Wellingtons was a mixture of navigation exercises, bombing, air firing and formation flying, with a limited amount of night flying. The bombing/air-firing range was in Devon. Crews often used towns and villages in the county as turning points on their navigation exercises, and they soon became accustomed to the sight of the white horse figures cut into the chalk hill slopes when flying in the vicinity of Harwell on the Berkshire Downs and in the adjoining county of Wiltshire. But the village of Cerne Abbas in Dorset, with its figure of a giant etched in chalk on the hillside, attracted aircraft like bees to honey. The figure is immense, as is his organ of reproduction. Legend has it that in earlier times infertile women would spend the night on the hillside in the belief they would become pregnant. RAF legend has it that any success in that direction was possibly due to the involvement of the monks from the nearly abbey – more probably a randy abbot was responsible for the whole concept! Whatever the truth, the giant certainly introduced added interest to cross-country exercises.

After completing fifteen hours at the controls by day and four hours twenty minutes at night, Geoff was certified as a qualified first pilot on Wellington aircraft. At the end of the five-week course he and his crew were posted to 99 Squadron, which operated from Newmarket, a satellite of the peacetime airfield, Mildenhall. With 238 hours 35 minutes' flying time he felt he was on a true wartime footing and a real pilot at last. Geoff left Harwell on 16 May 1940 with George Isbell, his rear gunner, in his car and joined 99 Squadron on Newmarket racecourse.

Newmarket, on the border of Cambridge, Norfolk and Suffolk and known primarily for its racecourse, is an attractive country town with green, leafy trees. In stark contrast to the peacetime RAF messes of Grantham and Harwell, the officers were accommodated on the racecourse and in the grandstand. They slept on camp beds and although the ablution arrangements were spartan, there was a great spirit in the squadron.

Raymond Lee wrote in *The Observer*: 'They were a queer conglomeration these men, some educated and sensitive, some rough-haired and burly, and drawn from all parts of the Empire, Great Britain, Canada, New Zealand, Australia.'

The airfield itself was the Rowley Mile and the take-off and landing runs were in one direction, regardless of the way the wind blew.

There was a pronounced hump running across the take-off path, probably a buried drain or cable, and aircraft were held down until the hump was reached, at which point they were more or less thrown into the air. Apart from these rough and ready features Newmarket turned out to be an excellent place to be stationed as the local population was friendly and hospitable.

The squadron had a disastrous start to the war when taking part in a daylight raid in December 1939 on German warships off Heligoland. Twelve antiquated Wellington 1As were set upon by a formation of Messerschmitt fighters, which found them easy game. The six aircraft which were lost probably persuaded the powers-that-be to confine future Wellington operations to night bombing, as such losses were clearly unsustainable. One feature of the Wellington 1As was the 'dustbin' turret which was lowered hydraulically beneath the aircraft when airborne. The idea was good as the turret could revolve through 360 degrees and had an impressive field of fire. Rumour had it that if you made too many revolutions in one direction the turret would 'unwind' and drop off!

'One feature which led to the turret being unpopular was that in the event of a hydraulic failure the undercarriage could not be lowered or the turret retracted,' said Geoff. 'The awful predicament of a gunner trapped in a turret and faced with a wheels-up landing did not bear contemplating. Actually, anyone unfortunate enough to be in such a situation could bale out, but even that was not an option pleasing to all and it was a relief when the squadron was equipped with the later Mark 1Cs with Fraser Nash turrets replacing the less effective Vickers type and no dustbins.'

Geoff, second pilot to Bill Thallon, a charming, dark-haired and flamboyant Irishman, was to carry out his first operation within three days of arriving on the squadron on 19 May 1940 in Wellington IA P9243. At the briefing, with a mixture of intrigue and expectancy, he watched as the CO, Wing Commander

Griffiths, revealed their target for the night. The purpose of the operation was to block the advance of the German Panzers by bombing a road and railway at Halle, southwest of Brussels.

> Some of the men were humming, some were singing, some were laughing, and others were standing serious and thoughtful. It looks like the dressing room where the jockeys sit waiting before a great steeplechase.
> – Max Hastings, *Bomber Command*

At dispersal Geoff lay on the grass smoking his pipe and chatting to some of the crew, then Thallon announced it was time to go.

With a strange unaccustomed feeling in the pit of his stomach Geoff took an extra pee, noticing the other pilots and crews were doing the same on the tail-wheel of their aircraft.

All went well until they came within sight of Brussels, when the aircraft was suddenly lit up by searchlights. And then he saw the red and yellow tracer – seemingly innocuous, but deadly. It shot up towards them, slowly at first and then faster, faster. He was at once fascinated and frightened.

Take evasive action! he said to himself, but immediately Bill dived and turned and corkscrewed to dodge the searchlights. In the early days the second pilot was also the bomb aimer. When nearing the target, Geoff lay on his stomach, looking through the perspex panel in the floor. He set up the bomb sight and when he identified the target he gave instructions to Bill.

'Bomb doors open left ... left ... left ... right ... bombs gone!' as he pressed the release and watched the bombs bursting on the target. Some time later he felt the aircraft shudder and knew they had been hit, but the big Wellington flew on into the dark night. Finally they were within sight of the English coast and, not long after, Newmarket.

'Looks like you've been hit, sir, but not too badly,' said one of the ground crew to Thallon as they clambered down the ladder. And when they looked up they saw stars through a huge hole in the port wing. As operations were carried out at a relatively low level in those early days of the war, pilots seldom flying above 3,000 feet, it was common to run into light flak from 20-millimetre guns and find holes in the aircraft on return. Unfortunately these operations turned out to be wasted efforts as the Panzers simply bypassed the damaged areas by taking to the fields.

This first mission for Geoff had been an easy blooding.

He felt hungry and made short work of the bacon and 'operational' egg which was served to all returned aircrew after de-briefing. (Eggs were in short supply in tightly rationed Britain and were always gratefully received.)

Geoff continued to fly as Bill Thallon's second pilot and the next few operations followed the same pattern as the first. On their fifth operation together on 29 May 1940 in Wellington 1A P9222, they bombed roads and buildings at Saint Omer. It was as they were turning for home that they ran into flak again. It burst all around them, glowing red and orange in the dark night sky. *Thwack, Thwack!* Just like fairyland on Christmas Eve, thought Geoff as the bursts lit up the inside of the aircraft.

The flak was so thick it was difficult to see out of the cockpit windows. They flew on, weaving in and out, trying to dodge the flak and the searchlights which swung to and fro from the French towns below. A loud explosion suddenly shook the left side of the aircraft.

We've been hit! Geoff thought as one of the engines in the Wellington coughed slightly, spluttered, and then amazingly revved into action again. They flew across the Channel towards the white cliffs, to safety. Not too far now.

'Diversion message from base, skip,' came the voice of the wireless operator. 'Weather clamped at Newmarket. Land at Mildenhall.'

At Mildenhall they landed and switched off the engines. As they climbed down they saw the ground crew gathered under the port wing. Geoff went over and once again saw stars through the large hole. This time the damage was much greater than on his first trip.

In May a new phase in Bomber Command operations began with the emphasis shifted to a strategic offensive against Germany itself. As the *Daily Telegraph* reported:

London, 16 May.
A communique issued by the Air Ministry today says: 'Each crew was given specific military objectives and instructions that bombs were not to be dropped indiscriminately. A few failed to locate their objectives and did not drop their bombs, but the majority found and bombed their targets with great effect causing widespread damage and many explosions.' This raid will please Bomber Command, which believes it can bring Germany to its knees by concentrated bombing of strategic targets within Germany.

The magnetic personality of Churchill, representing hope, inspiration and incredible energy, constantly encouraged the people to fight if necessary on the beaches, on the landing grounds, in the streets and in the hills. His voice was that of a man angry, defiant and utterly resolved. Newspapers made much of the success of the evacuation of the troops from Dunkirk, and London was a sea of sandbags and military uniforms. The *Luftwaffe* attempted to gain air superiority and the bombing of the fighter airfields in southern England now began in earnest.

On a beautiful soft summer's evening some two hundred aircrew were paraded in front of the grandstand at Newmarket to listen to an address by Wing Commander Griffiths.

'We have a most serious situation on our hands,' said Griffiths gravely. 'There is a strong possibility of an invasion and we are expecting to be attacked by German paratroops any time. If this happens you will be given short notice to fly to Ireland to refuel and then on to Canada, from where the war will continue.'

Geoff was stunned. A chill ran through his blood. England invaded! It didn't seem possible. Up until that moment it had all been a wonderful wizard show. He thought of Churchill's words: 'We shall defend our island whatever the cost may be ...We shall never surrender.'

Outside, the rain poured down. It dripped steadily on to the brilliant green leaves of the oak tree outside the window, this beautiful green country – somehow the war had to be won

at all costs. The talk by the Wing Commander had brought
home the seriousness of the situation and the vulnerability of
England. Then his thoughts turned to his family, whom he
would be leaving to the mercy of the Nazis. The room suddenly
felt cold and as he stood there looking at the rain splashing
against the window, he had a vision of squadrons of Wimpys
flogging across the cold Atlantic into the prevailing headwind.
(Wimpy was a nickname for Wellington aircraft, named after
the character J. Wellington Wimpy in the *Popeye the Sailor*
cartoon strip.)

It soon became apparent to his superiors that Geoff had
strong leadership skills. On his operations with Bill Thallon
he had shown enthusiasm, initiative and presence of mind in
dangerous situations. These strengths, coupled with an ability to
establish harmonious relationships and command respect without
demanding it, qualified him to be a captain. He was given his own
crew and their first operation on 29 June in Wellington IC R3197
was to bomb the Black Forest with incendiaries. The reason for
this strange target is unclear, unless there were fuel or ammunition
dumps in that area. Geoff was nervous as so much depended on
this first operation being a success. For all his outward confidence
he was a shy twenty-year-old, unsure if he was going to succeed
as a captain.

However, he tried to put these negative feelings aside and
concentrated on the job at hand. Fortunately, all went well and
the op was completed without interference from flak or night
fighters. As they were flying over the North Sea on the last leg of
the journey he congratulated himself on a job well done.

Not far from home now, he thought to himself, better just check
with the nav on our ETA.

The navigator worked it out by dead reckoning. 'Get me a QDM
(the magnetic course to base),' he said to the wireless operator.

'The bloody set's u/s (unserviceable),' the wireless operator
replied. The navigator related this to Geoff.

'Tell him to kick it!' replied Geoff.

'No go, Skip, he's tried that. I make the ETA another thirty-three
minutes. We're pretty short of fuel.'

What a right bastard! thought Geoff. Ditching in the North Sea wouldn't exactly enhance his chances of making a success of his career. They flew on, wireless blind.

'Front gunner to skipper, I think I can see a beacon on the port bow. It's very dim. Can you see it?'

'Roger, front gunner. I've picked it up. Navigator, I'm altering course twenty degrees port. Get your code sheet ready and when we can read the Morse letter you can tell me where we are.'

They flew on for another few minutes, the fuel getting lower.

'It's North Weald, captain,' said the navigator.

North Weald was a fighter station well south of their base at Newmarket but somehow luck was on their side, and with a flarepath operating at North Weald they landed safely.

The wireless set was repaired and after they had a good breakfast in the mess and the aircraft was refuelled, they flew the forty-minute journey back to Newmarket.

'Bang on. Good show,' they said as they congratulated each other on completing their first operation as a crew.

A tour consisted of thirty operations and it has been worked out statistically that losses in Bomber Command were such that one could expect to carry out twenty-five operations before 'getting the chop', as the expression went. In the early days, when both sides were engaged in learning processes, the risks from enemy action were far less than from the crew's own shortcomings in the way of faulty navigation, bad weather and lack of expertise. At that stage in the war Bomber Command was not as effective a force as it was to become later. Many targets were never identified and bombs were frequently dropped randomly or brought back.

Trying to identify targets from 8,000–10,000 feet by the limited illumination from parachute flares was almost impossible but we did have some successes as my Log Book shows that large fires were started at an airframe factory at Wenzendorf, near Hamburg after we bombed with incendiaries. We encountered fierce anti-aircraft fire and shrapnel severed an oil pipeline putting the front turret out of action.

Luck seemed to stay with Geoff and his crew. He was finding squadron life enjoyable. It was a huge boost to his confidence to have his own aircraft – *D Donald* – and crew and already he was developing a reputation for being a larger-than-life character. In the pleasant town of Newmarket the tall, red-haired captain with the enormous ginger moustache and the big personality and his gang of followers were a familiar sight. His initial lack of confidence had now been replaced with a strength of purpose which attracted people to him wherever he went. His positive nature, plus a tremendous sense of humour, made him not only popular on the squadron but also in the town. Nothing seemed to upset him. He had the world at his feet. This positivity had an infectious effect on his crew and they responded accordingly. It was all a bloody wizard show. Despite Geoff's devil-may-care attitude he made sure nothing was left to chance. His inherent sense of responsibility, which was why he had been made a captain in the first place, enabled him to make all the necessary preparations before going on operations, and, having done that, he would rush headlong into battle, knowing every eventuality had been covered.

When not on ops the men would lie on the grass smoking or dozing in the sun in their deckchairs, drinking long glasses of cold lemonade and discussing life and death and when the war would end. Music would be played on the gramophone and they would hum along to 'Deep Purple' and 'Hang out Your Washing on the Siegfried Line'. On days like these the war always seemed far away. When the time came to go on operations again, they would climb up the ladder into the fuselage of the Wellington, breathing in the now-familiar smell of fabric dope and, fighting down pangs of nerves, would prepare themselves for the next six or seven hours ahead.

In that glorious summer of 1940 Geoff could be found at either his friend George Long's farm at nearby Six Mile Bottom on the Cambridge road or at the Golden Lion in the company of his mates and some of the WAAFs from the station. However, it was a sort of unwritten law at the time that the WAAFS should not distract the pilots and the pilots thought hard before becoming deeply involved with these women. Although Geoff still saw Joan Terry occasionally, the relationship was coming to an end. He did not want a serious romance at that time and he managed to persuade her it would be best if they remained just friends.

One day came the news that both Freddy Harrold and Joe Ready, Geoff's first close friends of flying training school days, had been killed. With this tragic news the fun and laughter came to an abrupt end. Geoff was shattered. Little Joe Ready, who had coached him so successfully in engineering for his first examination, had been killed flying an Anson with Coastal Command. And Freddy with his film-star good looks, who had made flying his life, had been shot down in a Whitley. They would never be the Three Musketeers again. As if that wasn't bad enough, John Allen, Geoff's Spitfire pilot friend from Hornchurch who had had a distinguished career in the RAF, had been killed in the Battle of Britain. Up until then Geoff had never thought seriously that he or any of his close friends might 'get the chop'. In the back of his mind was always the thought that it would happen to other people's friends. He knew the statistics but they had failed to sink in. He was one of many young pilots who knew in a vague sort of way that perhaps ten, fifteen, twenty of them might die that night. It was a case of saying please God, don't let it be Freddy or Joe, my friends. Let it be somebody else's friends instead. As the war progressed they were all to change this way of thinking.

It is documented that a Church of England parson arrived in the sergeants' mess to become an air gunner and asked the whereabouts of his quarters. 'I wouldn't worry if I were you,' said Bill Magrath blithely, a hardened young veteran of twenty, 'You won't be here a week.'

With the passing of Freddy and Joe, Geoff became aware of his vulnerability. Some of the light-heartedness and the innocence which had been such a part of him was now gone for ever. Like many others, he became brutally fatalistic. Whenever he went home on leave – once every three months – he never mentioned anything of this to his parents, especially his mother, who he knew worried about him...

Ethel watched him closely that day he came home on leave. This son of hers was growing up too quickly. She knew what the odds were. Did all mothers feel the same when their sons were fighting for their country? Some of her gaiety was beginning to fade. There were little lines running along her forehead and the skin was stretched tightly across her cheeks. She tried not to show her anxiety, her dreadful fear, and it was all she could do not to reach out to him, to hold him tightly, and tell him to stay here with her where he would be safe. But she said nothing of her fears to him. How could she? Instead, she would pray silently when he had gone back on operations. 'Please God keep him safe.'

But for Commonwealth help, Britain was now entirely alone. There were only a few pilots and the persuasive eloquence of Winston Churchill to hold the tiny country together. Churchill offered words of hope to a nation that had none. Never had victory seemed more remote than during that summer of 1940. A grim cartoon by David Low in the *Daily Herald* showed a British Tommy, rifle in hand, standing defiantly on the Kent coast and looking towards mainland Europe. The caption said simply: 'Very well – Alone!'

Geoff could not help but wonder at the amazing resilience and versatility of this nation which previously had seemed relaxed, perhaps even bored. Now every man, woman and child lived under the constant threat of invasion, rationing, nights without sleep, falling masonry, wailing sirens and crashing bombs. Housewives mobilised their pots and pans, and garden railings were ripped up to go towards making fighter planes. And Britain was laying down a four-engine bomber programme which was to wipe out the cities of the Ruhr in 1943 and 1944.

On 13 July 1940 Hitler ordered preparations for *Operation Sealion* – the invasion of England. He had issued a military directive to the effect that Germany must gain air superiority over the RAF before an invasion could take place. He still hoped the British would offer peace terms but he was to wait in vain and when it became obvious Britain would not make peace, the *Luftwaffe* attacked in force.

It was mid-July. The Battle of Britain had begun in earnest. The *News Chronicle* reported:

London, 8 August
It is now a week since the *Luftwaffe* began its latest attempt to destroy the RAF in preparation for Hitler's planned invasion of Britain. In spite of relentless intensive fighting in the air over the Channel and along the south coast, on the evidence of today's battles it is still a long way from succeeding in that aim.

As the bomber formations with fighter escorts in close attendance roared in over the coast to attack harbours, naval bases and airfields, the Hurricanes and Spitfires of Fighter Command, carefully fed into the battle, took a terrible toll on the Germans. They lost 31 planes to the RAF's 17.

Now the blue summer skies of England were permanently etched by the vapour trails from Spitfire against Messerschmitt.

In between operations the pilots of 99 Squadron would lie on their backs, shandies in their hands, gazing into the cloudless sky as the sun beat relentlessly down on their heads. They would lie there each engrossed in his own thoughts, knowing they were in the midst of life one moment, death another, watching other people fight and die. They would listen to the drone of the aircraft engines high above them, watch the dog fights and the vapour trails and the kites ducking and diving and weaving in and out, and know each pilot was desperately trying to stay alive, and that he was entirely alone.

Some people were unaware of the immense importance of what was occurring over their heads. For them it was more like some sporting event, a cricket match for instance, when at the close of play one looked at the scores – how many German aircraft were destroyed against how many of their own.

Newmarket in 1940 was a hotbed of rumours and it was thought fifth columnists were active in the district. This idea may have some credibility in the light of the unfortunate experience of a VIP flight which left from an airfield in the area.

A member of 99 Squadron, Tony Payn, was detailed to fly as second pilot in a Wellington, captained by a Squadron Leader Samuels, which was taking Air Vice Marshal Boyd to Malta. Geoff recalled:

> The crew were waiting for suitable weather and were often seen in Newmarket and, despite the supposed secrecy of the operation it would have been simple for an eavesdropper at the bar of the Golden Lion to have learnt details. Whether or not these were passed on to the enemy I do not know but the fact is the aircraft was intercepted over the Mediterranean and forced to land on either Lampedusa or Pantellaria and the crew taken prisoner. Years later I met Samuels in Stalag Luft 1 where we were both incarcerated.

Rumours circulated in Newmarket that spies were in the town and posters everywhere warned people that walls had ears and to be careful. 'Careless talk costs lives' and 'Be like Dad, keep Mum', they said, and one or two incidents seemed to confirm this. Lights were seen in the grandstand on the July Course and on one particularly hot evening Geoff and an intelligence officer were sent to investigate. The night was inky black with just the odd star as they patrolled the seemingly deserted airfield. They were glad of their Smith & Wesson .38 revolvers as without torches or lights they could see nothing in front of them. An owl hooted close by, making them jump. As they approached a thicket of trees on the far side of the Rowley Mile they heard a faint sound. Geoff put his fingers to his lips, motioning the intelligence officer to be quiet. There it was again – like the sound of snapping twigs. They stood still, gripping the triggers of their .38. Stealthily they stepped forward, but not quickly enough. A shadowy figure moved swiftly away and out of range.

An inspection of the area the following morning found a pile of dry twigs and matches in the grandstand. A watch was kept for the next few nights but eventually discontinued as nobody was seen again. Not long after this incident Geoff and Bud Keller, a Canadian friend, had their camp beds moved out to an awning on the top tier of the terraces in the main stand. The beds had canvas covers which could be fastened at the sides with laces. Geoff always left the top laces unfastened but Bud tied all those on his bed. One night a loud explosion woke Geoff from a deep sleep. He looked across the racecourse and saw a vivid flash followed by another explosion ... and then another ... coming in a direct line straight towards them.

He leapt out of bed and ran down the grandstand steps to the air-raid shelter while the explosions continued towards the stand, without realising Bud wasn't with him. He rushed back and found him struggling to undo the laces on his camp bed. There was just time to help his friend before a bomb hurtled towards them. Geoff quickly threw Bud to one side. Badly shaken and gasping for breath, they collapsed wobbly-kneed into the air-raid shelter.

The next morning they found twelve bombs had been dropped, but even more amazing was that it had taken eight bombs to wake them.

No great damage had been done but the July Course was disfigured by twelve huge craters in a neat line.

The Battle of Britain continued day after day, hardly a lull in between. Full of courage and spirit, England appeared defiant in the face of adversity.

> We were just not going to let them get away with it. We were just not going to let them win, it was as simple as that. I have never known determination like it. I don't think there ever has been, before or since.
>
> – In conversation with Edith Heap, quoted in
> *Her Finest Hour*

The RAF fought back valiantly – every aircraft was on standby – but little did they know that worse was to come. 'Eagle Day', 13 August 1940, was the start of an intense *Luftwaffe* campaign to destroy the entire Royal Air Force. Hermann Goering, Hitler's Chief of the *Luftwaffe*, had a plan.

'The defence of Southern England will last four days and the Royal Air Force four weeks. We can guarantee invasion for the Fuhrer within a month,' Goring told his commanders.

But his failure to allow for the skills of Air Marshal Hugh Dowding, who was prepared for this battle, meant that large numbers of precious fighter aircaft were kept safely out of Goering's reach. Dowding fed his squadrons into battle with great economy.

During the defence of England, Bomber Command crews relied on their ground crews who serviced the engines, airframe and equipment, and every aircraft captain had the highest praise for them. Whenever there was a party in Newmarket, aircrew always made sure their ground crews were invited, and a good relationship was built up with them. These remarkable men worked long hours, in fair weather or foul. Sometimes it was so hot they could easily burn themselves handling metal parts which had been in the sun, at other times they were chilled to the bone. Geoff never heard a word of complaint from any of them.

'It's sad they received so little recognition for the excellent work they put in to maintain serviceability,' says Geoff.

Icing of airframes and engines was a worry to all bomber crews. It was no joke trying to control a heavily laden aircraft on which the build-up of ice had destroyed the smooth aerofoil surface which keeps the aircraft airborne.

On 29 October 1940 in Wellington IC T2541 on a raid targeting the German Air Ministry and Hitler's pride and joy – the Reichstag – weather conditions became extreme and cloud cover intense. Normally this type of sortie would have been aborted due to the danger of icing. However, on this particular evening *T Tare* had been specially chosen for an experiment with a de-icer known as snowdrop paste on the leading edges of the wings and tail plane. For two and a half hours Geoff's crew flew in these conditions, all the others having to return to base because of icing. Not only was the operation successful but *T Tare* was one of only four aircraft to reach the target.

After a bombing operation to Gelsenkirchen on 17 November in Wellington IC L7804 Geoff and his crew ran into extreme weather over the North Sea. They flew on, the clouds becoming thicker and the rain heavier. In a matter of minutes the weather had deteriorated to such an extent the downpour became torrential.

They tried to use the wireless to find out what the weather was like at base but it was unserviceable.

Geoff descended through cloud to 700 feet – a dangerous level in bumpy and turbulent conditions. Soon a thin coating of ice formed on the windscreen. He climbed once more to try to get above the cold front then set course for base. But he was still in thick cloud and five or six inches of ice had now formed on the engines, causing the carburettors to freeze up. Outside the temperature was minus 20 degrees. Suddenly the engines lost power, the Wellington lost height, becoming almost uncontrollable. He descended to 2,000 feet, 1,000, and then they broke cloud cover. To their enormous relief the weather was comparatively clear. On straightening out, Geoff found the Wellington could still be flown fairly straight and level as much of the ice had eroded in the dive. It had been a frightening experience but they made it safely back to Newmarket.

Each crew was allotted an aircraft which they guarded jealously and always flew when they were on ops. It was the custom to have an emblem painted on the front of the aircraft and when I was asked by the ground crew what we wanted on 'D for Donald' we decided on a character from a comic strip in the *Daily Mirror* – the Baron. He was evil-looking and had a hooked nose, turned up collar, and a hat pulled down over his face. We took a pride in keeping The Baron in tiptop condition and if anybody else flew the aircraft when we were not on the operational programme we would be in a state of nervous tension until we went down to Flights the next morning and found The Baron was safe and sound and undamaged.

By now the Battle of Britain had entered its most serious phase with the RAF barely holding its own. On 4 September 1940 Hitler declared, 'If the British Air Force drops two or four thousand kilograms of bombs, then we will in one night drop 150, 250, 300 or 400 thousand kilograms. When they declare that they will increase their attacks on our cities, then we will raze their cities to the ground...'

Night after night, night after night, the bombardment of London continues. I am nerveless and yet I am conscious that when I hear a motor in the empty street I tauten myself lest it be a bomb screaming towards me ... there is a lull now. The guns die down towards the horizon like a thunderstorm passing to the south. But they will come back again in fifteen minutes ... I have a sense of strain and unhappiness but none of fear. One feels so proud.

  – Diary of Sir Harold Nicholson, 19 September 1944

By the middle of September it was apparent the worst was over. The Battle of Britain had been won but only just. Large-scale daylight raids on London had dwindled away but the bombers still came back most evenings. Air raid sirens sounded every night, usually around 8 p.m., and people joked they could set their watch by them.

On a warm, soft evening in late September Geoff took off on ops as usual. The stars high in the night sky winked and blinked, casting a silvery-white brilliance in the late summer's night. They crossed the coast at Orford Ness and as he looked out of the cockpit window he saw London in the distance in the midst of a ferocious raid, aglow with red-orange flames. Smoke and fire rose above the city. He looked at the devastating sight and as he did so, feelings of panic and sadness such as he had never before experienced threaten to overcome him. The feelings were so intense it was all he could do to keep the aircraft steady and on course. Down there were his parents and sister, his precious family. He was sitting in an aircraft and flying away from the smoke and the devastation, but they and thousands of others were in the midst of something evil and dangerous. The sight was at once formidable and fascinating and he tried to stay calm and keep the bomber on course. It was a frustrating and dreadful situation to be in as he had no idea if his family were dead or alive. He felt powerless because he knew there was nothing he could do to save them.

'I thought those bastards, *those bastards!* They would get what they deserve.' And then suddenly he knew that what he was doing, however small, now, this very moment, was contributing to giving Hitler a good kick up the backside. Now more than ever he knew that he was fighting in a war in which it was abundantly clear there was a right and a wrong. He was on the side of the right and he would do everything in his power to prevent the evil he was fighting from ever achieving dominance.

Shortly after this incident he was home on leave and sitting in the garden with his family after supper. It had been a warm day and he was lapping up the last of the sun's rays, only half listening to Pat talking to her mother. The noise of the air-raid siren roused him.

'They're early tonight,' said Ethel as they scurried down into the Anderson shelter. The bombers approached.

'I bet they're Dorniers,' said Pat.

'No, they're Heinkels,' said Geoff. 'Listen. They have a distinctive sound which is different from other bombers.'

Hmmm, hmmm hmmm, they went. There was a whisper, then a faint whistle, rising to a shriek which seemed to fill the heavens, and then the *thud! thud!* as the bomb landed. They tensed automatically, half expecting the shelter to receive a direct hit and the earth to come cascading down on top of them and bury them.

Wave after wave came over that night and it was dawn when the all-clear sounded. They staggered out of the shelter in the half-light, tired and low in spirit, listening to the noise of ambulance sirens carting the dead and wounded to hospital, and smelling the acrid smoke of burning houses all around them. On the other side of the street an incendiary was burning steadily on the roof of a neighbour's house. The house was empty but Geoff knew if it was left to burn, the house would soon be engulfed by fire. He clambered on to the roof and managed to extinguish it with some sand and wet rags. His family watched him, knowing that although they had been lucky this time, the bombers would return the following evening, and the night after that.

The Observer reported:

In Britain rationing, high taxes and shortages have bitten deep into the average family's way of life. While expenditure on food, clothing and travel has been reduced drink and tobacco has doubled. Shortages of common items such as cigarettes, razor blades, torch batteries, vacuum flasks, cosmetics, prams and bicycles, has driven these goods on to the Black Market. Newspapers are reduced to four pages on several days of the month owing to shortage of newsprint.

On 8 November 1940 Wellington IC T2541 *T Tare* took off from Newmarket to bomb the marshalling yards at Munich, a distance slightly further than Berlin. At Ulm, northwest of Munich, they ran into an intense flak barrage.

Geoff circled the town to avoid the flak and as he did so he saw a large factory only dimly lit. Never one to let an opportunity go by regardless of danger, he switched on the intercom and explained to the crew what he intended doing.

'Let's have a go at this one, bomb aimer. Get ready. We'll drop just one.'

They descended to 5,000 feet, scoring a direct hit on the factory. They repeated the attack from 4,000 feet and once again hit the target, causing fires to break out. They flew on to Munich, clearly identifiable from afar by the intense concentration of searchlights, the marshalling yards visible in the bright moonlight. They dropped their bombs and turned quickly for home. But the night was not yet over. As they flew over Leipheim a flarepath shone brightly on an airfield – a good target and surely an opportunity not to be missed?

Geoff dived the Wellington to 500 feet, his gunners firing two quick bursts from both the front and rear turrets. The aircraft climbed to 1,000 feet as fires started below. They had probably hit dispersed aircraft. Nearing Ulm, they spied yet another airfield, undefended, and just waiting to be hit.

'What about it, Skipper?' said the front gunner.

'Why not!' said Geoff.

He again took the aircraft into a low dive while the gunners fired 4,000 rounds of ammunition on to the airfield. Flying over the factory at Ulm on their way home they saw it was still blazing merrily. 'We didn't half give that one a belting,' one of the crew observed.

With a feeling of a job well done they landed back at base after a trip of just over seven and a half hours. The following day Geoff was ordered to report to the CO, Wing Commander Ford. Apprehensive, he wondered if he should have dropped all the bombs on the main target instead of some on the factory at Ulm.

However he wasn't kept in suspense for long.

'Sit down, Rothwell,' Ford said pleasantly. 'I've read the intelligence report on last night's raid. It was a great effort and I think it's worthy of some recognition.'

Was he hearing right?

Wing Commander Ford went on: 'I intend recommending you for a DFC.'

A Distinguished Flying Cross! The feelings of wonder and surprise then gave way to exhilaration as he left Ford's office. The award of the Distinguished Flying Cross to Pilot Officer Geoffrey Maurice Rothwell was recorded in the *London Gazette* on 17 January 1941.

That day Maurice Rothwell was reading his newspaper when the name 'Rothwell' jumped out at him. Could it be? Surely not! But it was, indeed, his own son. It was typical that he and Ethel had to learn of their son's bravery from a newspaper, and this would happen again when he won subsequent medals. Geoff, although thrilled to receive the award, was a private person who shied away from glory. As far as he was concerned, the award should have gone to the whole crew – hell, it was a joint effort. He certainly had no intention of ever mentioning it to his family.

Not bad for a boy who was going to 'come to a bad end'.

6

OTU, PUBS AND PROMOTION

The moon hath raised her lamp above, to light the
way to thee, my love.
                    – Dion Boucicault and John Oxenford

December 1940
After four further operations at Newmarket Geoff was posted as
an instructor to Hampstead Norris, a satellite of the Operational
Training Unit at RAF Harwell, the RAF station where he had
carried out his operational training six months before. It had been
obvious to the authorities for some time now that the enthusiastic
and capable twenty-year-old would make a suitable instructor,
and they felt that a challenge such as this would bring out the best
in his character. At Hampstead Norris he was given the task of
instructing on dual-control Wellingtons without any prior training
in the art of teaching, but he was full of enthusiasm for this new
job and rushed headlong into it.

The airfield was a requisitioned farm on the top of a hill, ten
miles from Newbury in Berkshire; the runways and perimeter
tracks had been constructed in ploughed fields. The winter of
1940/41 was wet and cold and the ground was like a quagmire.
If a pilot's attention wandered for a second when taxying on the
narrow perimeter tracks, the aircraft would be axle-deep in mud
and often it would have to be towed out by a tractor. This was

a common sight as the unskilled instructors, unaccustomed to operating from the right-hand seat, were teaching equally unskilled pupils to taxi. It was all good fun, however, and there was an excellent spirit amongst the hard-working instructors. Geoff, who quickly adapted to instructing, was surprised to find he liked the work and enjoyed taking the young pilots under his wing.

The CO, Squadron Leader Bill Beaman, took an immediate liking to Geoff and would often loan him his private car to go down to a pub with the boys – a godsend as the men were restricted by lack of transport. Most evenings would be spent quaffing the local ale and playing darts and liar dice in the low-ceiling bars of pubs like the Bacon Arms in Newbury, where they were assured of a good meal, or The Hare and Hounds at Donnington a few miles away. This was run by an ex-police inspector with a waxed moustache and his wife who served delicious pickled onions with huge chunks of home-made crusty bread and as much cheese as the rations would permit – manna to starving young Air Force officers after they had drunk their fill of ale. At times they would roll around the floor in fits of laughter as 'Popeye' Lucas, a New Zealander, took out his false teeth and imitated the cartoon character after whom he was nicknamed. The local pub The Four Points – invariably referred to by RAF personnel as 'The Four Tits' – was not of a particularly high standard (an essential criterion for judging a posting) so was rarely visited.

After he had been at Hampstead Norris for three months, Geoff was posted with some of the other instructors to Moreton-in-Marsh in the picturesque Cotswolds where they were to start a new OTU. The Chief Flying Instructor at Harwell, Wing Commander 'Ginger' Cole, had been promoted to group captain and was now CO of the new station. Cole, a big man with a huge ginger 'RAF' moustache and a hearty sense of humour, was worshipped by his officers for his integrity and fairness. Geoff was still officially a pilot officer, although he was now due for promotion to flying officer on a time-served basis. However, he was never to wear the one thick stripe of a flying officer as shortly after arriving at Moreton he was promoted to acting flight lieutenant, so went straight from wearing one thin stripe to two thicker ones overnight.

He found it stimulating watching the new station grow from a handful of personnel to the arrival of the first course of pupils. The only aircraft on the station was an Anson, which was used to ferry the pilots to various maintenance units to collect new Wellingtons for equipping the OTU, and by the time they started instructing there was a fleet of aircraft. The OTU was situated in one of the prettiest parts of the country with many beautiful Cotswold villages within easy distance. Again, most evenings would be spent exploring the many good 'horsetilleries', as one of the flight sergeants would call the local watering holes, which abounded in the area. The Bell at Shipston-on-Stour became a home away from home, with the landlady, Mrs Scott-Dickson, known as Dicky, taking the young pilots to her heart and spoiling them.

There was many a time when, long after the other pubs were closed, the young officers were tempted to take further sustenance at The Fish Inn, which was situated at the top of a steep hill. This old pub was run by an Irish woman, Mrs Harrison, who, after hearing a knock on the door, would draw back the eye-level slide covering the grille and demand, 'Who would ye be and phwat would ye be wantin' at this toime o'noight?' When the inebriated young men had identified themselves, the door would be opened and in they would troop to carry on their drinking. Mrs Harrison was able to operate her establishment without fear of the law as the local policeman, equipped only with a bicycle and stationed in Broadway, was certainly not going to climb the hill after ten o'clock at night just to check whether the Fish was closed or not.

It was at the Bell in Shipston-on-Stour in April 1941 that Geoff, who adored dogs, acquired Wimpy, a springer spaniel puppy, from one of the regulars. Named after the indomitable Wellington, Wimpy was just a few weeks old and Geoff took him back to the station in the lapel of his greatcoat.

'Everybody loved Wimpy. I would take him down to the flights and the airmen would encourage him to follow them for a feed at their mess. The same thing would happen in the sergeants' and officers messes so in no time he became a roly-poly.'

Solly Burden, a Welsh warrant officer, was in the same flight as Geoff and the two became close friends. One day he invited Geoff and another friend to a weekend of Bacchanalian delight at his home in Treorchy, a village in the Rhondda Valley in South Wales. A framed religious text in their tiny but spotless bedroom warned them that 'The Day of Judgment is at Hand' (hardly the message wartime pilots needed). After a delicious meal cooked by Solly's mother, a charming, petite woman, Solly implored them: 'Come on, look you. It's time to take you both to the Red Cow to meet the tribe in the valley.'

The evening proved to be unforgettable. The Red Cow, unlike any other watering hole Geoff had visited, was a vast room with inches of sawdust covering the floor. Huge benches lined the walls, and large refectory-type tables stood at intervals. As soon as the Air Force officers entered the room they were greeted with a rousing reception, and the evening later turned into a musical occasion as they were serenaded with melody after melody, the beautiful Welsh voices swelling and filling the room, and the whole gathering joining in the choruses. They staggered home and fell into bed, secure in the knowledge that they did not have to wake early in the morning as the next day was a day of rest. How wrong can one be?

The next morning, Geoff was awakened by Solly. 'Come on, boyos, get your drinking boots on!'

He had one of the worst hangovers in his life and the very thought of getting up and drinking more was anathema, 'But Solly,' he said faintly, as even talking hurt. 'There are no pubs open on a Sunday.'

'We're not going to the pub, man. We're off to the Conservative Club, look you.' As Solly was well known for his extreme left-wing political views, he said in explanation, ''Tis the beer, Geoff boyo. The — sods keep the best beer in the village, man, so we have to overlook their political views.'

Altogether a weekend to be remembered.

'One of the cardinal rules in instructing is that instructors should exercise patience and never lose their temper,' said Geoff. That rule was in place before the arrival of Mucklethwaite, Geoff's pupil. Mucklethwaite and Geoff got off on the wrong foot right from the start as at their initial meeting it was his name that introduced an element of friction into their relationship. He had written Micklethwaite on the board.

> Instructing can be the most frustrating craft at times and the surprising feature of my association with Mucklethwaite was the speed at which he mastered the most critical part of flying – take-off and landing, eg full power for take-off, at 100 ft throttle back to climbing power, at 800 ft a 90deg climbing turn to port, level out at 1,000 feet with cruising power, 90deg turn to port downwind, when airfield disappears behind leading edge of the port wing make a 90deg turn to port, commence losing height, turn to port on to landing path, straighten up and land. However, Mucklethwaite seemed to have a mental blockage for everything in between the two operations. He thought nothing of ascending to 5,000 ft and would have kept on going if I had not taken control of the plane.

Geoff was to spend over nine hours instructing this pupil and on each occasion the same pattern would be repeated. On the last of these sessions Geoff gave vent to his bottled-up rage. In despair he went to one of the chief instructors, Max, who was one of the most capable instructors at the field. 'Would you like a second opinion?' he asked Geoff.

About twenty minutes later he saw a care-worn Max trudging across the tarmac looking very old. 'He came into the instructors' room and collapsed into an armchair and told me he didn't know how long I had lasted so long with this pupil as ten minutes had been sufficient to reduce him to a dithering wreck.'

Mucklethwaite was Geoff's only failure.

Geoff's twenty-first birthday was spent instructing in night circuits and landings. The usual procedure when the aircraft was due to land was for the pilot to signal the letter of the aircraft in Morse on the identification lamp and if permission to land was granted, the flarepath party would signal back with a green Aldis lamp. On this occasion instead of one green light, he saw hundreds of twinkling lights all over the airfield. Enemy aircraft must have dropped incendiary bombs. Quickly he grabbed the controls. 'We'll be sitting ducks if they're still in the area,' he told his pupil as he turned off the navigation lights and headed away from the airfield. Nothing further happened and as there was no sign of any enemy aircraft in the area, they circled the airfield and eventually were given permission to land. There they learned that the raiders had gone on to drop high-explosive bombs on nearby Little Rissington and Hullavington. Moreton, fortunately, received only incendiaries, causing little damage.

The next morning, amidst the resulting chaos of fire engines dowsing incendiaries and general hubbub, one of the Irish aircraft construction workers woke, still full of the local ale, and realised his bicycle had been moved. Completely unaware of what had happened during the night he yelled to all and sundry: 'And phwat would ye have done with me bleedin' boicycle.'

The year 1941 saw the situation steadily worsening for the Allies. Yugoslavia, Greece and Crete had fallen to the Germans in April and May and the *Afrika Korps* was winning in North Africa. On the home front on the night of 10/11 May London suffered one of its worst bombing attacks, which left a third of its streets impassable, an estimated 1,400 people dead and 1,800 badly injured.

It had taken eighteen long months of war before Bomber Command grasped a simple but remarkable truth about night bomber operations – that the airmen themselves were the last people to know what they had or had not achieved.

Throughout the war, part of the unique character of the bomber offensive was that the men who carried it out were totally dependent on their commanders for information about the success or failure of what they were doing. The bomber pilot, with rare exceptions such as the great fire-storms of Hamburg and Dresden, had to wait for the next bulletin from High Wycombe (Bomber Command Headquarters) to learn whether his colleagues were dying to good purpose or in vain. It was utterly necessary for him to believe that his

commanders' view of the bomber offensive was accurate. For
if it was not, then he was flying out each night to risk his life
and those of his crew for nothing.

– Max Hastings, *Bomber Command*

For Geoff this period at Moreton-in-Marsh was long and hard. He
missed living on a knife edge, the intensity of day-to-day physical
activity and the prospect of battle. Instructing was mostly tedious
and tiring, but more than anything he and the other instructors were
continually frustrated by their inability to return to operational
flying duties. Their answer was to play hard, and sometimes their
'play' would take the form of anti-social behaviour, such as the
time they broke up the mess furniture and threw glasses into the
fireplace. The trouble was they were like bored schoolboys needing
something to lift their spirits and alleviate the situation. Ginger
Cole, always supportive and understanding, turned a blind eye to
many of the indiscretions, realising they had to let off steam.

Sometimes they had collection sprees, keeping the loot in the
Flight Office, much to the consternation of Bob St John, the Flight
Commander, who came from Nelson, New Zealand. One of the
more extraordinary objects in the collection was a Belisha beacon
from London. There was also an array of Army officers' hats lifted
from coat racks when leaving a pub or restaurant. The relationship
between the RAF and the Army was never harmonious and this
type of behaviour did nothing to improve it. By contrast, the
Royal Navy and Royal Air Force always hit it off and it was quite
common to see the two services intermingling whenever they were
in the same pub.

'We were mad in those days,' says Geoff. 'We had a crest on
the door which some artist had painted on a wooden shield.'
Under the shield was a motto, *Nil carborundum bastardo zum* –
a variant of the more common *Illegitimi non carborundum* but
representing the same sentiment – don't let the bastards grind you
down. The shield featured a roll of toilet paper in one corner with
one sheet removed to represent 'tearing off a strip', the phrase
for a reprimand. In another corner were three trays – IN, OUT
and PENDING, with the IN and PENDING, piled high with

files and nothing in the OUT tray. A third pile had three dots like blackcurrants which were supposed to represent 'blacks' (misdemeanours). Ginger Cole was amused when he saw the crest but it's doubtful whether he would have reacted in the same way had he seen the stash of stolen property.

Another way of letting off steam was seeing how far they could drink their way around the Inner Circle line of the London Underground. This meant alighting at one of the thirty-odd stations, drinking a pint of beer at a pub, then going on to the next, and trying to cover as many stations as possible before closing time. The rushing up and down the stairs and running along the streets to find a pub, plus the fact that wartime beer was weak, helped to prevent them from becoming too intoxicated.

It was during these occasional visits to London that Geoff first saw the bombed-out refugees lying on mattresses or blankets in the Underground. They were packed like sardines and stretched from one end of the platform to the other, two or three deep. These indomitable Cockneys, most of whom had lost their homes and possessions, remained bright and cheerful in the face of privation and suffering. As they waited for a train, Geoff and his friends tried to keep up their morale by telling them they were bomber crews and were giving the Jerries more stick than they were giving London. Whopping lies, of course, because at that stage the British had no proof of any such thing.

It has been said that if Britain had understood in 1941 how powerful and how effortless was the German industrial machine, what enormous untapped potential it possessed, how widely its resources were dispersed, no one could have contemplated the overwhelming task of attempting to crush it by bombing. But the Air Ministry and the Ministry of Economic Warfare did not know this.

– Max Hastings, *Bomber Command*

One of Geoff's pupils at Moreton-in-Marsh was Ken Adams, a likeable Irishman. The two men struck up a rapport, so much so that when Ken got married he invited Geoff to the wedding.

Unfortunately, he was unable to attend as he was instructing that day so he did the next best thing – he 'beat up' the wedding reception which was held in the garden of the bride's home. Flying very low, he could see the startled expressions on the guests' faces. Shortly after his wedding Ken Adams was posted to Malta but crashed in Portugal and was killed. As soon as Geoff heard the news he wrote a letter of condolence to Ken's new wife, Pat.

> Writing condolence letters was a bloody awful job. I often think back to all those men who were killed, like Ken. When you served in a squadron you were like a family – you developed a camaraderie. You went on the piss together at the pub, played darts and shove-halfpenny, but you never got blasé and never developed a hard shell.

Every Operational Flying Control in the RAF had a large board on the wall with the numbers of aircraft and the time of take-off, ETA, missing, etc. Geoff recalled:

> No matter how tired you'd be when you got in from ops, which could be four or five in the morning, you would still check the board, and sometimes there would be a blank in the message space against a friend's name and crew. You would hope it was only wireless failure but you wouldn't know for sure until the following day. Then you would fall into bed and as soon as you woke up you would go down the corridor, look in his room, or go to the mess to check if he was there or not, and then on to the ops room, and there, you would see the dreaded word 'Missing'. And how many times have I seen that with my friends.

Unable to secure a posting back to an operational squadron, Geoff tried to relieve the monotony of life on an OTU by applying for courses, transfers or any job which might open up new opportunities and bring back a vestige of the glamour and excitement he had enjoyed whilst serving on a squadron. There was so much he missed about life at Newmarket – the smell of the dry grass on the landing strip, the thrill of going on operations, the pace of squadron life.

However, there had been a slight glitch in his previously unblemished copybook at Moreton-in-Marsh. He had decided at the last minute to beat up a football match while doing an air test as he thought it needed livening up. Unfortunately, Ginger Cole was standing on the touchline watching the match when Geoff appeared over the trees and proceeded to dive-bomb the field. This caused a certain amount of chaos amongst spectators and players alike, and Geoff was duly carpeted and received a good ticking off from Cole. To this day he believes it was this incident which finally got him a posting (not the one he expected) because he had been at Upavon on a short instructors' course for only a week when he was summoned to the Adjutant's office and handed a postagram. Incredulously he read: 'Report to No. 2 Personnel Dispersal Centre, Wilmslow, for allocation of transport to RAFDEL, Washington, for liaison duties in an Acting Squadron Leader post.'

Washington! Squadron Leader! It was all so totally unexpected. Not only was he overwhelmed by the fact that he had been promoted but he was also going into the unknown – his first experience of a foreign country. He returned to Moreton-in-Marsh to collect his kit and clear the station, and while he was doing this he was told to report to Cole.

'Thanks for all the work you've done, my boy,' said Cole, shaking Geoff's hand. 'I congratulate you on your promotion and wish you the best of luck in America. I quite understand your frustration – you've probably been instructing too long.'

Geoff knew he had been a pain in the arse. But under Cole he had risen from pilot officer to squadron leader. He had just over 1,000 hours' flying time and had consistently been given assessments of 'above average' as a heavy bomber pilot and an OTU instructor.

He was twenty-one years old.

7

NEW WORLD EXPERIENCE

Why do we fall in love? I do believe
That virtue is the magnet, the small vein
of ore, the spark, the torch that we receive
At birth, and that we render back again.
— Alice Duer Miller, *The White Cliffs*

March/April 1942
The bombing of Pearl Harbor in December 1941 caused a jubilant
Churchill to write later:

To have the United States at our side was to me the greatest
joy … so we had won after all! England would live, Britain
would live … Once again in our long island history we should
emerge, however mauled or mutilated, safe and victorious …

As Geoff had only four days' leave prior to his departure to
the United States there was scarcely time for anything other
than to make arrangements for Wimpy to stay with his parents,
sort through his kit and say goodbye to his family. There was
much excitement in the Rothwell home. When Ethel looked at
her tall, good-looking son she could hardly speak for joy and
pride. Her son, a squadron leader! And ten-year-old Pat, who
hero-worshipped him, wanted all her friends to see her handsome
pilot brother before he left for America.

Geoff telephoned Pat Adams, Ken Adams' widow, and told her he was coming to London en route for Manchester and America. They arranged to meet in an old pub, The Captain's Cabin near Piccadilly Circus. Pat, *née* Harrison, had been born in Malaya, where her father, an expert in anti-malaria control, had been the manager of a rubber plantation. The family had returned to England in 1928 and settled near Winchester. Now, determined to 'do her bit' for the war effort, Pat was driving ambulances in the Blitz on London.

They duly met, had a drink and a meal, then saw a movie. Geoff eyed her surreptitiously. Beautiful and slender with curly light brown hair and deep dark eyes, she was a real good-looker. She had a habit of speaking quickly with a clipped English accent, the words pouring out one over the other. He can't remember the name of the movie now, but all he recalls is sitting beside her in the cinema and knowing undoubtedly he had fallen in love with her.

'This being in love was such a strange feeling for me, so unexpected. I felt dazed and knew that Pat was totally different from any other woman I had ever met.'

For this to happen now, *now* when he was leaving for America, with no idea when he would be back... He was in a quandary, wondering if he should say anything to her as he had known her only a few hours. He wanted to ask her to wait for him, but it would be unfair – the timing was not quite right as she had so recently become a widow.

He decided to say nothing and tried to telephone her before he left England, but was unsuccessful as communication was difficult, with military matters taking precedence. In the end, he wrote to her quickly, explaining his feelings and saying he would quite understand if she decided she could not wait for him. It was a long time before he received an answer as overseas mail went by sea in those days. The reply, when it finally came to Albany, Georgia, made him jubilant. She was surprised by his declaration of love, but yes, she would wait for him. In the words of a popular song, it was ''S'wonderful, 'S'marvellous, that you should care for me.'

Geoff, in the company of two other squadron leaders, was posted to the South East Air Corps Training Center at Maxwell Field, Montgomery, Alabama. Their job was to educate Americans as to what was taking place on the European front. Most imagined the US Air Force was engaged in combat, despite the fact that, at this stage, it had flown no missions over Germany. Therefore it was to be their job to let Americans know the fallacy of this impression. Putting aside traditional English modesty, they were to embroider incidents or, as they say in the RAF, shoot a line. They were invited to talk to Rotary Clubs, Lions and Kiwanis and were also expected to introduce RAF training methods into the American system.

Several newspapers interviewed Geoff.

RAF PILOT, 22, Tells of Raids over Germany
Church Group hears of 37 personal 'Visits' Beyond Enemy
Lines
Britain's bombers are pounding the continent nightly and carrying the war to Hitler's own backyard, Flight Lt Geoffrey Rothwell of the Royal Air Force told members of the Fellowship Club of the South Highlands Presbyterian Church Thursday night following a dinner in his honor.

Painting a graphic picture of the Royal Air Force's bombing raids on the leading cities of Nazi Germany Lt Rothwell indicated he had paid some 37 personal 'visits' to Berlin, Emden and other German and German-occupied cities.

A robust, red-haired young man of 22 years, Lt Rothwell is a veteran of more than two years of combat flying and has been decorated by the King for distinguished service. He was in training with the RAF for six months before the outbreak of war and began flying in combat shortly after the start of hostilities.

Young Rothwell was one of the fliers who took part in the desperate and heroic efforts of the Royal Air Force to fight off German planes during the 'miracle of Dunkerque.' Much of the success of the evacuation he attributed to the British fighter command and the bomber command which smashed the advancing German columns and relieved pressure on the hard pressed rear guard.

Tribute was paid by the lieutenant to American planes which are being used by the Royal Air Force. Once he flew an American plane in after an air raid and when landing at the airdrome found a hole three feet in diameter in one of the wings, he said.

Describing many changes in his country, Lt Rothwell said that most of the golf courses now are converted into patches of cabbages and carrots.

The young officer told of seeing women and children killed and maimed in bombing raids over England, and related an instance when a comrade, forced to bail out of his burning plane over a German city was caught in the glare of a searchlight and his body was riddled with bullets.

In America only three weeks, the young flier's own impression of the country, he said, may be summed up in the word 'colossal'. And he commented on the many wooded areas which may be found in all sections of this country that he has visited.

The lieutenant who is stationed with an RAF training group at Maxwell Field, Montgomery was accompanied to Birmingham by Pilot Officer J. Gatiss who flew him here.

While at Maxwell Field Geoff took a flying medical test which included the lshihara Test for colour blindness.

'How many ops did you say you have flown in Bomber Command?' asked Harry Mantz, the medical officer.

'Thirty-seven. Why?'

'Because, my boy, you've failed and you wouldn't have been accepted for flying training by the USAAC. You're colour-blind.'

'Colour-blind my foot!' said an amazed Geoff. 'I've flown as many hours at night as I have day, and I would never have been able to identify the green or red Aldis lamp signal from the flarepath for landing if I'd been colour-blind.'

They concluded that the reason Geoff had been accepted by the RAF in 1939 was that in desperation to recruit aircrew, Geoff's slight colour-blindness had been overlooked.

A highlight of Geoff's tour of duty in the United States was when, in the company of English fighter pilot Johnny Freeborn, they visited Twentieth Century Fox film studios and met several stars, including Betty Grable and Tyrone Power. Power, acting in the film *Crash Dive* (a film Geoff was not to see until November 1988) had difficulty with one of his lines, getting a 'cup of coffee' to come out as 'cuff of coppy' and causing the scene to be shot over and over again.

'God damn it, man,' yelled the director. 'You're ruining me. This is colour film. You're costing me millions of dollars a day.'

News from Britain showed bombing techniques had been improved and Geoff was eager to be back in the fray. He had been away from England for over eight months, and although it had been an interesting posting it was time to move on. Even more than that, he felt he was remote in this part of the United States – somehow the war seemed far away. It was nearly the end of 1942 and the war had taken a turn for the better. 'It was the end of the beginning' and Geoff wanted to return to the action.

He had met people like Archie MacLachlan, the fighter ace who had lost an arm during the defence of Malta. Geoff had been detailed to see how he would cope with two throttles and a control column; Archie coped brilliantly by using his knees to hold the stick and constantly trimming the aircraft to fly 'hands off' most of the time.

Also he was missing Pat and although they had corresponded regularly and she had sent him her photograph and visited his family, he was desperate to get to know her better. He set sail from Halifax, Nova Scotia on the *Cavina,* a cramped and uncomfortable 3,000-ton banana boat, and got to know Anna Neagle and Herbert Wilcox who were passengers returning to England. The *Cavina* was part of a large convoy in the midst of murky, mid–winter Atlantic weather. A number of ships had been sunk in U-boat attacks and a few days out from Canada Geoff woke one night to the sound of depth charges exploding. Rushing up on deck he witnessed a Royal Canadian Navy destroyer circling astern and firing the depth charges on what must have been a submerged U-boat. Fortunately, it had failed to attack the *Cavina* although it was reported that two other ships in the convoy had been sunk. They reached Bristol safely and Geoff landed in 'the olde countrie' in December to cold, damp weather. With that he knew he was was truly back in England.

8

STIRLING WORK

We are going to scourge the Third Reich from end to end. We are bombing Germany city by city and ever more terribly in order to make it impossible for her to go on with the war. That is our object; we shall pursue it relentlessly.

– Sir Arthur Harris

December 1942
In the Western Desert the army of the Desert Fox, General Erwin Rommel, retreated back across the border from Egypt, and Benghazi fell to the Allies. The tides of war were at last starting to turn in favour of the Allies. Whereas in 1942 the Axis powers had been winning the war on all sides, now it was losing on every front. With the key battles of the Coral Sea, Midway, Guadalcanal, North Africa and Stalingrad having been fought and won the way was now clear for the Allies – only victory lay ahead.

On 6 December newspapers announced:

... the war in the air has reached a stage where German bombers hardly venture into British skies, while Bomber Command pounds German cities almost every night. It is, however, a time of some concern for the RAF. Bomber losses during the year have been high with 1,453 aircraft lost and 2,724 damaged in action.

Geoff was thrilled to be back in England and even the winter weather, shortages, restrictions and blackouts could not curtail his delight to be in his own country again. He could hardly wait to meet up with Pat Adams again and they arranged to meet as soon as they both got leave. He wondered how they would feel towards each other after an absence of nearly a year. He was both nervous and excited at the thought of meeting her, but the reunion was everything he had wished for and more. She hadn't changed and they discovered they had much in common. Within a short time he began to realise this was the woman he wanted to marry. He still could not discuss this with her as he felt it was too soon after Ken's death and he knew she wasn't ready for such a huge step. And there was always the thought that she might lose him as she had Ken.

It was a strange feeling, this being in love – to want to spend every waking moment with her. What was the French expression we borrowed, that first intense feeling of love at first sight? – *un coup de foudre*, a lightning strike – and it was true. There was no other feeling like it in the world. Now he knew what his mother meant when she had replied to his 'How do you know when you are in love, Mother?'

'You know you love that person when you know all their faults but still love them.'

Not that he could find any fault with Pat. She was his Sweet Pea, or SP for short. There was a complete lack of class-consciousness about her, despite her privileged upbringing. He loved her sense of fun, her vulnerability and the way she cried at sad movies, her sweet nature and her extraordinary resilience in the face of tragedy. She was kind-hearted to all creatures and her sense of patriotism and devotion to duty epitomised everything that was decent in a world gone mad.

She wanted him to meet her family and that was the beginning of a lifelong friendship between Geoff and the Harrisons. They had three daughters – Pat was the eldest, Nancy, training to be an actress, then Ann – and one son, Chris, or 'Chibby', as he was known from his initials C. J. B., who was at boarding school. Geoff would often stay at their home, the Old Rectory in Kingsworthy, and days were spent going for long walks in the country, and evenings talking quietly together before a roaring fire, Pat's parents discreetly leaving them alone.

She was starting to fall in love with him. It wasn't just the glamour of his job, perhaps it was his voice that made her love him. It was deep and clear and radiated strength and promise – promise for the coming day. He had a gift for reassurance and he was always making her laugh. There was a self-assurance about him, a confidence, which she embraced completely. She had already gone through so much, but she knew instinctively this man would never let her down, that somehow, despite what might happen, she would have him forever. It was impossible to be depressed around Geoff for long. If she felt a little down he would look at her with a twinkle in his eyes, laugh that hearty laugh of his and squeeze her arm.

At the end of January 1943 Geoff was posted to RAF Stradishall, near Bury St Edmunds in Suffolk, in No. 3 Group, to convert on to Short Stirlings. The Stirling was not a glamorous aircraft like the Lancaster or Mosquito, which all pilots wanted to fly, and it was unable to reach the altitude at which those aircraft operated. Mosquitoes cruised at altitudes of 18–20,000 feet but the Stirling was limited to around 10–12,000 feet. Consequently it was vulnerable to flak, which was more accurate at the lower level. The mighty four-engined Short Stirling III had a wingspan of just under 100 feet and an all-up weight of 70,000 pounds. Its cockpit was so high off the ground a pilot could suffer from vertigo. The casualty rate of Stirlings was quite high. However, they were manoeuvrable, with reliable Bristol engines, and Geoff enjoyed flying them. It was unfortunate they had a complex electrical system, which gave endless trouble, and a poor serviceability record.

On the conversion course Geoff was allocated a crew in which there were three New Zealanders – Jacky Drawbridge, the navigator, a diminutive teetotaller from Wellington, Wal' Fielding, the bomb aimer from Christchurch, a real 'smoothie' who was a hit with the ladies, and Ian Entwistle, known as 'Whistle', the wireless operator, who came from Hawera and looked as though he should still be at school. Right from the beginning they all got on well and Geoff looked forward to operating with a keen crew who rapidly began to take on a professional air

The course finished in February and when the postings came through he was delighted to find they were going to 75 (New Zealand) Squadron, at, of all places, Newmarket. It was the first Commonwealth squadron to be formed in Bomber Command and was to gain great distinction throughout a prodigiously active operational service, achieving the fourth-highest number of sorties in Bomber Command and a Victoria Cross winner, James Ward. For Geoff, returning to Newmarket, where he had completed his first tour, was like a homecoming. He remembered the kindness and generosity of the local people and he was again given a warm reception.

Their first operation together on 1 March 1943 in Stirling I BF451 involved them in one of the heaviest attacks on Berlin in the war so far. As they were turning for home and two hundred miles from the target, Geoff looked out of the cockpit window. Even at that distance he could still see the glow from the incendiaries. On to Osnabruck, and suddenly the night sky was lit up like a carnival. They had run into intense flak. Shells burst with deadly accuracy all around the Stirling, causing air flow disturbance and making the huge aircraft lurch from side to side. *Whoosh! Thump!* Geoff hauled back on the control column to climb away from the flak, and as he did so he heard a thumping sound and the controls were almost wrenched from his grasp.

'What the hell was that?' yelled Ginge Negus from the mid-upper turret as anti-aircraft shells burst under the aircraft, hurling it aside as though a titanic hand had shaken it. The engines screamed an octave above their normal tone before the Stirling steadied itself.

'Are you all right, Captain?' asked Ginge as Geoff dived the aircraft to try to escape from the barrage of predicted heavy flak.

'I'm fine. We've taken a couple of knocks but the controls are working.'

It was then that he saw the Junkers 88 on the port beam. With its grotesque black shape, it reminded Geoff of a giant insect waiting to pounce.

Its engines reputedly sang a duet – one in the voice of a tenor, the other a vibrating bass. He could see the aircraft's wing shining in the bright moonlight and in that split second he knew they were going to be attacked and he knew quite calmly he could defeat it. He took the Stirling into another manoeuvre, the customary 'corkscrew' – diving, banking and climbing as the gunners swung their turrets around to follow the enemy aircraft.

The Junkers fired but it was a near miss. He hauled back on the control column so the nose shot up and the aircraft hung on its propellers, whilst Ginge, in the mid-upper turret, fired furiously into the darkness. The enemy aircraft passed over the Stirling, its black and white cross on the fuselage clearly identifiable. For a second he was transfixed by the sight. 'I'm going to fight this beast,' he thought. 'We're going to get out of this, and we're going to shoot it down. We'll shoot the bugger down, that's what we'll do.'

The perspiration was dripping off his forehead as he tried to keep the aircraft steady. He was angry now and then scared. 'You're not going to get us, you bastard,' he yelled. The Junkers swooped and dived and danced and fired one more burst, this time missing the Stirling by a mile.

'Either he's a lousy shot or he can't see a bloody thing,' said little Jacky Drawbridge, who had left his navigator's seat and was standing in the second pilot's position.

Geoff stared at the huge machine with its secret radar aerials. Suddenly, he felt confident. 'There's nothing to worry about,' he said. 'There's nothing to worry about at all. We're going to get him.'

The Junkers climbed steeply, veering away to the right and continuing out to sea. It must come back again, surely, they thought, but they never saw it again that night.

'Holy Mother of God,' whispered Jacky. 'That was a close shave.'

But they were not to escape unscathed. Suddenly, over the intercom came: 'One-one-oh closing dead astern just below!' from Jock, the rear gunner. This time it was a Messerschmitt. And each time Geoff played his game. 'Come closer, you bastard, come into our web,' he said, manoeuvring the Stirling as he saw it clearly in the moonlight. The black and white crosses on the fuselage and rudder danced and swayed in front of his eyes. *Come closer, said the spider to the fly, as they chased each other around the sky.* Ginger Negus let out a squeal of joy. 'I've got the sod!' He watched the Messerschmitt plummet into the darkness, orange flames shooting out of the nose of the machine and trailing black smoke. Like a dying eagle, it dipped its wing and dived towards the sea.

They had strayed a little from their track and Geoff found it difficult keeping the aircraft on course as the flak grew more intense. We're not out of the woods yet, he thought. The sound of the windscreen shattering cut into his thoughts. A blast of cold air struck him in the face, causing him to don the goggles on his flying helmet. The flight engineer stuffed an engine cover into the hole. There were numerous holes in the wings and fuselage but the crippled Stirling struggled on home, and after a journey of eight and a half hours, Geoff's longest flight to date, they finally landed at Stradishall.

Operations continued to the Ruhr Valley and to the port of Hamburg. Briefed for an attack on Nuremberg, they had to turn back owing to the failure of one engine. It was more difficult flying a Stirling on three engines than Lancasters and Halifaxes, but after jettisoning 300 gallons of fuel to reduce weight they managed to return with their load of bombs.

On 9 March they set off to Munich in Stirling I BF443 with an incendiary bomb load. All went well and the attack, which started large fires in the target area, was successful. On the way home they congratulated themselves on a successful trip but they couldn't relax, not even for a moment. There was always the thought that the enemy would still be after blood, even though the attack was now complete. They had been airborne for almost eight hours – another long, tiring trip.

'Getting dangerously low on fuel, Skip,' said the flight engineer. With any luck they would have just enough to get back, otherwise they would be ditching in the North Sea. On they flew through the dark night, nearer and nearer to home. Finally, they were over England and approaching base. As they came within sight of Newmarket Geoff called up on the radio.

'V Victor. Angels three. ETA two minutes. Short of fuel. Request emergency landing. Over.'

'Roger, V Victor. You're cleared for immediate landing. Call when on approach. Over.'

'Roger, out.'

The dim lights of the flarepath came into sight on the southern side of the town.

'V Victor. On approach. Over.'

'Roger V Victor. Clear to land. Out.'

Undercarriage down ... 500 feet ... flaps down ... 400 ... 200 ... blast – he wasn't properly lined up with the flarepath. He pushed the throttles forward to overshoot and as he did so, both outer engines cut out, and with that he knew quite clearly a crash landing was inevitable. It would be impossible to maintain height with flaps and wheels down and only two engines functioning.

'Stand by for a crash landing,' he told the crew.

The ground was coming up now in front of him, shining clearly in the moonlight. He hauled back on the control column and the huge aircraft was down and came to an abrupt stop.

'V Victor. Landed safely. Whereabouts unknown.'

'Roger, V Victor. We can't see your navigation lights. Turn on your landing lights.'

Ginge Negus came up to the control deck. 'A wizard landing, Skip,' he said.

Eventually they were spotted and the driver of the transport sent to collect them greeted them with: 'You chose an odd place to land, sir.'

Incredibly, they had landed on Newmarket Heath, parallel to the Cambridge to Newmarket road and with the nose pointing straight down Newmarket High Street! It had all been a wizard show, but they had had a narrow escape, especially as an inspection the following day revealed that the starboard wheel had actually passed over the rim of a concrete gun emplacement pit. Had it travelled a foot to one side, it would have been a different story, as the undercarriage would have collapsed and a serious pile-up would have occurred. Later, the ground crew told them there were only five gallons of petrol left in the tanks.

Close friendships were made in 75 Squadron. One particular friend of Geoff's was Fray Ormerod, a tall, lanky New Zealander known as 'Slim', who rivalled Geoff for height.

Fray recalls that although Geoff had a reputation for 'creating chaos and hoopdedoodle', his unshakable courage and devotion to duty had a profound effect on all of them. 'He worked hard and played hard – his enthusiasm for life was infectious and this helped to ease tensions.'

Relaxation was vitally important as they were living in extremely stressful times. At this stage of the war the casualty rate was exceptionally high and death never seemed far away from them all.

'The line between the living and the dead was very thin,' wrote Flight Lieutenant Denis Horsney from 76 Squadron. 'If you live on the brink of death yourself, it is as if those who have gone have merely caught an earlier train to the same destination. And whatever that destination is, you will be sharing it soon, since you will almost certainly be catching the next one.'

Some people expected bomber aircrew to behave in a sombre and reflective way at all times, and were puzzled and mildly disapproving of anything indicating high spirits. Officers should behave with decorum and dignity, they said, and any other type of behaviour was unbecoming.

'Thank goodness there were men like Geoff who encouraged us to let off steam,' says Fray. 'He never exhibited any signs of depression – his example was very positive indeed.'

There were many times when the two men took part in off-duty escapades in which the stimulus of alcohol played a large part. According to Fray, Geoff was the first to recognise the potential of the red lanterns which sat on top of the massive concrete tank barriers beside the roads, by throwing them into the trees and shouting out 'Light flak!" It took all the application of alcohol-inspired imagination to see the resemblance but they loyally applauded his efforts to develop this fascinating new technology. Not surprisingly, the number of lanterns on display dwindled a bit and Geoff, accepting the need for conservation, found a new use for them. He would bring one home to the mess and go around the bedrooms, irrespective of the time, looking for sleeping figures. When he found one he would sit down companionably, pull back the bedclothes, hold up the lantern, and say:

'Slim, old boy, have you seen the light? If not, it's high time you did!'

But high spirits in which Geoff was involved often meant trouble. Their mess was in Sefton Lodge, a requisitioned private house on the other side of Newmarket from the racecourse. One evening Geoff decided to have a few beers in the Golden Lion before dinner with Archie Marsden, a squadron intelligence officer. After a few drinks they set off for Sefton Lodge on Archie's bike, Archie sitting on the crossbar whilst Geoff sat on the saddle and pedalled. There were no lights on the bike but as the traffic at night virtually ceased they weren't worried. That is, until they met a policeman on his bicycle, going the opposite way. He yelled at them to stop and made a U-turn to follow them.

To hell with that! Geoff pedalled furiously and raced into the drive of Sefton Lodge well ahead of their pursuer. They threw the bike into the bushes and rushed through the French windows into the dining room, where a few officers were finishing their meal. They collapsed into some chairs, gasping for breath and nearly hysterical with laughter. They had the sense to grab some coffee and a morsel of cheese and biscuits in the hope of giving the impression they were just completing their dinner in case they were followed. Not a moment too soon, for a few minutes later the dining room door opened and the mess secretary entered, followed by the constable. After an intense scrutiny of all present and not recognising the errant cyclists, the constable left to search elsewhere, whilst Geoff and Archie congratulated themselves on their quick thinking.

One day they brought a racehorse into the mess from the stables adjoining Sefton Lodge via the French windows. The horse had been encouraged to enter the mess by giving it a bowl of the morning's breakfast cereal, which the men regarded as unfit for human consumption. The pranksters hoped the animal would leave some evidence of having been in the anteroom but fortunately this did not eventuate. Then someone thought up the idea of leaving the horse in Eric Fowler's bedroom, Eric being a fellow flight commander of Geoff's. They had just managed to get the horse up a few stairs when a visiting wing commander came into the mess, realised the danger to the horse and persuaded the men to return the poor animal to the stable.

One day the men were sitting in the anteroom after lunch reading the papers when, for no reason at all, a cushion fight started in which Bill Scollay, the squadron navigation leader, and Slim Ormerod were leading participants. It reached the stage when the strain was too much and the cushions burst, shedding feathers over the entire room. It was like a snowstorm and became even worse when someone introduced water into the act. The mess was indescribable and it took many hands to clear it up and restore some order, but the room retained a damp and soggy look for days. To this day Geoff wonders if the owners were adequately recompensed for the damage sustained to their elegant home at the hands of exuberant Air Force officers.

After briefing, crews would be taken by bus back to Sefton Lodge for what was morbidly called the last supper, afterwards they would be returned by bus to the airfield. It was common on the journey to the airfield to see queues of people waiting outside the local cinema, and Geoff would kneel on the window seat, shake the bars of the bus windows and address the amazed crowd. 'Let me out! Let me out! I'm not mad! They're taking me away! I don't want to fly! Please help me! I'm too young to die!'

Many years later in 1978, Geoff attended a grand reunion of 75 Squadron at Cambridge and whilst there a speech was made by Air Chief Marshal Sir Douglas Lowe, who referred to the incident. Lowe had been a sergeant pilot in Geoff's flight.

Geoff was a natural leader who had the gift of instilling positivity and confidence in his men. His crew thought the world of their skipper, trusting him implicitly and knowing he was a good pilot – one of the very best.

> The decisive factor in the morale of bomber aircrew, like that of all fighting men, was leadership. At first, it is difficult to understand what impact a leader can have, when in battle his men are flying with only their own crews over Germany, far out of sight and command. Yet a post-war 8 Group medical report stated emphatically: 'The morale of a squadron was almost always in direct proportion to the quality of leadership shown by the squadron commanders, and the fluctuations in this respect were most remarkable.'
>
> – Max Hastings, *Bomber Command*

Inevitably, the stress of operations took its toll on many in Bomber Command, but because they were young and fit and resilient they recovered enough to live life to the full by wining and dancing and making love to pretty girls. It was essential to have a vestige of normal life around them, to divert their thoughts from killing and avoiding death. The strain of nights with little sleep, waiting at dispersal for the order to take off, and then night after night flying for six hours or longer in the biting cold of a bomber, all took its toll. Without stating the obvious, most knew it was a case of 'Eat, drink and be merry, for tomorrow we die.'

Geoff flew almost every day and entries in his log book for 1943 testify to the high workload. He flew on 26 and 27 of February, the 1st, 3rd, 5th, 8th, and 9th of March – seven sorties in twelve days. The average flying time of these trips was over six hours to targets such as Hamburg, Munich and Berlin, which were near the limit of the Stirling's range and endurance.

In his smart Air Force uniform, many women on and off the station found the good-looking squadron leader attractive. When Pat Adams was unable to get leave, Geoff would occasionally take out girls like Lucille Smith, who loved horses and who lived close to his family. He would enjoy the company of other women but there was only Sweet Pea for him. Their leaves together were precious and they would make the most of them as there was always the thought that it might be the last time they would see each other. They would hold each other tightly while dancing at Odininos in Piccadilly to the haunting lyrics of 'The More I See You' and other popular songs. Sometimes he took S.P. to visit his family, and Ethel would look at her son and see the happiness on his face and pray it would last, and that they would all survive this terrible war, somehow.

At the end of March 75 Squadron was inspected by the base commander, Air Commodore 'Square' McKee, a New Zealander serving in the RAF, later to become Air Marshal Sir Andrew McKee. 'Hello, Rothwell,' he said, on being introduced to Geoff. 'Where are you from?' expecting Geoff to say some town in New Zealand.

'From England, sir.' There was a pause.

'I'm terribly sorry, my boy,' McKee said apologetically, 'but it's the New Zealand Government's policy to staff senior posts with New Zealanders. It's nothing personal but I'm afraid I'll have to post you.'

Geoff was dismayed but then McKee went on to say that he would be able to retain his crew wherever he went. A few days later the posting came through to 218 (Gold Coast) Squadron at Downham Market in East Anglia. New Zealander Squadron Leader Dick Broadbent took over Geoff's flight.

'It was a daunting prospect taking over Geoff's flight,' Broadbent remembers. 'A real leader, Geoff had a reputation of doing a first-class job. Not only did he get on with the job in hand, but he had the extraordinary ability of being an extremely able pilot as well as a proficient flight commander. All this, coupled with the fact that he was well-liked and respected and the squadron was really sorry to see him go.'

At the time when Broadbent took over at Newmarket morale was at an all-time low. With the high casualty rate and the many near misses, with aircraft finding it increasingly difficult to land and take off from the unsuitable airfield, few finished their tour of operations. An additional hazard was Devil's Dyke, a bank which ran across the end of the take-off path and was hit by several aircraft which failed to become airborne soon enough. The squadron eventually moved to RAF Mepal.

Two days before his twenty-third birthday Geoff and his crew bade a sad farewell to 75 Squadron. Despite the dangers and near misses it had been a happy time for him.

'I wouldn't have missed being at Newmarket for worlds. I met a grand bunch of fellows, we completed nine operations, and I made many friends – some for life.'

9

TARGET FOR TONIGHT

Weary, we dodge the heaven-splitting flame.
Then, with no certain victory to impart,
Out of the dawn we drop from frosty height,
Welcomed alone by those who saw us start
And watched and waited for us through the night.
– P. Heath, *We, The Bombers*

The veteran 218 (Gold Coast) Squadron at Downham Market in Norfolk was so named as it had been adopted by the people of the Gold Coast in West Africa in 1941. At first the squadron operated with twin-engined Vickers Wellington bombers, but from February 1942 it was equipped with the Short Stirling. By the time Geoff and his crew arrived in April 1943 the Stirlings were a familiar sight over Downham Village.

At the end of April 1943 an investigation was carried out by Bomber Command to try to establish the cause of 218's high loss rate. No. 3 Group had the highest losers with eight failures to return, the New Zealanders of 75 (NZ) Squadron being particularly unlucky with four missing crews, while 90 Squadron made up the numbers with a single loss. After an extensive examination of all available information the eight-page report concluded that the major cause of the losses was light flak and sheer bad luck! The squadron topped the group for sorties during April with 127 and this produced a new record of 708 flying hours. It also topped the table for monthly mine-laying sorties with 26.

RAF Station Downham Market was a charming location, close to the village, which had a very old and attractive village church. The officers' mess was housed in the rectory in beautiful grounds, and the airfield was situated across the road, surrounded by a profusion of apple trees and blackberry bushes. Geoff enjoyed renewing his acquaintanceship with the new CO, Wing Commander Don Saville, the Australian with the pencil moustache whom Geoff had encountered at Kemble in November 1939 on a cross-country exercise. At thirty-nine years of age he was probably the oldest RAF pilot still flying on operations and in the next few months he became extremely popular. 'You always knew where you were with him and the troops loved him,' says Geoff.

In *St Vith to Victory*, Steve Smith wrote about Wing Commander Donald Saville DFC:

Born in 1903 in Portland, New South Wales he joined the RAAF in May 1927. He was granted a short service commission in the RAF in February 1928 and served with a number of fighter and bomber squadrons in the UK until his transfer back to the RAAF in Feb 1932. On leaving the RAAF he became a flying instructor with the Tasmanian Aero Club and in 1937 joined the Australian National Airways where he remained until the outbreak of war. On re-joining the RAF Saville was posted to No. 2 Ferry School where he could utilise his vast experience of 8046.35 flying hours. In August 1941 he was put in the front line and after completing his course at 21 OTU at Moreton-in-Marsh, he was posted to 12 Squadron at Binbrook to fly Wellingtons. On Dec 2 he was posted as a flight commander to the newly-formed 458 RAAF Squadron at Holme-on-Spalding Moor, and in early 1942 was given command of a detachment of the squadron sent to the Middle East.

When 458 was handed a new role he was posted to command 104 Squadron at Kabrit. He was awarded a Bar to his DFC and by the completion of his tour in February 1943 he had 47 ops to his credit.

Inexplicably Saville was not screened from ops for the usual six month rest period and within weeks of his arrival back in the UK the tough, no-nonsense Australian was commanding 218 Squadron. Some found his style of leadership refreshing, while others thought he was a typical Aussie, loud, rude and self-opinionated. However, all agreed he was a first rate pilot and a true leader of men.

The target on the night of 4 April 1943 was Kiel. Geoff and his crew were detailed to fly Stirling III BK650. 'Target ahead, Skip,' said Jacky Drawbridge. It was difficult to see anything as there was 10/10 cloud cover. Geoff could hear the heavy flak tearing and slicing into the aircraft. To escape further damage he put the aircraft into a steep dive. He looked at the altimeter; they had lost 800 feet and were still losing height. He had to pull out of the dive and quickly. He eased the stick back and slowly the nose began to rise. He closed the throttles as the airspeed had increased alarmingly but they were not out of danger from the flak, which was now bursting above them. They ran up on the target, dropped their bombs and headed for home.

On the return journey Geoff's thoughts were interrupted by the voice of the flight engineer on the intercom.

'Fuel supply low, Skip. One of the tanks must have been hit when we ran into that heavy flak.'

'Roger, Mike. What's our ETA at the English coast, navigator?'

'Another twenty minutes, Captain,' said Jacky Drawbridge.

'Roger. Get Whistle on the intercom and write out an SOS message.' Then 'Whistle, get on to base, and ask for a QDM.'

The flight engineer was perpetually monitoring the fuel gauges, and they registered just above empty. Geoff had enough to climb to 3,000 feet and tell the crew to bail out if they made landfall, then fly on until the engines cut, and bail out himself.

A sliver of cold sweat ran down his neck as he made his decision, and his fingers felt cold and stiff inside his gloves. So it had finally come. He had always wondered what it would be like, his last few minutes of life. Would his life flash in front of his eyes? Maybe, maybe, if he just held his present course and altitude for another ten or fifteen minutes until the coastline came in sight. The crippled Stirling flew on and then suddenly he saw the first grey, choppy waves of the East Anglian coast beneath him. Nearly there now. If he could hold on a little longer. He sat there flying the Stirling, looking down at the sea swirling below, and as he did so he heard the unmistakable sound of one of the engines cutting out … and then another … The starboard outer engine spluttered … So near … and then a reprieve. The engineer switched tanks and one engine picked up again.

Somehow Geoff managed to keep the aircraft on course and then a solitary searchlight shone vertically, flicking on and off, before dropping to the horizontal, guiding him to the nearest airfield. A second searchlight repeated the performance, enabling them to be handed from one to another until they saw the Coltishall flarepath ahead. Flying Control was ready for them, flashing a green light to make an immediate landing. He brought the Stirling down with immense care and set it neatly on the runway. As he was taxying clear of the flarepath, the other engines cut.

'Bloody marvellous show, sir,' said one of the ground crew when he climbed down. 'Cut it a bit fine though, didn't you?'

'Got hit in the tank…'

One evening, Geoff and his crew were returning to the airfield at Downham Market in the flight van after a visit to the local pub. He found it difficult negotiating the road as the van's headlights were covered with a slotted hood to conform with blackout regulations, and the narrow footpath to the airfield was crowded with returning airmen and women in varying stages of intoxication spilling over on to the road. Geoff felt a bump but did not realise anything untoward had happened until some time later, when the WAAF flight officer came storming into the anteroom where they were enjoying a nightcap.

'Squadron Leader Rothwell!' she said indignantly. 'I believe you have knocked over my oldest and dearest WAAF and I'm going to report this to the CO immediately.'

A concerned Geoff found out later that the flight officer's indignation was due to the fact that when the side of the flight van had bumped the WAAF's shoulder, she had stumbled and her false teeth had shot out of her mouth and were shattered by the van's rear wheel. To make matters worse a visit was expected from the king and queen, and who was going to be presented to their Majesties? The oldest WAAF, of course. And now she had no teeth! It took a great deal of fast talking on Geoff's part to prevent the WAAF officer reporting him.

Another time, returning ravenous late at night from a local hostelry, Geoff and his crew decided to raid the group captain's asparagus beds. They climbed the stone wall into the garden and were busy pulling up the spears when the shutters on the first floor of the house flew open, revealing an irate CO in his pyjamas in the bright moonlight. They all took to their heels, hoping they had managed to avoid being identified. No such luck as Geoff was summoned the next day to appear before the Station Commander.

'You're a disgrace to the Air Force Rothwell,' he said, 'and what's more, if anything else goes wrong in the neighbourhood such as a WAAF being knocked down or pubs being set on fire, I only have to look at you and your crew to discover the culprits.'

The ultimate result was a week as station duty officer as punishment.

For several months while the bombing of London was at is most intense, Ethel and Pat Rothwell had been evacuated to a farm in the village of Tring, Hertfordshire, while Maurice remained in London. It was a delightful spot as it overlooked paddocks and a large cricket field where young Pat could run wild. Night after night the two women would sit in the farmhouse in the blackout, just the two of them and Wimpy huddled in front of the glowing embers of the fire, listening to the steady drone of engines of hundreds of bombers on their way south. They knew in all probability that Geoffrey could be part of that bomber force and that he was risking his life nightly with only their prayers for company.

When Pat had gone to bed Ethel would lie awake in the cold bedroom for hours, unable to sleep. Eventually she would get up and put on her light dressing gown and a shawl around her shoulders, as a thin shaft of moonlight shone dimly on the photos of Geoffrey, so handsome in his uniform. She would try not to look at them. Instead, as a way of passing the time, she would consciously will herself to be with him in the bomber as if in some way it would keep him alive. She imagined she was sitting up in the cockpit beside him keeping him company, helping protect him from the flak, from the shells and from enemy aircraft.

She would still be there many hours later in the icy room when dawn would cast its freezing fingers on her. She did not notice the cold or the stiffness in her legs or her extreme tiredness, and she would count the bombers returning – eleven, twelve, thirteen, fourteen...

And sometimes in the cold light of the following day there would be a reprieve, something magical and wonderful. She would be busy in the kitchen and would hear a familiar noise, a rumble in the distance which grew louder and louder, and Pat would yell out: 'Mother! Mother! It's Geoff! It's Geoff!'

And the two of them would run outside, rushing frantically into the middle of the cricket field in case they should miss him, and there they would see a mad Air Force pilot diving on the farmhouse, breaking all the rules, and her heart would leap and swell with happiness. Sometimes he would fly so low Pat would actually see him waving madly out of the window and almost see the grin on his face.

One day when they heard him coming, Ethel ran into the field just in time to see an elderly man with his little grandchild running for cover to a hedge at the edge of the field. The terrified man thought it was a German plane until an embarrassed Ethel called out it was just her wonderful daredevil son. Ethel and Pat kept quiet about the identity of the pilot to the local farmer who owned the farmhouse where they boarded. He was not so impressed and would throw his hands up to the sky. 'That bleedin' low-flying bomber has upset me cows again and made their milk curdle,' he cursed.

'That courageous brother of mine even beat up the village school where I was a pupil,' says Pat. 'We were out on the sports field and I, bursting with pride said: 'That's my brother up there – he's a bomber pilot.'

Sometimes a battle-weary Geoff would get forty-eight hours' leave and he would go to the farmhouse with its pale ochre walls and welcoming smells of wood and freshly baked bread.

Oh, the delight in having her hero brother home again! He would smile down at her, telling her how much she had grown, and ask her about school and her friends. And he would tell her something of his life in the Air Force, of the pranks they played, and the people he met. It was all so wonderfully exciting to Pat. She wished she was older so she could join the Air Force too. She couldn't wait to grow up to be part of it all.

She would sit watching him for hours, watching the firelight dancing on his head as he dozed exhausted in an armchair by the fire. When he woke she would talk to him and hang on to every word he said. She would ask him all kinds of questions, many of which he could not answer. But he, always good-natured, would try to answer as best he could. And then later, much later – after they had talked long into the night and Ethel would implore them both to get some sleep – she would creep into his room and cuddle up to him, laying her golden-red head against his darker red. And there Ethel would find them the next morning.

Geoff sat in the stuffy briefing room on 14 April 1943, letting his mind wander. On one of the walls was a notice: 'It is better to keep your mouth shut and let people think you're a fool than to open it and remove all doubt.' The air was thick and heavy with the distinctive smell of serge battle dress and the scent of sweet tobacco from the scores of pipes and cigarettes. He wondered if each man was thinking that perhaps he might never see the English shores again, that tonight might be the night. But it was not likely to happen. It would surely be a piece of cake...

Just a few nights ago they had celebrated his twenty-third birthday. It had been a great night, with Whistle entertaining the patrons of the Red Lion by performing a solo haka, a ceremonial Maori war dance, in the middle of the saloon bar. Everyone knew that whenever Rothwell's Ruffians were around, a good time would be had by all. He wondered how little Jacky Drawbridge, the teetotal navigator from Wellington, had avoided becoming waterlogged by all the lemonade he had drunk. They had all put five bob into the kitty and left Jacky in charge as he was the only one likely to be in a trustworthy condition by the end of the evening. However, it also required him to drink pint for pint with the crew, whose capacity for beer was legendary.

Geoff's thoughts jolted back to the present with the arrival of the briefing party. All eyes focused on the target – Stuttgart. It would be a long trip, but not as exacting as Happy Valley (the name the Bomber Command crews gave to the Ruhr Valley). The very thought of again having to fight through lanes of flak and searchlights to reach a Ruhr target made his stomach sink. Stuttgart was a welcome change.

'We are trying new tactics tonight,' said Wing Commander Saville. 'Total effort will fly to this point on the coast of Belgium at ten thousand feet. The new plan is designed to confuse Jerry radar and involves the main force splitting into three – Lancasters will climb to twenty thousand feet, Halifaxes and Wellingtons remaining at ten thousand, whilst Stirlings will drop to ground level, climbing to bombing height just before reaching their target. Flying low will be no problem for the Stirlings as there will be a full moon.'

It was certainly an innovative idea and a buzz of excited discussion began after the briefing ended. All the same, Geoff's stomach tightened into a knot, the familiar signs of the strange mixture of fear, uncertainty and excitement, the dry mouth, the wet hands and the urge to go to the toilet.

Some hours later Stirling III BK650 *T Tare* took off with sixteen other Stirlings from Downham Market, the full, bright moon shining on their wings. They pinpointed their position over Orford Ness on the East Anglian coast, and set course for the enemy coast.

'Now don't forget, anything remotely resembling a target – let 'em have it,' Geoff told his gunners.

At first all went according to plan. The huge Stirling flew over the North Sea to the Belgium coast, towards Germany and Stuttgart. The night was almost too bright – they would be easy targets for enemy aircraft. They flew very low over France and

Luxembourg, hedge-hopping above the ground as the crew looked everywhere for possible targets. Wal Fielding, the front gunner, let rip into a train, a signal box, river locks and barges, a hutted military camp and, of all things, a casino. How they decided it was a casino, Geoff has no idea. Then the town of Junglinster came into view, a railway line and train travelling slowly towards them. 'Here's a good one, Skip,' said Wal. 'Looks like an ammo train.'

'You're getting bloody trigger-happy, Wal,' said Geoff into his mouthpiece. And the resulting laughter relieved the tension.

Geoff moved the control column forward, dropping the aircraft even lower, all the time watching the yellow and red tracer hit the engine of the train, and steam gushing from the burst boiler. He shifted his gaze to the front, and it was then he saw it, a large electricity pylon dead ahead of them. He thought he was dreaming, everything was in slow motion. Climb! Quickly! He instinctively pulled back hard on the control column, and the nose of the great aircraft reared upwards like a huge angry bird. For a minute he thought they had cleared it.

It was too late.

There was a tremendous crash as the belly of the aircraft hit the pylon and metal bit into metal at 150mph, ripping a six-foot section off the bomb bay. There was a vivid display of blue and white sparks and flashes as live wires shorted. There was no power to a large area northeast Luxembourg until the following day. Oh, my God, thought Geoff, this time we have really had it, as the Stirling shuddered as it approached the stall. But with the throttles rammed forward against the stops, the Hercules engines delivered maximum power to the propeller and, gradually, the aircraft climbed away. The drama was not yet over.

'Incendiaries have caught fire in the bomb bays, Skip!' shouted Wal.

Immediately Geoff opened the bomb doors and pulled the jettison toggle, adding to the fireworks below as the incendiaries cascaded down.

'What's the damage?' he yelled into the mike

'Can't see much but the fire hasn't spread, Skip. Get us home quick,' replied Wal.

He set course for home, crossing his fingers in the hope that damage had been minimal. He looked at the altimeter. It registered their height as 5,000 feet.

He concentrated on keeping on course, trying gentle turns left and right. There seemed to be little or no damage but there were vibrations from the port inner engine. They weren't out of the woods yet – the English coast was more than two hours away.

The Stirling flew on through the night, all the time getting closer to Downham Market. Then Ginge Negus, the mid gunner, let out a yell, 'A Junkers eighty-eight on port beam, Skip! Turning in now.'

'Corkscrew port, corkscrew port, go!' yelled rear gunner Jock Howat, his voice half drowned in the noise of his guns as he opened fire with his Brownings, the smell of cordite wafting down the fuselage.

Geoff pushed the stick hard forward and with full aileron the Stirling went into a steep dive to port.

'OK, Jock, I've got 'im,' said Ginger.

Geoff could see the Junkers on his left. In the moonlight it looked huge and black and shiny, as if it had been recently polished. Suddenly, tracer was coming from a different direction from another enemy aircraft. A long burst ripped through the canopy over his head, then a piece of shrapnel flew straight through one of the holes, slicing into his neck before embedding itself in the back of his seat. He pulled back hard on the stick, not noticing the blood pouring from his wound, and took the aircraft into a steep climbing turn to starboard. A near miss from the Junkers' guns saw tracer pass harmlessly over the Stirling. This time he let the aircraft skid down in a violent sideslip as Ginge let rip in a frantic burst from the mid-upper guns. The Junkers climbed steeply, desperate to escape the Stirling's guns. Too late. Out of the corner of his eye Geoff watched, light-headed but fascinated, as the great black machine shuddered and then descended, burning and breaking up as it fell in a rapid downward spiral of black and orange flames.

'Nice work, Ginge,' said Geoff. 'Now let's beat it for home.'

He hung grimly on to the wheel, not noticing the strange thumping of his heart. By a miracle all the instruments were working. If he could hold his present course and altitude ... He brushed aside Whistle's anxiety over his wounds. A freezing draught swept through the damaged fuselage, stinging the men's faces and numbing their fingers. Their fleece-lined flying boots were barely keeping them warm.

'Send a message to base, wireless operator, advising we're damaged and one engine's dicky. Ask for permission for an emergency landing.'

'OK, Skip. I've got base on the line now … We're cleared to land immediately on one of the shorter runways,' said Whistle. This would be because in the event of a crash the damaged Stirling would block the main runway for the returning squadron.

There was the coastline with the surf breaking on the shore … not far to go now … 2,000 feet … 1,000 feet. The airfield was dead ahead. A green Very light, fired from the Flying Control tower, lit up the sky as they approached.

'Undercarriage down,' Geoff instructed the flight engineer.

The green indicator lights came on as the undercarriage locked down. 'One third flap.'

'One third flap Skip.'

Then the starboard outer engine cut.

'Switching tanks, Skip,' said the flight engineer.

The engine picked up and Geoff applied full throttle to maintain height. Now he was certain he could make the airfield. 'Give me full flap!'

And as the flap went on they crossed the airfield boundary. Now down, *down* … and the two main wheels of the huge Stirling squealed as they hit the tarmac runway. He applied full brake, coming to a stop just before the end of the runway. The fuselage echoed with cheers from the crew and Wal was heard to say, 'Every landing you walk away from is a good one. Bloody fine show, skip!'

Geoff turned off the engines, sweat pouring down his face, only dimly hearing the noise of the ambulance and the fire engine racing across to the aircraft. 'Well, you've gone and done it this time, haven't you, sir,' said Corporal Stan Hurd, his rigger. 'Hope you got the bastard who did this to you and to our lovely aircraft.'

'Hit a pylon,' he replied as he was helped down off the plane and taken to the ambulance.

'Bloody marvellous show in getting home,' said Saville later, congratulating him as they inspected the damage. There was a huge gap in the fuselage from the bomb doors to the rear entrance hatch on the port side as though it had been ripped open with a tin-opener. The bomb bay itself had suffered the most damage, with a great jagged tear starting from the bomb aimer's panel and extending back to about six feet inside the bomb bay. The Pitot head fairing had been bent back parallel with the fuselage, and the propeller on the port inner engine had scarring and dents with the tip of one of the blades bent back. The canopy above the pilot's seat was shattered and the bomb compartment showed some fire damage.

They patched Geoff's wound and he was given a spell of leave and spent it with his family.

'How did it happen?' asked young Pat, seeing the dressing on his neck.

'I ran into a spot of bother over Germany, but don't worry about it, darling, it's nothing at all. You know I'm indestructible,' he said, ruffling her curly red hair.

The *Daily Telegraph* duly reported the incident of the Stirling's collision with the pylon.

Germany, 15 April
Bomber Command attacked Stuttgart last night, despatching 462 aircraft to deliver what is officially described as 'a very keen attack' on one of Germany's largest armament and industrial centres.

Halifaxes and Stirlings dropped 4,000 pound and 8,000 pound bomb 'factory-smashers' and 'blockbusters' and thousands of incendiaries. The raid, the heaviest yet against Stuttgart, lasted for 45 minutes. Some of the huge four-engined aircraft, filled to capacity with bombs and petrol, flew very low, with gunners shooting up targets in the bright moonlight. One Stirling collided with an electricity pylon and had to jettison part of its load when the incendiaries caught fire. Some 23 of the Allied aircraft are missing.

'We were so proud to have Geoff flying our aircraft,' says Stan Hurd,

> ... although we weren't too carried away when he brought them back with lumps missing. In my estimation, and always denied by a modest Geoff, he was the best flyer of a Stirling, he bloody well must have been to have brought the aircraft back after hitting the pylon! He maintains Wing Commander Saville was better, but I cannot agree. The ground crew support me in this, although on test flights he would try to frighten us to death. His favourite trick was to fly between and below the level of twelve tall chimneys of the London Brick Company's works in Peterborough. However, he always managed to bring us back safely without any loose bricks becoming attached to the aircraft.

Some months later on a visit to the Short and Harland factory in Northern Ireland, which made Stirlings, Geoff's attention was drawn to a notice board on which was pinned a Ministry of Aircraft Production leaflet headed: *Stirling Bulletin No. 13*.

> Flying low in moonlight, going to Stuttgart, a Stirling collided with an electric pylon near a big power station.
> Broken wires filled the air with blue flashes and the Stirling's fuselage was stabbed and gashed underneath with holes. The incendiaries in its bomb-bays caught fire...
> Hastily the pilot jettisoned his load, set course for home and made a safe return.
> That air-crew will not forget what they owe to the builders of their Stirling.

The war in the air had now reached a new peak of intensity with Bomber Command fighting 'The Battle of the Ruhr'. The *Daily Mail* reported that 'hundreds of bombers go out almost every night to attack armament and industrial factories in what the bomber crews cynically call "happy valley." The *Luftwaffe* is equally aware of the dangers posed by Allied bombers and has decided to concentrate on producing fighters for the defence of the Reich by day and night.'

The battle of the Ruhr started in March 1943 and lasted for four months. It was to be a major test of the skill, determination and courage of the participants. On the one side there was the Commander-in-Chief of Bomber Command and the personnel of his squadrons; on the other side stood the German civilians and the flak and night-fighter units which attempted to defend the cities. The levels of death and destruction were to mount dramatically. Bomber Command statistics for the period 5/6 March to 24 July (141 days/nights) show that operations took place on 99 nights and 55 days. A total of 23,401 night sorties were carried out from which 1,000 aircraft were lost.

The day started for the bomber crews with attendance in the Flight crew-rooms at 0900 hours. Shortly the Flight Commander or his deputy posted on the blackboard the crews and aircraft which were on stand-by for the night's operations. Those involved boarded the crew bus which made a circuit of the airfield, stopping at each dispersal point for crews to disembark. If repairs had been carried out on the aircraft it was taken up for a short air test, otherwise the various members went to their respective posts in the aircraft and checked that their equipment was good. Satisfied that all was in readiness they lay in the grass smoking, reading, telling lies to each other, writing letters on their knees, or dozing in the sunshine – it there was any!

After lunch the crews detailed for operations congregated in the Briefing Room to await the arrival of the heads of the different sections, led by the Station Commander and his Squadron COs. On the dais at one end of the room the briefing officers seated themselves, and the Intelligence Officer rolled up the blind covering the large map on the wall. Loud moans came from the aircrews when they saw the red thread showing the route led right into the heart of the Ruhr industrial area. The IO grinned and would say: 'Yes, chaps, it's Happy Valley again tonight.'

Now that the target was known and the details of the briefing occupied their attention there was a noticeable lessening of tension amongst the crews who would be involved in the raid.

They dispersed to get on with their various tasks, the navigator being the one member whose ground work would be most vital in the actual flight. It was his job to ensure the aircraft maintained its correct position along the track to the target. Any errors in navigation could put the aircraft outside the safety of the mainstream of bombers and liable to be picked off by night fighters. When they had worked out their courses the navigators usually checked with each other to make sure no mistakes had been made inadvertently.

Most crews would agree that the worst period in the entire operation now began. 'There would be a wait of perhaps eight hours or more before the time for take-off. There was little we could do to relieve the boredom and bridge the hiatus except read, sleep, or listen to the wireless,' said Geoff.

Night flying meals were served in all the messes, after which transport ferried the crews to their flights where they prepared for their forthcoming trip. There were visits to the Parachute Section and Crew Locker Rooms where woollen aircrew sweaters, flying suits, and boots lined with lamb's wool were donned. Pockets were emptied of all material which, in the event of capture, could be of assistance to the enemy.

At the dispersal points last cigarettes or pipes were smoked and bladders were emptied under the tail plane in what was known as the 'operational pee'. The captain ordered his crew to take up their positions and once the hatches and doors were secured he started the engines. Committed as they now were, there was a general air of relaxation.

Tension reached a higher level as the pilot lined up the heavily laden bomber with the flarepath lights. This was one of the most critical times as a swing off the tarmac runway on to the soft ground, or an engine failure before they became airborne, could spell disaster. Once take-off speed was reached and the wheels left the ground the undercarriage was raised and the long climb commenced. Once again, the feeling of relaxation returned as the first hurdle was overcome, which lasted for the best part of an hour until the navigator's microphone was switched on.

'Navigator to pilot, ETA enemy coast five minutes, skipper.'

'Roger, navigator, I can see the shore line and there's some searchlights over to starboard.'

The route to the target had been carefully chosen so as to avoid the more heavily defended areas, but the crew knew they were being tracked by German radar and there was constant danger of attack by night fighters.

The Pathfinder Force had dropped indicator markers at the turning point so added watchfulness was necessary as it was a virtual certainty the enemy night fighters would have congregated over the markers. Sure enough tracer was seen on the starboard bow followed by an explosion and fire which lit up the stricken aircraft seen in silhouette to be a four-engine Halifax.

Anti-aircraft shells burst under the aircraft, hurling the huge plane aside as though a titanic hand was shaking it. Searchlight beams illuminated the cockpit, showing up the tense looks of pilot and flight engineer.

Even after the release of their bomb load and with a much lighter aircraft their troubles were not over as they had to fight their way out of the target area in conditions not dissimilar from those they had experienced on the way in.

For those aircraft lucky enough to make it back to base the crew tumbled out of the aircraft, limbs stiff from the cold and sitting in one position for so long, completely drained of any emotion, and overcome with fatigue. Before they could even think of sleep however, crews had to be debriefed and then they made their way to their different messes for the 'operational egg' breakfast. Dawn was approaching as they fell into their beds.

On 13 May 1943 Geoff and his crew were detailed to search for a crew reported to have ditched in the North Sea. Although the weather forecast was favourable there was cloud all the way, with a thick sea mist in the search area.

'It's like looking for a bloody needle in a haystack,' said Jacky Drawbridge as they searched for five hours but failed to find the crew. On returning to base they went straight to the ops room. Geoff's heart sank. They were due to fly that night in Stirling III BK688 on a raid on Bochum in the Ruhr Valley. It meant another five hours' flying and Bochum was a real hot spot. He wished he had taken a Benny (the drug Benzedrine) to keep him awake. 'I'll have to manage without it,' he thought.

It was cold in the Stirling, so cold it had brought on the inevitable urge to go to the toilet. That was the trouble on long-distance flights; the extreme cold at altitudes of 12,000–15,000 feet always produced urgent signals from the bladder. Unlike Avro Ansons which had a funnel and tube leading out of the fuselage into the slipstream, the Short Stirling had an Elsan chemical toilet about the size of an ordinary lavatory pan situated midway down the port side of the aircraft. For a moment he debated engaging George, the automatic pilot or getting one of the crew to take over the controls. George was temperamental at the best of times and had been known to put the aircraft onto a steep climb or dive for no apparent reason. He could not take the risk.

'Take over from me, will you Wal?' he called out to the bomb aimer and then made his way to the Elsan, worrying the whole time that enemy fighters or flak would engage the Stirling. Trussed up in Mae West and parachute harness and with icy hands he removed his flying gauntlets, silk and Chamois gloves, trying to find his zip fastener and open the flap in his thickly-padded flying suit; now to negotiate his battle dress fly-buttons and find the opening slot of his underpants and release an organ which because of the intense cold had retreated into his scrotum.

Mission accomplished he returned and took over the controls. He gripped the wheel, looking straight ahead at the instrument panel and trying to stay alert by concentrating on what he was doing, and thinking of nothing except flying the Stirling. Its powerful motors droned on and on and he found his thoughts turning to Sweet Pea. He had seen her just two days before, when she had a spell of leave and had come to Downham Market. They saw each other so rarely nowadays. It had been a wonderful visit. Of course they would write, but sometimes he would be so involved in the day-to-day workload of running a flight – the operations, flying, fighting the enemy or writing to the next-of-kin of dead comrades. All this would sap his energy, leaving him little time for anything else.

She will probably be asleep now. They will all be asleep now. Sleep, he mustn't think about it. His eyes felt sore and itchy and he put up his hand to rub them. He looked through the cockpit window and saw the sky full of searchlights. They looked like long fingers of light, moving this way and that, as if there was a strong wind blowing them. Left, right, left, right like the metronome which sat on top of the piano at home in his parents' drawing room. It was all he could do not to let his head fall forward on to the control column. Christ, concentrate on the instruments. Fly straight and level, out of the reach of the searchlights. They were weaving in and out like a game of hide-and-seek. One, two, three – coming, ready or not. Run and hide. You're not going to find us!

He needed to focus on something. 'Come on, you lot in the back,' he called over the intercom. 'Sling some of those beer bottles down below.' This practice started early in the war when Geoff was in 99 Squadron before the days of radar. Flak and searchlights were operated on the sonar principle and it was believed that the whistling noise from a falling bottle would upset the system.

The flak was all around the aircraft. It came up from the town below in a thick veil, bursting like logs crackling on a fire. He struggled to keep control of the aircraft. Then suddenly he was wide awake and quite cool and confident, sitting there in the cockpit, flying the aircraft and watching the flames and the searchlights as he guided the huge Stirling through the curtain of flak. It was so thick it did not seem possible that one could fly through it. A Wellington on the port side of his aircraft went down in flames, falling through the air like a stone.

'Get out, get out,' he screamed silently to the crew inside.

But no parachutes appeared. He needed light relief, and his thoughts turned to Ginge. Ginge, who always brought a handbell which he had lifted from somewhere to ring over the R/T on raids. 'Bring out the handbell, Ginge. Let's give the bastards a call.' Then he turned on the R/T. '*Achtung! Achtung! Der Fuhrer*. The Bell Boys are here again. Why don't you pack it in?' And Ginge rang the bell.

On the run-up to the target they managed to avoid the searchlights. The bomb aimer reported he had dropped their load on one of the green target indicators. As they headed for home a solitary searchlight picked them up, and immediately they were coned by dozens more. By twisting and diving Geoff managed to escape, but they knew the absence of flak meant there were fighters operating and he warned the gunners to be vigilant.

Back at base, 'Rothwell's Ruffians' provided the following report on the raid for the intelligence officer.

> A really good show. Huge explosion over target area when a/c [aircraft] was well on way home. Wizard prang. Defences (AA) [Anti–aircraft] practically nil. Bags of searchlights. Called up Fuhrer on TR9 and told him he might as well pack it in.

Geoff had Squadron Leader Maw alongside him in BK803 HA-D over Dusseldorf when they ran into searchlights while closing in on the target. For five minutes the Stirling was bracketed by flak, and Geoff used every ounce of his experience as a pilot to escape it. Finally, after surrendering 3,000 ft of altitude he managed to slip away but it had been a close call which would be self-evident in the cold light of the following morning, when twenty holes would be found in the winds and fuselage, some of them the size of dinner plates.

On returning from a raid on Dusseldorf on 24 July they learned Wing Commander Saville had bought it. Don Saville, the dapper little Australian with his loathing of humbug who had endeared himself to everybody on the station, and given Geoff an 'Exceptional' rating as a pilot in his 'Assessment of Ability'. It was typical that he had volunteered for a difficult and dangerous raid on Hamburg. His aircraft had come under extremely heavy attack and, knowing it was going to blow up, the courageous pilot had managed to hold it steady for the crew to bale out but was unable to get out himself. He had served with distinction and was posthumously awarded the Distinguished Service Order in addition to the DFC won previously.

It was bad timing. Not only had Geoff lost a good friend and CO but his tour of operations at Downham Market had come to an end. Ian Ryall, who had been a fellow flight commander of Geoff's at Moreton-in-Marsh, flew Geoff and his crew to Westcott, where they were to take up duties on an operational training unit again.

'One had to be a bit mad in order to survive the war in Bomber Command, and Geoff was liberally endowed with this quality,' says Ryall. 'He treated the whole thing as if it were one big game. We all had our own way of dealing with it; this was his, and he seemed to me to be indestructible.'

Geoff and his crew had tried to avoid the posting to an OTU as they wanted to continue as a crew on operations. But it seemed there was nothing to be done. However, some weeks before his tour finished he received a letter from the adjutant of 617 Squadron, of Dam Buster fame. The squadron was recruiting crews. Would he like to join them?

The Dam Busters!

He dashed off a letter saying he would be overjoyed to join the squadron, but before committing himself there were just two things he wanted: confirmation that he would hold his acting squadron leader rank, which he had held for sixteen months, and that he could take his crew with him. He was bitterly disappointed. There was no vacancy for a squadron leader and therefore he would be reverted to flight lieutenant if he accepted the offer. Furthermore, he would not be permitted to bring his present crew. He declined.

Geoff's stay at Downham Market had been one of the happiest times in the war. He made many friends and his days were filled with laughter, companionship, camaraderie and nostalgia. His sad departure was not without pathos. On 10 September 1943 he was awarded a Bar to his DFC for his tour with 75 and 218 Squadrons.

'For my gallant and courageous crew who had accompanied me throughout the tour – nothing!'

August 1943

The war was into its fourth year and Geoff felt it had been going on forever. Victory seemed far away, somewhere in the distant future, if at all. *Victory,* Germany defeated, no more bombing raids, prisoners of war returning home to their loved ones and life returning to normal again. He thought longingly of what he and Sweet Pea would do when it was all over. And in the midst of the nation's feelings of gloom and depression came the voice of Winston Churchill over the wireless, telling everybody how splendidly they were doing.

By the time Geoff was posted to the OTU with his crew to command a flight at Oakley, the satellite of Westcott, he could not shake his premonition of despair and was unable to rid himself of the 'black dog on his shoulder', as Churchill called depression. But he was pleasantly surprised to find a good atmosphere at Oakley and met up with friends from the old days at Desford. Many of the instructors were New Zealanders and this was a bonus to Geoff as he had always got on extremely well with Kiwis. The weather was warm and pleasant and the days passed quickly, lulling him into the thought that perhaps he could settle down there after all. But after three months he was transferred to the parent station, Westcott. There, with the first cold winds from the east blowing into the station, his earlier premonition of despair and depression recurred.

This period was to be the most unhappy and frustrating of his service career. For a time he served under a remarkable CO, Group Captain Dick Shaw, but he was eventually posted and replaced by an austere disciplinarian, Peter Stevens, who was universally disliked. Geoff also had the humiliating experience of having to serve under a chief instructor, Clive Scott, who had been a pupil pilot officer on an OTU course when he had been a flight lieutenant. Geoff would not have minded so much had Scott been a likeable man, but he was one of the rare breed of New Zealanders who was disliked by everybody, including his fellow countrymen. There were continual arguments over Scott's treatment of instructors as he was out to exploit them and impose unnecessary restrictions on them, whereas Geoff insisted on them being given a fair deal.

In addition to the antagonism Geoff felt towards Scott, he and Stevens had taken an instant dislike to each other. As there was a big difference in rank it was always Geoff who came off the worst. One day he was summoned to Stevens' office.

'Listen, Rothwell,' said Stevens, 'your code of dress is a bloody disgrace. Your shoes aren't regulation for a start (this was true, Geoff's shoes were brown brogues dyed black) and neither are your socks. (Geoff's grandmother had knitted them in Air Force blue rather than regulation black.) And what's more, your tunic has only one RAF button on it.'

'Actually, sir,' said Geoff, determined not to be outdone, 'the button is, in fact, a WAAF one.' This habit of swapping buttons with other services was fairly common and most officers had a Polish, Czech, New Zealand or some other Air Force button somewhere on their tunic. This was too much for Stevens, who gave Geoff a week of being station duty officer as punishment for insubordination.

January 1944 and Bomber Command was losing 6.11 per cent of aircraft dispatched to Berlin. Casualties continued to climb, with further raids culminating in a loss of some 7 per cent of the force dispatched, according to the *Daily Sketch*: 'a rate which cannot for long be accepted. At a briefing for last night's raid, crews "gasped with horror or disbelief", according to an observer, when they saw Berlin was again the target.'

In early April Geoff made a determined effort to get away from the OTU and Stevens. He regularly applied for postings, all of which were turned down by Stevens, who took great delight in tearing up the applications in front of Geoff. He was now on the point of despair, feeling there was no way out of the situation. He commiserated with his good friend Jack Parker, a New Zealand · instructor who wanted a posting as much as Geoff. One day Geoff suggested Jack should contact the RNZAF liaison officer, who was attached to the High Commission in London. Jack took up Geoff's proposal and within a few weeks a posting came through to 161 Squadron at Tempsford RAF Station in Bedfordshire. This was a strange posting as neither of them had heard of the squadron or station, and to their knowledge there were no Bomber Command units in that county. The whole affair began to assume a rather unusual aspect.

A few days after Jack's departure a four-engined Halifax landed at Oakley. 'Hey! Parker's just landed,' came a shout from Dan

Godfrey, the flying control officer. On hearing this, some of the men piled into the flight van and drove out to the dispersal point, where Jack was just shutting down the engines. They swarmed all over the aircraft.

'What's that for, Jack?' they said, pointing to a large hatch covering a hole in the floor of the fuselage at the rear. 'Bugger off, you sods,' said Jack. 'You're not supposed to be in this bloody aircraft, so get to hell out of it!'

It was a strange business and Geoff hoped to find out more about the mysterious posting. But all the pumping in the world did little to persuade Jack to give anything away. He would say only that the sister squadron at Tempsford was commanded by a Wing Commander Speare and that there was a vacancy for a flight commander.

'I know Dicky Speare,' said Geoff. 'He was an instructor at Harwell when I converted on to Wellingtons in April 1940. You owe me a favour, old son. Will you see Dicky and tell him I'm interested in that job and to hold it open for me until I can get to Tempsford to see him?'

Jack readily agreed and Geoff flew over to Tempsford, where he met Speare. Did he remember Geoff? Of course he did. However, Speare explained he was unable to reveal more about the nature of the work of the squadron except that it involved low flying in moonlight, and that the flight commander's job was his for the asking.

Geoff immediately accepted. Speare told him to go back, say nothing to anyone and he would arrange for a posting at once. Feeling on top of the world, he flew back to Oakley. It was a magical spring day of pale cloudless skies, and looking down on the still countryside spread beneath him he felt light-hearted for the first time in many months. At last, at last, he was getting away from the OTU and the dreaded Stevens. But his euphoria was not to last for long.

A few days after his interview with Speare, Stevens strode into Geoff's office, curtly telling the other instructors to leave. When they were alone he took out of his pocket a Bomber Command postagram sending Geoff to 138 Squadron. Finally! His heart leapt for joy but just then Stevens tore it into shreds.

'You can forget all about the posting,' he said. 'I've arranged for it to be cancelled.'

What a bastard the man was. What spleen the man had. But Geoff would fight to the death for this. I won't be beaten, he thought. I'm going to beat this bastard at his own game. As soon as Stevens' car had disappeared he telephoned Dicky Speare and told him what had happened.

'Don't worry, Geoff,' said Speare. 'I'll fix Stevens. I'll get my CO to arrange for an Air Ministry posting. Let him try and stop that.'

Geoff learned later that the CO at Tempsford was a Group Captain Fielden, who had taught the Prince of Wales to fly and was the current Captain of the King's Flight. Fielden was obviously a person with good connections.

He felt honoured that all this in-fighting was taking place over a mere squadron leader's posting and was grateful he had the support of people like Speare and Fielden on his side. Despite this assurance he lived on tenterhooks until the great day arrived. Stevens appeared at his office door as before and when they were alone he produced an Air Ministry postagram. He threw it on Geoff's desk.

'Well, Rothwell, you've beaten me,' he said. 'You've got what you wanted. Now I'll give you forty-eight hours to get off the station.'

'That won't be necessary, sir. I intend to leave within twenty-four hours,' said Geoff, impertinent as ever. He did not bother to get the usual Assessment of Ability on Posting in his log book as he could not get away from the place fast enough. To this day he wonders what would have been written.

It was almost a year to the day before he saw Stevens again. Having just landed in a Flying Fortress at Ford, a reception unit for returning POWs, who should come strutting across the tarmac but his erstwhile scourge, Stevens. However, he failed to recognise Geoff in the crowd of ex-prisoners and Geoff certainly made no attempt to introduce himself.

Of his other comrades, Geoff later learnt that:

Flying Officer Herbert John Drawbridge (Jacky) of Lower Hutt was killed whilst crewing in a Lancaster of 97 Squadron on his 21st operation on 20/21 April 1944. The aircraft was brought down by anti-aircraft fire and crashed in France where he is buried in the Clichy Cemetery, Paris.

Wireless Operator 'Whistle', Flying Officer Ian William Entwistle of Hawera, New Zealand was a member of a Lancaster crew of 115 Squadron, which failed to return from an attack on Gelsenkirchen on the night of 12/13 June 1944. It was his 39th operation and the International Red Cross reported that F/O Entwistle is buried in the Nast Cemetery, Gelsenkirchen, Germany.

Mid-upper gunner Flying Officer (Ginge) John Negus, from Harlow, Essex, England was killed in action.

Jock, Sergeant Adam Howat, the rear gunner, was killed with Wing Commander Saville over Hamburg.

Flying Officer Walter Fielding, always known as Wal, from Christchurch, New Zealand, survived the war. He would meet Geoff forty-five years later at a reunion of 75 (NZ) Squadron in Cambridge, England.

10

SPECIALLY EMPLOYED

We saw a simple duty to stand up against what was plainly
bad, and followed where that duty called us...
– M. R. D. Foot

You were a member of a team which, by its faithful service
to your comrades behind enemy lines on the battle fronts
of the world, enabled nations to gain their self-respect and
made the allied task so much easier. You have reason to be
proud of your contribution to victory.
– Brigadier Nicholls

RAF Station Tempsford had a motto: 'Stay low, stay on track, and
stay alive.' It was one of the most secret and important RAF bases
during the Second World War and operated in liaison with the
Special Operations Executive, or SOE. Some of the most daring
and historic missions of the war originated from Tempsford. Two
Special Duties Squadrons – 161 and 138 – were devoted almost
entirely to SOE operations and were equipped with Halifaxes,
Hudsons and Lysanders, which carried out sorties to France,
Belgium, Holland, Norway, Denmark, Poland, Czechoslovakia,
and Germany itself on rare occasions.

Everything about Tempsford was top secret. The entrance to the
station was guarded around the clock by patrols armed with Sten
guns. Even on the base nobody talked about 'ops' and the locals

knew little, if anything, about the missions originating from the airfield down the hill.

The Germans knew of the existence of the airfield but never seemed to spot it, as it was a long way off the A1 main road to the north and down a lonely and steep country lane.

> The existence of the Moon Squadron was well-known in Berlin. Neutral Dublin was a sounding board for the Nazis and it is possible that the hint came from there, No one will ever know. But its activity had become a thorn under the finger-nail of Hitler himself and it was his dominant wish to find and destroy what he called, with an original turn of phrase, 'this nest of vipers'.
>
> Jerrard Tickell, *Moon Squadron*

The Special Operations Executive, a small British fighting service set up in July 1940, was an independent body separate from the British Secret Service. Known as a 'dirty tricks department', it was employed in sending agents (known as 'Joes'), arms, food, explosives and supplies into enemy-occupied countries. The agents were usually dropped by parachute to the Resistance receptions, but some went by sea and others by Lysanders which landed on reception fields. Supplies of arms packed in containers and panniers were dropped by parachute.

Until then there had been no hard and fast rules for encouraging sabotage and subversion behind enemy lines. No organisation existed for conducting irregular warfare. Previous operatives in irregular warfare such as Lawrence of Arabia who had died in 1935 were past the recruitment age at the time the Second World War began.

However, on 1 July 1940 Dr Hugh Dalton, Minister of Economic Warfare, had written to Lord Halifax:

> What is needed is a new organisation to co-ordinate, inspire, control and assist the nationals of the oppressed countries who must themselves be the direct participants. It should be comparable to the Sinn Fein movement in Ireland, to the Chinese Guerrillas now operating against Japan, to the

Spanish Irregulars who played a notable part in Wellington's campaign or ... to the organisations which the Nazis themselves have developed so remarkably in almost every country in the world...

The motivation behind SOE was to stimulate and support resistance activities clandestinely in the hope they would ultimately shorten the war. Churchill had been the driving force 'to set Europe ablaze'. He had written in a memo to his personal representative to the Chiefs of Staff: 'How wonderful it would be if the Germans could be made to wonder where they were going to be struck next, instead of forcing us to try to wall in the island and roof it over!'

Most operations from Tempsford took place in the 'moon period' although some were carried out when there was no moon by using special equipment and techniques. As a senior officer of SOE put it much later, 'for at least two years the moon was as much of a goddess as she ever was in a near eastern religion'.

For Geoff, who knew nothing about Tempsford or SOE, the months spent on the station were to be the most enjoyable of his war service. When he learnt that he would be involved in cloak-and-dagger operations he was reminded of all he had read as a small boy in his avidly devoured *Boy's Own* papers.

The CO of 138 Squadron was a charming Canadian, Wing Commander Wilf Burnett, who had taken over from Dicky Speare. He and Geoff took an instant liking to each other. Although the work would be extremely dangerous, it would be a relief to be out of the bombing war, to be doing which seemed more directly beneficial to the war effort. Whilst on active service with Bomber Command he had tried not to dwell too deeply on what he was doing on operations, otherwise it would have been difficult to carry on, to go out night after night, seeing the appalling destruction caused by 4,000–pound and 8,000-pound blockbusters and the firestorms created by incendiary bombs. It was a matter of concentrating on the job, he was responsible for the safety of his crew and this was the motivating factor. Besides, after all the destruction he had seen in London, it was a question of kill or be killed. It was impossible for any member of Bomber Command not to be awed by the sight of cities ablaze and there was always an awareness of the suffering of the civilian population.

Max Hastings in *Bomber Command* writes that most surviving Bomber Command aircrew felt deeply betrayed by criticism of the strategic air offensive:

> After surviving the extraordinary battles they fought for so long against such odds and in which so many of them died, it is disgraceful they were never awarded their own campaign medal ... The aircrew of Bomber Command went out to do what they were told had to be done for Britain and Allied victory, and subsequent judgements on the bomber offensive can do nothing to mar the honour of such an epitaph.

At Tempsford all crew members were on their second or third tours and there was a profusion of decorations. Group Captain 'Mouse' Fielden, MVO (Member of the Royal Victorian Order), Air Equerry to the King, was the station commander. Fielden, a dapper little man who looked more like a senior Army officer with his close-clipped moustache, had formed 161 Squadron. Geoff was on his third tour with a DFC & Bar; his navigator, Roddy McKitrick, a big well-built man from Northern Ireland with thick dark hair, had a DFC; Derek Shaw, an immensely capable flight engineer, a DFM; William Walton, known as Wally, was the rear gunner with a BEM; and good-looking Roger Court, self-effacing and quiet with a delightful personality, was the map reader. Tall, fair-haired Bob Wilmott from the North Country was the dispatcher, and the wireless operator, Flying Officer Howell, had been working for Special Duties for some time and had been shot down by a Junkers 88.

Geoff itched to get stuck into his new job but first he had to serve as senior officer at a court martial, the president of which was his new CO, Group Captain Fielden.

'Er ... er ... Rothwell,' said Fielden, scratching his moustache with his thumbnail, 'do you have, er ... a writing machine?'

Puzzled, Geoff asked, 'Do you mean a pen, sir?'

'Yes, yes, of course,' was the reply.

Before Geoff took over A Flight from 'Scruffy' Wilding, he had to convert on to the Halifax, which was different from any aircraft he had flown, not only did it have a 'Joe' hole, but the front turret was replaced by a perspex nose with a seat so that the map reader had an uninterrupted view of the countryside ahead and to the sides.

The night of 18 May 1944 was cold and brilliant as Geoff prepared for his first SOE operation as second dicky to Wilding. The purpose of the sortie was to drop five agents and containers to a reception in France. The trip was expected to take around six and a half hours. The two men were driven in a flight van to a corner of the airfield, where there was a collection of buildings known as Gibraltar Farm. There they greeted the agents who were dressed in bulky overalls over their French attire, parachutes strapped on to their shoulders. Then the agents who were 'going into the field' were driven to the entrance door of the aircraft and greeted by the dispatcher. He would look after them in the event of a diversion to another airfield if the operation had to be aborted for any reason.

At 8.30 p.m., Halifax V DG285 took off, the heavy aircraft flying over the Channel. They were flying at a height of 500 feet as they met the French coastline, below radar, but low enough for the German light flak below to send them the traditional welcome to all visitors to France. The tracer came uncomfortably close, but Wilding went into a steep diving turn, levelling out at around 100 feet, too low for the anti-aircraft guns to focus on them. They were soon clear. The flight continued without further incident until they approached the dropping zone (DZ).

Far below them in the French countryside, members of the Resistance and the Maquis with rifles or Sten guns strapped to their backs were busy preparing for the agents. The night with its huge orange moon was strangely peaceful and silent. Quietly they worked away, chopping small pieces of wood for the bonfire. Any minute now they would hear the drone of the aircraft overhead. There it was! The drone became a steady rumble and a minute later they could see the Halifax approaching from the north ... The bonfire burst alight.

'Reception ahead,' said Wilding.

They were right on time and as they circled they watched for the correct signal in Morse code from a torch in the field below. The letter '*L*' flashed immediately. Dot, dash, dot dot … it was the right signal.

In the back of the aircraft the agents checked the straps on their parachutes and felt for the cyanide pills sewn into the cuffs of their sleeves. They desperately hoped the people far below them were indeed the Resistance and not the enemy.

The dispatcher opened the Joe hole hatch and the wind rushed in, cold and damp. The field, glowing softly in the pale moonlight, stood out clearly in the blacked-out French countryside. The agents' parachutes were checked one by one, and the static lines were attached so they would be pulled automatically out of the pack when they jumped. The tension in the aircraft was palpable – a strange mixture of excitement and terror as they sat with their legs dangling over the hole, waiting for the dispatcher's warning light to come on. The green light flashed …

Now go! They felt a gentle boot in their backsides and one by one they dropped through the hole, all five of them, down into the cold night, the static line connected to their parachutes going taut at first and then automatically releasing them down into the darkness, the wind flapping against their overall legs, their faces stiff with cold. Mission accomplished, the Halifax zoomed back over the field for the last time, dipping its wings in farewell. Then quickly it gained height and climbed away into the darkness, heading for home. At Tempsford a message awaited them from the Resistance circuit – the operation had been a success.

'A right little piece of cake,' Scruffy told Geoff.

In fact it was anything but. They were dangerous missions, requiring the highest levels of skill, particularly in navigation. A high level of commitment was demanded from the Special Duty crews as it was a huge responsibility delivering agents and supplies safely. It took skill to fly an aircraft at just the right height so supplies and containers would not drift away from the reception on the ground or drift outside the dropping zone or become entangled with trees. Apart from these obvious skills, Tempsford pilots and crews had the knack of making the Joes feel welcome and safe. As agent Yvonne Basedon wrote in *Moon Squadron*:

> I immediately felt happy about the whole thing. They made us welcome and looked after us as if we were their special friends. Not only were the men of the Moon Squadron efficient at their jobs. They transmitted their confidence to us.

Flying crews on Special Duties were always fully conscious of the risks they were taking, especially flying low over enemy occupied territory. But they joked about it and lived life to the full, determined to enjoy what time they had left.

The Resistance circuit *Ventriloquist* along with all the other circuits had been warned that *Le jour de libération*, D-Day, was close at hand and they should be on standby to carry out railway demolitions and communication disruption tasks allotted to them by High Command. Consequently on 5 June 1944 members of the *Ventriloquist* circuit gathered around their secret radios to receive the following message from the BBC: '*Et maintenant, les messages personnels. Mesdames et Messieurs, le chat de Louise est mort.*'

To the Germans who were monitoring the wireless transmissions Louise's cat might have died but to the Resistance workers it meant: 'Prepare for action.'

Adjusting the ancient valve wireless and straining to pick up any message through the static, the resistance leader heard the announcer's crackling voice, the message he had been waiting for: '*Tout est perdu sauf l'honneur.*' All is lost except honour. The words of Francis I announced that the Great Day had finally arrived.

Across the English Channel in rural Bedfordshire some hours later Geoff puffed on his pipe as he contemplated the map on the wall of the inner sanctum of the Intelligence Section of RAF Tempsford.

On the morning of 6 June 1944, Geoff had woken to a quiet rain gently falling outside his window. It was the day of the invasion of Europe, 'Operation Overlord'. The Allied assault on the strongly fortified coast of France was the greatest combined operation of all time. It was made at a time when the Germans were fighting for their lives on the Eastern Front, and when the Allies had won air and sea supremacy.

The maps of Europe had coloured pins marking the position of every resistance circuit. Stretching from the English to the French coast were pinned two black ribbons, parallel to each other. In thick red lettering, between the two ribbons, were the words: 'DANGER! KEEP OUT! YOU HAVE BEEN WARNED!'

The room rapidly filled with meteorological and intelligence officers and the squadron and flight commanders from the two Tempsford squadrons. Geoff jostled his way through the throng to greet Wilf Burnett and discover what had occurred the previous night. (Wilfred Burnett, DFC took over command of 138 Squadron on 9 May 1944.) The wing commander and his crew had dropped dummy parachutists, nicknamed Ruperts, in the Bayeux/Caen area behind the beaches where the Allied forces were scheduled to land at dawn the following day. Attached to the dummies were explosive charges and fire-crackers which were designed to go off at intervals to confuse the enemy and give the impression of a greater force than the one that had actually landed.

A black curtain screening the door of the small room was pulled aside and the station commander, Mouse Fielden, strode to the rostrum. There was silence as the men waited for up-to-date news, then Fielden confirmed what had been announced on the BBC, that a beachhead had been established on the Normandy coast and the operation was progressing satisfactorily. Then the waiting crews were given their instructions for the evening. The operation for Geoff and his crew on this most vital day, codenamed 'Hubert', was to drop containers of arms and ammunition to a resistance reception in France.

Later that night, Geoff lined up Halifax V LL416 for take-off. He waited for the green Aldis lamp signal from the Flying Control caravan parked at the beginning of the runway, then he pushed the throttles forward.

'Saint Pierre en Port,' called out the map reader. They were on track and descended to 700 feet in the brilliant moonlight. Some time later, there were the two islands in the River Loire, their pinpoints on the port bow. The river glistened in the moonlight.

'Bang on, Roger,' said Geoff.

The reception party had laid out three dim lights with a fourth forming a letter 'L' from where the signaller would operate. As soon as he saw the lights ahead of them he flashed the code letter on the identification lamp. The correct signal was given and they descended to 600 feet.

'Running up to the reception now, Roger. Bomb doors open.'

Now to line up the lights, which should be into wind ... 500 feet, 400 feet. Roger Court pressed the bomb release and away they went ... the containers dropping from the bomb bays, the parachute opening, hopefully to land beside the lights and be collected by the reception committee. Now to get away as fast as possible as their presence was a danger to the Resistance. Already the engine of the Halifax was like thunder, waking the tranquil countryside. In a farewell gesture, he flashed a 'V for Victory' sign and received one in return. He set course for base, and then down below in the moonlight were gun flashes and lights from vehicles speeding on the road approaching the field. It must be Germans. His first instinct was to fire at the lights but then he remembered that the Resistance often used transport to carry away containers. In an endeavour to identify the vehicles, he dived. Just as he did so, figures in the vehicles – now distinct as German transport, stood up and fired at the Halifax.

'OK, Wally. Let 'em have it!' and the rear gunner opened fire as the aircraft passed over the vehicles. 'Now let's beat it for home and hope the Resistance is all right.'

At debriefing a message was received to say that the Gestapo had been tipped off that a drop was due to take place and that they were on their way to the field when they were sighted by the crew.

On the night of 1 September 1944 there were two operations. The first, codenamed 'Rummy 1', involved dropping an agent with a parcel at a large country house in North Holland, and the second, codenamed 'Bob', was to supply containers to the Resistance at another reception on the Dutch/German border, dangerously close to a German fighter airfield, which meant a high chance of detection by radar.

'We're on course, Skip,' said McKitrick, the navigator, 'Reception dead ahead.' Outside, the night was brilliantly clear. The dispatcher tightened the straps on the agent's parachute, hooking the static line, then opened the Joe hole. At 400 feet, they could clearly see fields and trees, houses and windmills dotted here and there. Lower still and there was the target, a house, white and gleaming in the moonlight, but no sign of any reception waiting in the grounds.

Stirling IV LK192 climbed again to 500 feet, then turned around and made another run – still no luck. 'What's going on?' asked the agent to the dispatcher.

'No contact yet,' said Wilmott, listening intently on the intercom.

'I'm going to give it one more try,' Geoff told Roger Court.

'OK, action stations,' yelled Wilmott to the agent. Third time lucky.

Down below in the moonlight a dim and lone light streamed from the door of the house, enabling the crew to identify a figure flashing a torch in the grounds.

'Right, sonny, out you go!' yelled the dispatcher over the noise of the engine, and out went the agent, spectacles secured to his temples and bridge of his nose with sticking plaster. Clutching the parcel to his chest, he dropped silently through the hole.

Following the second operation, when they dropped the containers on 'Bob', the Stirling suddenly broke into a steep climb. Looking through the small circular windows, Howell, the wireless operator, caught a lop-sided view of the town, but a few seconds later it had disappeared, and all he could see was a star-speckled sky. They dived faster and faster. Then all at once they were flying straight and level again. They were under attack by a Messerschmitt. For a few more minutes the two aircraft chased each other around the sky and then as suddenly as it had appeared, the fighter disappeared.

'Bloody fine show, Skip,' said Derek Shaw. 'You shook him off easily.'

They thought no more about it until they reached Tempsford some hours later when the ground crew showed them the damage – just two machine-gun bullets. However, they had hit a vital part of the undercarriage and the aircraft was put out of action for some time.

Some weeks later Geoff had to drop two tough-looking Joes, reputed to be ex-Foreign Legionnaires, deep into French mountainous country close to the Swiss border. This was to be the longest in flight time – over nine hours. When they arrived over the field the reception was perfectly laid out, but when Geoff flashed the Morse challenge letter on the identification light, he was given an incorrect one from the ground. Some latitude was allowable as many of the Resistance workers were unskilled in Morse but this was nothing like the letter. He could not chance it. It was no go. Three times they flew over the reception but each time the reply to the challenge was faulty. Orders were that no drop was ever to be made in the event of a wrong signal response in case the Germans had compromised the circuit. There was nothing for it but to abort the operation and return the agents and supplies back to base.

In the meantime the Joes in the back were turning nasty. 'What the bloody hell's the problem?' said one of them to Wilmott, the dispatcher. Wilmott listened through the intercom for a moment and then closed the Joe hole.

'We've had the wrong signal from below. We've been circling your dropping point for nearly half an hour. There could be a bust-up down there but we don't know for sure. If you drop you could be landing straight into the hands of the Germans. It's absolutely nothing doing, I'm afraid.'

One of the agents eyed the Joe hole. They could make a run for it.

'Look,' he said, 'we're going to give it a go anyway. We know that's the bloody field. We're jumping anyway.' And they tried to force their way past the dispatcher to the hole.

'Skip,' said Wilmott on the intercom, 'I think we're in for trouble as I've had difficulty preventing them from jumping every time we passed over the reception'.

'Right, send one of them up here,' replied Geoff.

When the Joe stepped into the cockpit, Geoff saw he had a Smith & Wesson in his hand. 'You'd better drop us or else,' said the man nastily, pressing the gun to Geoff's head.

There was no doubt the agents meant business. They were unscrupulous and nothing would stop them. But Geoff banked on the fact the man would not pull the trigger. If he did he would be putting his life at risk. He decided to try some diplomacy.

'You'd better not do anything stupid,' he said. 'If that gun goes off, you put all our lives at risk. I quite understand your frustration, but the Germans have infiltrated Resistance circuits in the past and if I let you jump I could be endangering your lives. Look, the risk is too great. You're in my care. I'm under orders, and I'm sorry we've got no choice but to turn back. We'll try again on another night after we know everything is all right on the ground.'

This diplomacy seemed to calm him down and grudgingly the man accepted the situation. Derek Shaw, who had been standing behind the agent with the fire axe in his hand and ready to strike, let out a sigh of relief. That had been a close one. It was possible the agent may have been bluffing but the situation could have turned out very differently. Geoff never did find out if the reception committee had been taken over by the enemy or if they had mistakenly been given the wrong code letter.

In his book *Wings of Night*, Alexander Hamilton wrote:

By virtue of the nature of public morale, the raids undertaken by Bomber Command made daily headlines. The Ruhr, Bremen, Hamburg, Hanover and countless others became well known to the embattled people of Britain. The deepening interest lay, not in the names of remote German cities under bombardment, but in the number of British aircraft which 'failed to return'. Of those engaged from RAF Tempsford never a word was spoken, with each mission clouded in absolute secrecy and the pilots, crew (except those being inserted into enemy territory by the small two-seater Lysander) and the Joes setting out in to the complete unknown, steeped in unqualified danger. Tempsford pilots and crew were soon to become acquainted with both bravery and intense danger.

'You're dropping a VIP woman agent into France tonight,' said Wilf Burnett to Geoff. When he was introduced to 'Isabelle' (her real name was Madeleine Lavigne, she died in Paris in February 1945), a tall, attractive woman, he noticed she was very heavily made up and perfumed.

'Did you notice her make-up?' commented Geoff to Bob Willmott when they were alone.

'All these women Froggies make the 'ole bloody aircraft smell like a bleedin whore's boudoir!' he complained.

Major Charles Tice, the Army Liaison Officer, told them Isabelle was going back into the field for the second time and was to be dropped near Reims in the Ardennes in Silversmith, the codename for the Resistance Circuit in that area. On her first trip she had been captured by the Gestapo, who had tortured her by stubbing out lighted cigarettes on her face. The make-up covered the scars. She had made a daring escape from her jailers but incredibly had volunteered to return to France.

The Stirling climbed steadily. Forty minutes later they were flying over the English Channel. Derek Shaw glanced out of the cockpit window. Not a break was to be seen in the thick white carpet of clouds.

'Looks like pea soup down there, Skip,' he said to Geoff. 'We didn't expect this. Why don't those Met fellows get it right for once?'

Then without any warning a loud *crack* sounded in the middle of the aircraft, followed by another lightning strike at the nose. Geoff looked at the instrument panel, it glowed in a strange red colour. He rubbed his eyes and eventually they returned to normal as his sight cleared. He called up the wireless operator on the intercom.

'Any damage amidships?'

'My set's out of action, Skip,' replied Howell, 'otherwise, everything's OK.'

The Stirling flew on, Geoff hoping no serious damage had occurred.

Navigator Mac came on the intercom, 'ETA at reception five minutes, Skip.'

Geoff called up Roger Court, the map reader. 'Can you see the railway crossing pinpoint?'

'It's just over on the starboard side. Steer 070 degrees for four minutes and the reception should be straight ahead. I'll go down to the bombing panel now, OK. Skip?'

'Roger, map reader. I can see the pinpoint,' replied Geoff.

At the end of the four-minute run, Geoff could see the reception lights ahead and a torch flashing the letter 'L', the correct reply to the challenge.

'Open the Joe hole, dispatcher, and get the agent ready,' he told Wilmott.

'She's all ready and waiting, Skip.'

'Right, love, it's action stations! GO! Good luck!' and Wilmott pushed Isabelle, who was sitting on the edge of the Joe hole, out of the aircraft with his foot. Down she dropped, floating 500 feet above the ground, the slipstream nearly knocking the breath out of her. The lights of the reception came closer and closer, and the noise of the Stirling receded into the night.

As well as supplying the resistance movements in France, Holland and Belgium, there were also operations to Norway and Denmark for Geoff and his crew. The Danish Resistance circuits were the most pleasant as they meant low flying in bright moonlight over delightful countryside with no heavily defended areas to worry about. Also there was no need to circle a dropping zone two or three times, as in France, as agent Tablejam, the head of the Danish Resistance, had asked them to drop agents and containers on the first run and straight on to the reception field without waiting for a recognition signal.

However Norway was a different story. It was particularly difficult because of its mountainous terrain, and Geoff was relieved when the trip was over. One particular operation, codenamed Crupper 7, on 29 August, was to drop two Joes to a reception deep in a valley surrounded by mountains. Fifty minutes after take-off, George, the automatic pilot, became unserviceable, and the aircraft had to be flown manually for the rest of the seven-and-a-half-hour trip. It would have been much easier if George had been operable as the flight home over the North Sea was long and cold. The reception was not far away now, about 2,000 feet below the mountain tops. Geoff could see tiny dots of light far below him, beyond which was the shape of a huge mountain. It was a dangerous situation to be in and called for all his piloting skill as he had to dive down and level out over the reception to drop the Joes. Silently he cursed the reception committee.

'Can you see the reception down below, Roger?'

'Yes, I've got it, Skip.'

'I'm going to dive and flatten out – try to get rid of the lot in one go. Engineer, give me one-third flap.'

'One-third flap, Skipper.'

The familiar cold sweat trickled down his back ... He reduced power on the engines as he had to lose height quickly to about 50 feet above the top of the mountain. The snow glistened in the bright moonlight, its glacial coldness glowing. How many people had succumbed to it, he wondered. He had to reach that reception somehow, carry out the drop and get away without crashing into that mountain on the other side, put the nose down, level out...

'Containers gone, Skip!' called Court through the intercom.

'Joes gone too, Skip,' said Wilmott.

The bomb doors closed. He gave the engines full bore and applied port aileron to put the aircraft into a steep climbing turn, the Stirling's reliable Hercules engines screamed as the huge aircraft just avoided hitting the mountain slope ... 1,000 feet ... 2,000 ... 3,000 ... They had made it, and they all let out sighs of relief. Now for the long haul home.

After the war, Geoff discovered that losses on Scandinavian operations had been high and his friend Mick Brogan had disappeared on a mission over Denmark. Mick Brogan, the good-natured Irishman who was liked by everybody and had joined 138 Squadron as a flight commander at the same time as Geoff, had been the target of so many of Geoff's practical jokes. Newly married, he had spent every available minute with his wife Audrey in Bedford. Geoff was always pulling his leg, and once had written a postagram posting Mick to Burma. He had left this on Wilf Burnett's desk when he was away flying, and when Wilf returned he had picked it up, read it and then called the adjutant to send for Mick. When Mick read the postagram his face fell. 'But sir,' he said, 'I'm married. Couldn't they send Rothwell, who's single?'

'Sorry, old boy,' said Wilf. 'Orders are orders. You've got forty-eight hours to pack.' Geoff, who was peeping through a slide hatch in the next office, realised the joke had gone too far and decided to come clean. It was just as well, as Mick was going to telephone his wife to give her the sad news. Rothwell was not the most popular man on the station that day in Mick's estimation.

One day at Tempsford a container marked medical supplies burst open on hitting the ground, revealing supplies of sanitary towels, groceries of various descriptions and many packets of condoms. To the Resistance these were the necessities of life for which many hundreds of bomber crews were risking life and limb.

Nobody, not SOE including the agents and Special Duty crews, had any idea how dangerous the situation was in the Netherlands. Long before Geoff had been posted to Tempsford, the Germans had been transmitting to London on seventeen captured agents' radio sets. The operation, codenamed *Nordpol* (North Pole) or *Das Englandspiel,* is the story of how Herman Giskes of the Abwehr broke into SOE's intelligence in Holland. This travesty caused the capture of fifty-eight Dutch agents, of whom fifty-seven died in Mauthausen Concentration Camp, the deaths or capture of numerous Special Duty air crews, plus a great loss of supplies. All dropped straight into the hands of the Germans.

Sixty-one agents fell into German hands through compromised circuits before the gaff was blown on 1 April 1944, when the Germans realised they could no longer keep up the subterfuge. The German counter-espionage officer responsible for operation 'North Pole', Oberstleutnant Giskes, sent a message over the transmitters they had captured:

To Messrs Blunt, Bingham & Co., Successors Ltd, London. We understand that you have been endeavouring for some time to do business in Holland without our assistance. We regret this the more since we have acted for so long as your sole representatives in this country, to our mutual satisfaction. Nevertheless we can assure you that, should you be thinking of paying us a visit on the continent on any extensive scale, we shall give your emissaries the same attention as we have hitherto, and a similarly warm welcome. Hoping to see you.

II

LUCK RUNS OUT

Mothers! you who wait in anguish,
Watch with dread for news each day,
White-faced mothers, worn with weeping,
Think of one thing when you pray...
                              – Private King, 1915

8 September 1944
In a stunning ten-day display of style and vigour, British,
Canadian and Polish forces have raced across northern France
and into Belgium to liberate Brussels and capture the key port
of Antwerp. The Canadians are besieging the Channel ports
of Boulogne, Calais, and Dunkirk, where the Germans are
clinging on in order to deny the Allies port facilities close to
the front lines.

Hitler is desperately scrambling together new infantry
divisions by drafting the elderly and disabled who have been
carrying out guard duties in rear areas.

                              – Daily Telegraph

Geoff never really expected S.P. to turn up to the dance – he
thought it unlikely she would get leave – but when he saw her his
heart leapt. She came across the smoke-filled room towards him a
little shyly, dressed in ATS uniform, a cap perched jauntily on her

freshly washed curls, her face aglow. For a moment he was unable to speak. It was such a long time since he had seen her and he had almost forgotten how beautiful she was. He held his hand out to her and pulled her to him, kissing her gently, smelling her sweet smell, not caring if anybody saw.

He looked down at her, smiling into her dark eyes. 'You smell delicious,' he said. 'Chanel No. 5?'

'Yes, what you gave me for my birthday. Oh Geoff, I just want this war to end, to live in a normal world again.

'It's what we all want. It can't be long now.'

She looked at him without appearing to, looking for changes, noticing the lines of tiredness around his eyes. She knew he had been transferred, knew deep in her heart he was doing something dangerous and was unable to tell her anything, not that she would have asked. Part of her did not want to know, she worried enough about him. It helped that she kept busy. She never ceased to be amazed at his kindness and consideration towards her, and consequently her love for him had strengthened. He was prepared to do anything for her, including travelling far to see her whenever he could get leave. But the sadness of frequent partings was intensified by the uncertainty of whether they would survive to meet again.

That last meeting had been a long time ago and now he had completed his seventieth operation at Tempsford. He was to be promoted to Wing Commander to take over the squadron as Wilf Burnett had been posted to Bomber Command Headquarters. Although delighted at the prospect of promotion, he knew he would be faced with much more administrative work and therefore would be unable to operate to the same extent. Could he get in one more op before being chained to a desk, he asked Wilf. 'Sure thing, Geoff,' said Wilf.

And Geoff put himself on programme for that night.

There were only two jobs, 'freshman' ops, and both in the Dutch Alkmaar district – easy operations usually given a new crew. He felt a little foolish and mentioned it to Wilf.

'This is your last opportunity for a while,' said Wilf, patting Geoff on the back. 'Take it and go!'

According to the met officer, they should have a trouble-free flight across the North Sea, as apart from a few isolated storm clouds the weather was perfect. In addition to supplies they would be taking two Joes, Draughts and Backgammon, and a load of homing pigeons stowed in small cardboard boxes attached to miniature parachutes. Strapped to the pigeons' legs were capsules containing questionnaires on important military information in the district, which hopefully would be found by patriots. It was usual practice after completing the questionnaire for the patriot to roll up the rice paper, put it in the capsule on the pigeon's leg and release the bird, which would then return to its home loft somewhere in Bedfordshire. However, in the strictly rationed enemy-occupied countries of Europe, the prospect of a plump pigeon for supper was sometimes too much to resist, even for the most fervent patriot.

At dispersal, Geoff and his crew had a last pipe and cigarette. It was a beautiful late summer evening with a clear full moon, perfect weather for flying. He watched idly as a few feet away a crow pecked at a worm in the grass, then rose screeching into the air. He glanced at his watch – it was time.

'Right, chaps,' he said. 'Get aboard.'

At Gibraltar Farm the two agents, Pieter de Vos and Tobias Biallosterski, were being prepared for their flight. They were returning to Holland to join the Dutch Resistance in the field.

'There should be no worries,' said Bunny Warren, the conducting officer, to the agents. 'You're being taken by one of the best crews in one-three-eight Squadron.'

As the crew climbed into the Stirling, the agents, dressed in civilian clothes, alighted from a car with blacked-out windows. Warren introduced Geoff to the men and Geoff shook their hands. 'Don't worry,' he said. 'This trip's a piece of cake and I'll get you there without any trouble.'

Stirling IV LKZOO, *U Uncle*, was soon airborne and the agents settled down on a pile of engine covers in the back of the aircraft for the journey. It was not going to be a long trip, no more than perhaps three or four hours. The aircraft headed east towards the coast.

Ethel Rothwell, unable to sleep, heard the noise of the aircraft as it passed overhead. Of course she did not know it was his aircraft; all she could hear was the throbbing of a four-engined bomber which grew louder and louder as it passed over the cottage.

It was not easy having a son in the Air Force, knowing that most nights he would be flying over enemy territory, that there was nothing she could do about it, and knowing all the time that something could happen to him, and that if something did, part of her would die too.

'Please God,' she would pray silently. 'Look after him. Please keep him safe.'

He would come home from leave and he would always be the same and yet not the same. He would have the same tall figure and the wavy red hair, and he would smile at her as he stooped to kiss her, and she would notice the dark shadows under his eyes and the little lines deepening on the sides of his mouth. She would settle him in a chair while she cooked a meal, and he, always hungry, would wolf it down, and she would sit and watch him as he ate. Then she would clear the plates from the table and as she did so, she would look at him without him knowing, as if she was trying to remember every little detail about him, in case, in case ...

They were half-way to their ETA now, and looking in the direction of the Dutch coast lying dead ahead Geoff saw a giant cumulonimbus cloud directly in their path. He silently cursed Taffy Jones, the meteorological officer, who had assured him there were no weather problems to worry about. Little did he know that the other sortie from Tempsford had aborted and returned to base – wise fellow. He debated whether to climb over the cloud, thereby giving the German radar warning of their approach, or attempt to fly straight through it. In the end he realised it would be impossible to gain sufficient height to fly over the cloud and decided to climb from the present level of 500 feet and enter the cloud at around 6,000 feet.

It was rough going, so rough that the agents in the back thought the heavy turbulence was caused by flying over a flak barrage off the Dutch coast. 'This will be another failed attempt to get back to Holland,' thought Backgammon. The strain of the whole trip was beginning to play on his nerves, following, as it did, a sortie the previous night aborted through bad weather.

Geoff followed the plan for flying through storms, which was to maintain straight and level flight. However, it was contrary to his instinct and all he had learned in his years of operational flying. The turbulence was so great that the huge aircraft was tipped from one wingtip to the other, plunging up and down. *Straight and level ... straight and level*, he told himself.

Eventually, fearing structural damage if he remained in the cloud, he decided to drop down to sea level and try to fly underneath the storm. He descended to 150 feet in driving rain, and switching on the landing lights he saw 'a tempestuous sea' beneath them. Then just as suddenly as it arrived the storm abated and they were in brilliant moonlight again. They made landfall over a horseshoe-shaped bay on Vlieland, a small island in the Frisian group, with scrubby grass and sand dunes. In the glistening moonlight the dunes looked low and flat. From Vlieland they set course for the end of the causeway which stretches across the vast expanse of water, forming an inland sea and joining the peninsula of North Holland with Friesland on the east side.

Switching on his microphone, Geoff called up the map reader, Roger Court. 'That's Den Oever coming up on the starboard side. Roger. If we fly due south you should pick up a good pinpoint on that road from Slootdorp.'

'Roger. Skipper. What's our ETA at Mandrill, Mac?'

'Another twelve minutes.'

'Roger. Am I right that this canal leads us straight to the target?'

'That's right, Skip. Just follow it. I'll get the bombing panel set up, if that's OK with you.'

'Sure, that's OK, Roger,' said Geoff. 'Dispatcher, get the Joes ready. We'll be over the reception in a few minutes.'

'Roger, Skip. I'm opening the Joe hole and they're ready to go,' said Wilmott, lifting the hatch over the Joe hole and checking the static lines on the agents' parachutes. They sat on the edge, their feet dangling in the slipstream, breathing in the cold of the night. A light flashed the Morse code letter 'A' – the signal for the drop to go ahead.

The bomb aimer pressed the light switch.

'Let 'em go, Bob,' he said.

The green light flashed on the panel above the Joe hole and Wilmott pushed first one and then the other with his foot, watching the courageous agents disappear below the aircraft.

'Joes gone.'

'I can see them right on the lights of the reception,' said Wally from his rear turret.

The Stirling flew on for a while and circled once over open country to confuse the Germans in case their radar had picked up the aircraft. By now the wind had strengthened and shifted, but soon both agents were in a warm farmhouse drinking glasses of Bols to calm their nerves. As soon as possible, Draughts sent the following message to London.

9 September, 1944
From Draughts via Plym.

Safe landing all MJEE is OK stop Balder shot two months ago stop Love Eva.

Meanwhile back on board the Stirling, the containers of arms and ammunition were dropped and the carrier pigeons were thrown out in their cardboard boxes on the way back. The job well done, the aircraft returned to the pinpoint on the causeway, and Geoff altered course to bring them over Vlieland again.

'Vlieland directly ahead,' said Roger. 'We're a little to port.'

They were still flying at a height of 300 feet and Mac, the navigator, always meticulous, came up to the cockpit to see for himself. Just as he looked through the windscreen the Stirling staggered as though it had hit some solid object.

Geoff looked at his instruments, saw they had picked up speed and instinctively hauled back on the control column with all his strength but then knew they were going to stall.

'Give me an emergency course to base, Mac!' he yelled.

'Steer two-seven-oh to start with,' came the reply.

As soon as Geoff saw the air speed indicator, he knew the hopelessness of their situation. It was inoperable, the needle had dropped to the bottom of the scale. It registered 250 knots and made him think the Stirling was in a dive, then the starboard inner propeller flew off and fire broke out in the engine, rapidly spreading to the wing. Fuel pressure was lost on three engines. They were still flying over water and too low to bale out. He gripped the wheel, fighting to keep the Stirling on a straight course, but they were rapidly losing height. There was no time to be nervous or to feel despair. There was no time to think of anything, to say his last prayers, or to wonder whether he and the crew would survive. Quite coolly he knew they were going to crash and there was nothing he could do to prevent that happening.

'Ditching stations, everybody,' he yelled over the intercom.

He thought they were going to crash in the Waddenzee, but as the Stirling dropped like a stone, he could see they were over sand dunes and then a hillock into which it appeared certain they would crash head-on. He heard Mac yelling that the starboard wing was stalling. Seconds later *U Uncle* hit the ground with a gigantic thud and the land and the moon, dancing madly, spun all around him. He was aware only of being hurled against the control column, the sickness rising in his stomach and the noise of splintered metal as the Stirling disintegrated, before he was picked up and thrown like a rag doll violently through the cockpit roof. Then all receded into blessed oblivion.

Some time later he reached up to the edge of consciousness and grasped it tightly lest he lose it for ever. There was a sensation of being pulled down, of there being no light, only darkness, and of drowning in a black void. It could have been an hour or a few minutes before he gradually started to recover consciousness, and then he realised he was unable to see. For a moment he wondered if he was blind. It would be so easy to lie here, he thought. It was warm and safe and he didn't have to think any more – didn't have to make any more decisions. That was the best part. There was nothing, absolutely nothing to do any more, and it would be so easy to go back to sleep.

But then he began to suffocate and slowly realised that there was sand up his nose, in his eyes and in his mouth, and if he didn't lift his head, he would surely die. And as he did so, he became aware of a pain in every part of his body. Lifting his head was like trying to lift a lump of lead. His chest felt as if it was clamped down, and he had a raging thirst. There was something wrong with the co-ordination between his body and his brain. Perhaps he had died and was in some transitory place between Heaven and Hell? There was no recollection of the crash itself. Then the answers came slowly, slowly.

Too low to bale out, he had looked down and seen the sand dunes, and then the Stirling had hit the ground.

I'm alive! As he said these words, he felt astonished, as if he did not expect to be. The thoughts kept coming... *Get up, you've crashed. Don't go to sleep. Find the others. They may still be alive. Get help.* And with that thought he made a supreme effort to sit up, this simple action causing him to cry out from the pain in his chest. *Must have broken some ribs.* He looked down and saw he was wearing only one shoe and his helmet was nowhere to be seen. He brushed the sand out of his eyes and as his vision started to return he could see he was in a sand dune amidst the wreckage of his aircraft, which was strewn everywhere. The starboard wing was blazing furiously, having broken off from the fuselage which was buckled and crushed.

He got up slowly and stood there looking at the wreckage, trying to take in the enormity of what had happened. It was then he saw Mac. He was sitting with his head in his hands, a deep and nasty gash on his shin and his thumb hanging loosely. There was no sign of the others.

'Jesus, what happened?' he said when he saw Geoff. And then: 'Are you all right?'

'Yes,' said Geoff, and looking at the hole in his shin: 'Does that hurt?'

'Of course it bloody hurts,' replied Mac.

'Don't worry. Stay here and I'll find the others.'

Not far away Geoff found Derek Shaw, close to the disintegrated fuselage. He seemed to be unconscious, his breath coming in great gasps. Blood was pouring from a severe head wound. *Better not move him.* Bob Wilmott was sitting on top of a sand dune a short distance away, one of his legs sticking out at an odd angle. When he went closer Geoff could see a fragment of bone sticking out. He was conscious and moaning quietly, and was otherwise unhurt.

'You've got a broken leg, old son,' said Geoff. 'I can't move you – it's too dangerous. Try to hold on. Help will arrive soon.'

'I'm OK, Skip' said Bob faintly. 'I'll be all right. You get away.'

There was no sign of the rest of the crew. Geoff hated leaving Bob, knowing the Germans would have seen the flames from the blazing aircraft by now and would soon be on the scene. He stumbled back to where he had left Mac. The fire from the crashed Stirling was burning fiercely and he was afraid the petrol tanks would explode. There was nothing he could do about Bob and Derek. When the Germans came they would take them to hospital.

'We've got to get away before the Germans come,' he told Mac.

They were both in a state of shock, concussed and with raging thirsts, but they knew they had to pull themselves together. With no idea where they were, but assuming they were on Vlieland, they started walking across a field, and as they did so, an idea started to form in Geoff's mind. Maybe they could find a boat and get down the coast, as the British Army was believed to be on the Belgian/Dutch border somewhere to the south.

He kept thinking of the injured men and what had become of the other members of his crew. Mac's leg wounds had to be treated and they needed to find somebody who could tell them about the current situation on the island. With difficulty they trudged across the field, Geoff with only one shoe, and Mac limping and in pain from his wounds. They shivered; the night had grown chilly and a cold wind hit through their clothing. Lights flickered ahead. It could be transport. This seemed strange as it was supposed Vlieland was unoccupied.

Mac unexpectedly produced a language card and apprehensively they knocked on the door of the first house they came to. It was opened furtively and they were just able to make out the dim figure of a man lurking in the doorway. As soon as he saw them he abruptly stepped back and tried to close the door, but Geoff's foot was in the way. With the aid of a cigarette lighter they scanned the language card but the only applicable phrase was: 'Where is the enemy?' The Dutchman pointed to the way they had come, so they felt they were heading in the right direction.

It was difficult not being able to speak Dutch but they were able somehow to convey that they were desperate for a drink, so the man closed the door and in a few minutes returned with a cup and a jug full of delicious water. They drank every bit, and a second jug.

With a *danke* they decided to try their luck at the next house along the road in the hope that somebody there might speak English. All seemed quiet in the house but when they looked through a wide picture window a commotion broke out – men shouted, women screamed and children cried. They must have disturbed a family sleeping in the room, so they retreated quickly. As they went around the back of the house they found a tiny shed into which they managed to squeeze.

By now both of them were suffering from exhaustion, in considerable pain and could not have walked any further. There was just enough room for them to collapse on to the floor with their knees drawn up to their chest. As they were about to nod off they heard a rustling sound from somewhere above them. Geoff shone his cigarette lighter and saw some rabbits huddled together on a shelf.

Some time later they were roused by the noise of the back door of the house being unbolted and opened. Maybe it was somebody coming to render assistance, but the footsteps suddenly stopped. They could hear the sound of someone relieving himself on the cobblestones. They called out and the person ceased urinating abruptly, banged the door shut and bolted it.

In London a message was being sent to Draughts.

9 September, 1944
To Draughts Via night Plym.

Delighted with news because aircraft did not repeat not come back stop. Did you have reception and were containers dropped Good luck.

Just as dawn was breaking, they were awakened by the sound of knocking at the door of the shed and they pushed it open. A man beckoned to them to go through a hedge. They followed him into the house next door, where they were ushered into a warm kitchen. The man's wife indicated for them to sit down. For the first time since the accident Geoff was able to attend to Mac's injuries, using the first aid dressing pack he carried. There was a nasty gash in his broken thumb in addition to the one on his shin. He put a plastic bag filled with sulphanilamide powder over the thumb and a dressing on the shin. Geoff himself had a nasty pain in his side, indicating broken ribs.

It was getting lighter all the time and the Dutch woman was hovering silently in the background. They produced one of the escape maps and asked the couple their whereabouts with the aid of the multi-language card. To their surprise they found they were at a place called De Cocksdorp on the island of Texel, and not Vlieland, as they had assumed. When the aircraft had been hit it must have swung around on to a westerly heading and Geoff, preoccupied with keeping the aircraft airborne, had not noticed what had happened.

The Dutchman and his wife were not unfriendly but clearly uneasy having two Allied airmen in their house. Suddenly the man produced a large box which Geoff thought could contain a wireless set. He strapped the box on to the back of a bicycle and set off down the road, pedalling furiously. The men guessed the couple were afraid that the Germans would be searching for them and as they had no wish to put the couple in any danger, they thanked the woman and left.

They were in an invidious position. They had left the injured crew, needing urgent medical treatment, back at the crash site although by now it was highly likely they had been found by the Germans as the blazing wreck of the Stirling would have been seen by all and sundry. They could not speak a word of Dutch and so far had not met anyone who could speak English. Now on the run, they needed to escape; it was the duty of every airman. The longer they were at large, the more danger they were in, as with every passing minute the Germans would be coming closer and closer to finding them. Their best bet was to keep going in the hope they would find someone who would shelter them until they could find some means of escape from the island.

The September day was grey and overcast, with a little watery sun trying to squeeze through the clouds. It was still early in the morning and there was no traffic. They kept off the road, walking behind a hedge, but had to duck down as a German transport passed, until they came to a farmyard where there was a man working on a haystack.

'We are RAF aircrew,' said Geoff in English. 'Can you help us to find a boat to get off the island? Is there a resistance movement here?'

The man understood English and spoke it well. He told them his name was De Graaf.

'It is impossible to escape,' he said. 'All boats have been confiscated. The Germans have already found your aircraft and know some of the crew are missing. They are searching for you now.'

Obviously the transport they had just seen and the one after the crash were German patrols on the way to the crash site. Nobody could help them and now it was only a matter of time before they were found.

De Graaf took them into the farmhouse and after some discussion they decided there was no alternative but to give themselves up. It was a heartbreaking decision, but the only one they could make in view of their poor physical condition. At least they knew the survivors of the crew would be receiving the necessary medical attention. They gave their pistols – two Smith & Wesson .38s – to De Graaf and told him to take them to the nearest German unit as an official sign of surrender. Although apprehensive about taking the weapons De Graaf told them he would come back with a soldier.

A document released in 1993 to a Dutch historian, Dr Theo Boiten from Groningen University, states that De Graaf was interviewed after the war about the details of the crash of Stirling LKZOO. The text of the interview includes a passage on the surrender of Geoff and Mac to the Germans.

De Graaf now was given the two revolvers by the two flyers, and was told to bring them to the Germans as an official sign of surrender. So De Graaf went on his bike to the German garrison on the Island, and handed over the two guns to the German commander of the garrison. Thereupon the commander said to De Graaf: 'With these old shit guns we were shooting a hundred years before Christ,' which was bluff of course.

They sat in the farmhouse waiting for De Graaf's return, with their heads in their hands. What would happen next? Would they be well-treated by their captors? For Geoff, his morale was the lowest it had ever been. They started to doze but were awakened by the sound of heavy boots crunching in the farmyard. Two German soldiers armed with rifles appeared.

'*Raus! Raus! Komm! Schnell, Englische Terrorflieger!*' they shouted as they roughly propelled the two men through the kitchen door. When they noticed Geoff had only one shoe they commandeered a clog from the farmer. With heavy hearts they set off down the road into a bitter wind until they reached a type of guardhouse manned by naval personnel. There they were given a cup of filthy coffee floating with seeds and debris. This was the standard brew in wartime German-occupied Europe and also in the Fatherland.

They still had not met anyone who spoke English, apart from the farmer, but their captors made themselves understood by gestures. They were made to turn out their pockets and were searched, and when their belongings were eventually returned Geoff noticed that a beautiful Parker pen, a twenty-first birthday present from his parents, was missing. He immediately complained but never saw the pen again.

In the afternoon they were taken somewhat incongruously in a horse-drawn open coach to a small seaport. They sat on a seat facing the rear whilst a German with a rifle sat opposite them as they progressed at a leisurely pace, driven by a Dutchman. On the way they passed the field they had walked through the previous night. On the perimeter was a large board with the inscription *ACHTUNG. ACHTUNG, MINEN.* They had walked through a minefield.

At the port they boarded a ferry and were taken to the mainland harbour of Den Helder, where there was a convoy of coastal shipping vessels flying barrage balloons, presumably for protection against attack by low-flying intruder aircraft. While they waited in an office Geoff asked the English-speaking *Luftwaffe* officer about the fate of the rest of his crew but it was immediately obvious that any speaking was *verboten*.

'Nein information! For you the war is over! If you escape you will be shot!' It was a message they were to hear many times before reaching Stalag Luft I, their POW camp on the Baltic coast.

Speculation as to the cause of the crash continued for years. The Germans seemed to have no idea as no flak batteries had been in operation and there were no night fighter aircraft airborne.

The following day the convoy in Den Helder harbour was attacked by low-flying Beaufighters led by a New Zealander, Bill Tacon, who crashed at the opposite end of Texel from where Geoff crashed. Tacon survived the crash and died in Auckland in 2003.

Immediately after the Liberation in May 1945, De Graaf and his elder brother were arrested by the Dutch military, which had taken over the command of the island of Texel from the Germans. They were locked in the Roman Catholic school in their village because, they were told, 'they had disarmed Allied flyers and handed them over to the enemy,' for which they could be shot. This was a tragic situation, because shortly before the Liberation, De Graaf's father and another brother were killed in the uprising of the hundreds of Russian prisoners of war on the island (which was suppressed by the Germans, killing almost all the Russians and lots of islanders in the process).

After the war the balance sheet of Special Duties was compiled: 138 Squadron carried out 2,562 sorties whilst stationed at Tempsford; 995 agents, 29,000 containers and 10,000 packages were dropped. Seventy aircraft failed to return and the agents suffered six casualties on deployment, usually from being dropped too low, although two were Joes who jumped without the static lines being attached to their parachutes.

12

GUESTS OF THE THIRD REICH

Freedom is the only thing worth living for. While I was
doing that work I used to think that it didn't matter if
I died, because without freedom there was no point in living.
— Nancy Wake, 25 October 1968
Sydney Morning Herald

Trier, Germany, 11 September 1944

American forces resuming their advance in the central sector
today crossed the Germany/Luxembourg border north of
Trier and began probing the Siegfried Line defences. In the
north, other American forces crossed the Dutch border at
Maastricht and are poised for a thrust on Aachen.

Daily Telegraph

On the day following the crash Geoff and Mac were transported
in an open Volkswagen vehicle to the very point on the causeway
they had so recently used as a pinpoint on their last operation.
There they were taken to an underground control room that
operated the sluices of the dam. They sat there for a long
time; the waiting was interminable. Where was the evidence of
German efficiency?

Depression started to seep in as they were suffering from fatigue, cold and hunger and it was a long time since they had had a decent meal or any sleep. Would their wounds be properly treated? What would the treatment be like for them in POW camp?

Some of their questions were soon answered. In the late evening they were ushered into a Mercedes-Benz car, which travelled at high speed across the causeway and dropped them at a hospital in the town of Harlingen. There they were examined by a German doctor, who could not understand why the Air Force raincoat Geoff was wearing had no badges of rank. 'You are British spy,' he kept saying to Geoff.

To satisfy him Geoff took off the raincoat and showed him the stripes on the shoulder of his battle dress blouse, and when the doctor compared them with a chart of German badges of rank and found he was the equivalent of a major, he expressed disbelief.

'You are lying!' he exclaimed. 'You are too young to be a major.'

Geoff was convinced the doctor thought he was an impostor. For an awful moment he wondered if he would be thrown into prison and treated as a spy. But the doctor carried on examining him and strapped his ribs. Mac was taken to a room and given a bed, and as Geoff was thinking how nice it would be to settle down between clean sheets and rest his weary body, he was taken out of the hospital and back into the car again. With Mac gone he was alone.

Later they came to some kind of military establishment and he was taken into the guardroom, down a corridor and into a cell. He lay down on a wooden-slatted bed, too tired to take stock of his surroundings, and drifted into oblivion. The following morning he was awakened by a guard bringing him a cup of the filthy ersatz coffee he had drunk the previous day and a thick slice of black bread which looked as though it had a good proportion of floor sweepings in it and a thin scraping of something like lard. He wolfed it down, too hungry to notice the taste.

Whilst trying to come to terms with captivity he heard a voice calling out in German in the next door cell and a knocking on the wooden partition.

'*Sprechen Sie Deutsch?*' called the voice.
'*Nein.*'
'*Qui êtes-vous?*'
'*Je suis un aviateur anglais.*'

His unknown fellow prisoner told him the reason for his imprisonment was that he had been drunk the previous night. He directed Geoff's attention to the partition and then a cigarette was pushed through a small hole, followed by a match – kindness in captivity.

Lunch consisted of a bowl of watery soup with a fragment of greyish meat and another slice of the inevitable black bread. An air-raid siren sounded, causing a rushing of feet down the corridor. His cell door was flung open and he was hurried into an underground shelter with a guard. He sat on the bench, feeling conspicuous with a crowd of *Luftwaffe*, including some women in uniform. They chattered away, for the most part ignoring him. A burst of machine gunfire sounded close by. What was the target for today? The all-clear sounded and he was returned to the cell block, after discovering he was being housed at a German Air Force base at Leeuwarden and the attacker had been a Mosquito strafing the airfield.

He had been in the cell for two days when he was taken early one morning into the guardroom. The duty NCO climbed on to a chair and took a bottle of what looked like furniture polish from the top of a cupboard. Uncorking the bottle, he thrust it at him saying: '*Trink, trink.*' Geoff took a swig and felt the liquid warming him. This was his first introduction to schnapps and the kindness of his captor. He was ushered outside into the cold morning air, and to his delight saw Mac sitting in the back of a truck.

'Mac!' he cried. 'Any news of the crew?' And Mac told him that Derek Shaw had been brought unconscious into the hospital, but he knew nothing of Bob Wilmott and the others.

At dawn on 11 September the two men, guarded by a *Feldwebel* (sergeant) with rifle and pistol, boarded a train at Leeuwarden. The journey finally ended at mid-morning the following day, at Frankfurt-am-Main. As they crossed into German territory the country was flat and green. On the platform while waiting to change trains at Leer on the Dortmund–Ems Canal, they had a chance to look at the civilian population for the first time. They were grey-looking, down-at-heel, and with an air of defeat. Their shabbiness and depression was at once distressing and tangible. But there was no doubt they were the enemy and the RAF officers were prisoners in their land. Now they had crossed the border there was no possibility of escape. Up until then there had always been a slight hope they may have been rescued by the Dutch Resistance.

Fortunately, Geoff's old resilience surfaced. He knew the hopelessness of their situation, but nothing could keep him down for long. Perhaps if he struck up a conversation with their *Feldwebel* guard, who seemed to be pleasant, it would make the journey less unpleasant?

'Ach! Germany can never win this war!' said the guard resignedly. 'I hope it will be over soon.' Geoff endorsed this wholeheartedly.

Their journey took them south, along the River Ems, and Geoff, sitting by the window in the company of Mac and the *Feldwebel*, looked out at the passing countryside, his thoughts a long way away. He closed his eyes and listened to the noise of the train on the tracks and the click of the wheels, with every mile getting nearer to his destination – a prisoner-of-war camp in Germany. It was a grim prospect. His thoughts turned to home. What would they be doing now? He would have been posted as missing, the squadron and his family not knowing if he was alive or dead, or if he was a POW. Who would take over the squadron from Wilf Burnett now he was out of the running? His family would be going about their everyday life, not knowing yet what had happened.

They reached Hamm, the target of so many raids, in the afternoon. They looked for damage but saw little. They continued on their way, the train stopping at most stations, with the *Feldwebel* lowering the window and calling to what appeared to be groups of Women's Voluntary Service workers pushing trolleys with big tureens of soup. The soup was good and the women dished it out in bowls free of charge to the servicemen, and Geoff and Mac wolfed it down.

The train pulled into a station in the early evening. An air raid was in progress and they were hustled down some stairs into a tunnel which ran under the tracks. Grim-faced Germans sat sullenly in the shelter. As the Allied bombers thundered overhead they looked at the POWs menacingly. *Englische Schweine*, they muttered angrily, looking in their direction. The atmosphere in the shelter was stiff with hatred and Geoff and Mac were fearful for their safety. Suddenly several of them made threatening moves towards the two men but before they could do anything the *Feldwebel* drew his pistol and said '*Halte Dich zurueck, ich bin verantwortlich fuer die Gefangenen*' (Get back, I'm responsible for these prisoners), and they retreated. But the two men felt vulnerable and breathed sighs of relief when the all-clear sounded and they could get back to the safety of the train.

Not all prisoners' safety was automatically assured. After the war it was learned that on Wing Commander Don Saville's last mission to Hamburg in 1943, three of his crew who had managed to parachute from their flaming bomber had been lynched and hanged from lamp-posts by the local German population. As the intensity of Bomber Command's raids on Germany grew, so did the hazards of parachuting over enemy territory. In Frankfurt an RAF gunner was attacked by a mob and only saved by a *Luftwaffe* patrol who pulled him into a basement, later smuggling him out in a German tunic.

Finally in the early hours of the following morning they pulled into Frankfurt station, where there had been a heavy raid during the night. A short tram journey took them to the *Luftwaffe* Interrogation Centre at Oberursel, a small village on the outskirts of Frankfurt. The camp was nestled at the foot of a delightful wooded hillside and consisted of some six or seven buildings, above which numerous model farms had been built among the trees. This picturesque scene was enhanced by an old church, its tower protruding from the woods. A charming bridle path led to the top of a hill from where Frankfurt could be seen on the right and Bad Homburg on the left. In spite of the beauty of his surroundings Geoff felt apprehensive. The scene on the train had made him fearful and now at the interrogation centre this feeling was reinforced by the interrogator, who launched straight into a tirade of abuse, accusing them of being saboteurs.

'Tell us which country you are spying for and the names of your friends,' he screamed. 'You British are nothing but spies and the penalty for such subversive activity is death! You are criminals who have finally been caught in your own web!'

Geoff, weak and starved from lack of food, lashed out at the man.

'How could we be spies when we're RAF airmen, you bloody idiot?'

The German's face went scarlet. He jumped up and down. 'You will pay for this insolence! The Geneva Convention does not apply to vermin such as you as far as we are concerned.'

'That would be typical, coming from swine like you,' said Geoff, determined not to be outdone.

It was the last straw. Mac glanced nervously at Geoff as the German pressed a buzzer under his desk and two men, the same height as Geoff, came into the room. Without a word one grabbed hold of Geoff whilst the other punched him as hard as he could in the stomach. The force and pain of the blow almost knocked him over. It was excruciating with his injured ribs. Waves of faintness engulfed him, but he had no time to get his breath back as the burly henchman let fly with a right cross and Geoff sank to the ground. Mac protested and started to move forward but the other man grabbed him and frogmarched him out of the room.

Geoff was dragged to his feet, forced to walk down a long dark corridor and thrown into a cell numbered 8B. His body was racked with pain and he staggered over to a wooden slatted bed on which was a sack filled with straw. There was no other furniture in the icy cell. He pulled a scruffy threadbare grey blanket over himself, trying to fight the strange chilly feeling which was now engulfing him. For the first time in his life his freedom had been taken away from him and he had no idea how long he would be there – it might be hours, days or weeks. The pain was starting to pulsate throughout his chest. *They have probably broken more ribs,* he thought. To make matters worse, he was lousy with some vermin picked up from the filthy blankets he used after he was taken captive.

After what seemed like ages, he roused himself and took stock of his surroundings. The cell measured 8 by 5 feet. There were bars on the window and a radiator from which no heat could be detected. There was no water or bowl to wash himself. Alongside the door on the wall was a knob which, when turned, allowed a metal strip on the outside to drop and clatter. This was to alert a guard when a prisoner needed to go to the toilet. The guards took their time and prisoners were often left waiting.

The hours passed, and just when he was resigned to the fact he might never see food again, there was activity in the corridor and the cell door was suddenly opened, a guard announcing *'Das Essen! Das Essen!'* He looked down the corridor and saw guards with rifles over their shoulders pushing a trolley. They gave him a bowl of watery soup and the door was slammed shut. This was the standard German ration and would never vary the whole time he was in solitary confinement.

The next morning he awoke to a strange feeling of warmth. At first he thought the radiator must be turned on as the room became hotter and hotter. He removed first one and then more items of clothing and soon he was bathed in sweat. There was no air in the room as the window was sealed. He had no idea that the Germans used this 'heated cell treatment' as a means of softening up their captives. Then as suddenly as it began, the heating was turned off and the cell reverted to its icy self once again. Geoff endured this torture for the next two days, which passed in a blur of pain, hunger and stupefaction. Each morning he was given two slices of black bread with a splodge of something akin to red jam and a cup of odd-looking liquid containing bits of sticks, leaves, seeds and some kind of vegetable matter found under a hedge. This was referred to as *'Der Tee'* by the guards. This was to be his unvarying breakfast for the next fortnight.

It was while waiting for his meagre rations that he noticed his neighbour for the first time. He was standing in the doorway of 103. The man was stockily built, with fair hair, a high forehead and a long Roman nose. They exchanged no conversation. He was immediately suspicious as the man was dressed in what appeared to be 'best blue' and not the usual 'battle dress' which aircrew normally wear on operations. These suspicions were heightened by the fact that he did not have a flying badge over the pocket on his left breast. Perhaps he was a German 'plant' infiltrated to pick up information? It was to be some weeks before these suspicions were allayed.

One morning the cell door was thrown open and he was taken to an office, where he was photographed with a placard around his neck bearing his rank, name and number. He was told to sit at a table opposite a *Leutnant*, who produced a form for him to fill out.

'It is necessary for you to do this so you will receive Red Cross food parcels,' he was told. He filled out his name, rank and serial number, and read the rest of the questions.

Number of squadron?

Name of CO?

Name of airfield? Target, bomb load?

And a host of similar inadmissible questions, which he struck out.

'Sign the form,' said the *Leutnant*, and Geoff tore it up and gave him back the bits!

He thought the man would have a heart attack and had grave fears for his own safety. Surely he had gone too far this time. The *Leutnant's* face turned an unhealthy kind of puce. '*Bringe der Gefangene ezurueck in die Zelle!*' (Take the prisoner back to the cell) he yelled in a shrill voice to the guard. And as a parting shot said to him in English, 'Five years in a German prison camp will show you!'

Geoff was now officially POW No. 5865, or, as the Germans put it, Kriegsgefangener Nr. 5865. He was destined for Stalag Luft I at Barth, near Stralsund on the Baltic coast, north of Berlin.

On the third day a man of medium height with brown hair and a pleasant open face arrived at Cell 8B wearing civilian clothes. Speaking in faultless English with an impeccable Oxford accent, he shook Geoff's hand immediately. 'Terribly sorry, my dear fellow, for not seeing you sooner, but I've only just heard of your arrival.

I must apologise for the way you've been treated and you must let me know if there's anything you need.'

This man must be in the Gestapo, surely, Geoff thought. I'll play him at his own game. 'Apart from being beaten up by your bloody thugs, I haven't had a bath or a shower for a week and I'm lousy,' he replied.

'Good God, old man! I'll make arrangements for you to have a shower immediately,' said the German, and he opened the door of the cell. Geoff heard him barking orders to the guard. Shortly after the man left he was given a razor and a greyish tablet which looked like soap but didn't lather, then he was taken to the ablutions. To his astonishment the bathroom was full of POWs showering and shaving, two Germans guarding them with rifles.

'Who are you?' Geoff asked his nearest neighbour.

'*Nicht sprechen! Nicht sprechen!*' yelled one of the guards. However, beneath the sound of the running water Geoff managed to find out his fellow prisoners were paratroopers and glider pilots who had been captured on an operation at Arnhem in Holland.

This conversation, although short, did much to lift Geoff's morale. Although he did not know it then, on the day he crashed – 8 September 1944 – British, Canadian and Polish forces had raced across Northern France and into Belgium to liberate Brussels, capturing the key port of Antwerp. At the same time, Hitler, in desperation, was scrambling together new infantry divisions by drafting the elderly and the infirm. In the same month London prepared for the bright lights of peace by fitting a pre-war globe to a lamp in Piccadilly Circus. The end was in sight at last.

Later in the day he was taken out of the cell and down to the basement where a large boiler stood in the corner. The guard was not unfriendly and spoke with an American–English accent, telling him to undress for his clothes were to be fumigated and disinfected.

'Where did you learn your English?' asked Geoff.

'I was a butcher in New York before the war,' replied the guard, and went on to tell him something of his life there. By the time Geoff dressed again his clothes were scalding and he had to wave them about to cool them down first.

Geoff and his mother Ethel in 1938.

Geoff in a
de Havilland
Tiger Moth,
with the
mess in the
background,
taken at
Desford in
August 1939.

Joe Ready at
the controls
of an Anson,
Grantham,
1939.

The Spitfire was the plane Geoff initially really wanted to fly.

A Hawker Hurricane at RAF Station Duxford, December 1939.

May 1940: Geoff Rothwell as a young pilot, aged nineteen at 99 Squadron, based at Newmarket.

The Vickers Wellington was the bomber Geoff piloted with such skill that he was decorated for his efforts.

'The Three Musketeers': Joe Ready, Geoff Rothwell and Freddy Harold at Flying Training School, RAF Station Grantham in 1940.

Left: Geoff and Joe Ready in 1940. Geoff's comment referring to their height difference was: 'I'm standing in a hole!'

Below: Geoff's crew, with Geoff in the front row, second from the left; the picture was taken at Newmarket in 1940.

Right: Flight Lieutenant Roddy McKitrick, a big well-built man from Northern Ireland, had a DFC when he and Geoff met at Tempsford. He was Geoff's navigator.

Below: This picture, taken in America in 1942, shows Geoff, centre, interviewing a candidate who is sitting facing him.

RAF Pilot, 22, Tells Of Raids Over Germany

Church Group Hears Of 37 Personal 'Visits' Beyond Enemy Lines

Britain's bombers are pounding the continent nightly and carrying the war to Hitler's own backyard, Flight Lt. Geoffrey Rothwell, of the Royal Air Force, told members of the Fellowship Club of the South Highlands Presbyterian Church Thursday night following a dinner in his honor.

Painting a graphic picture of the Royal Air Force's bombing raids on the leading cities of Nazi Germany, Lt. Rothwell indicated he had, paid some 37 personal "visits" to Berlin, Emden and other German and German-occupied cities.

A robust, red-haired young man of 22 years, Lt. Rothwell is a veteran of more than two years of combat flying and has been decorated by the king for distinguished service. He was in training with the RAF for six months before the outbreak of war and began flying in combat shortly after the start of hostilities.

Young Rothwell was one of the fliers who took part in the desperate and heroic efforts of the Royal Air Force to fight off German planes during the "miracle of Dunkerque." Much of the success of the evacuation, he attributed to the British fighter command and the bomber command which smashed the advancing German columns and relieved pressure on the hard pressed rear guard.

Tribute was paid by the lieutenant to American planes which are being used by the Royal Air Force. Once he flew an American plane in after an air raid and when landing at the airdrome found a hole three feet in diameter in one of the wings, he said.

Describing many changes in his country, Lt. Rothwell said that most of the golf courses now are converted into patches of cabbages and carrots.

The young officer told of seeing women and children killed and maimed in bombing raids over England, and related an instance when a comrade, forced to bail out of his burning plane over a German city, was caught in the glare of a searchlight and his body was riddled with bullets.

In America only three weeks, the young flier's one impression of the country, he said, may be summed up in the word "colossal." And he commented on the many wooded areas which may be found in all sections of this country that he has visited.

The lieutenant, who is stationed with an RAF training group at Maxwell Field, Montgomery, was accompanied to Birmingham by Pilot Officer J. Gatiss, who flew him here.

H. G. Turner, president of the Fellowship Club, presided at the meeting. The distinguished young visitor was greeted at the Municipal Airport by William Pitts, President Turner, H. G. Mann and Steadham Acker.

The ribbon under Squadron Leader Geoffrey Rothwell's Royal Air Force insignia is for the Distinguished Flying Cross—given him by King George two days before his 21st birthday. His total trips to Germany and enemy territory: 37. He's over here to give British cadets-in-training the benefit of his experience.
—Staff Photo.

A graphic picture of the Royal Air ing cities of Nazi Germany was give Club of the Highland Presbyterian Ch RAF officer, Flight Lt. Geoffrey Roth with an RAF training group at Maxw

Declaring that Britain's bombers w ly, Lt. Rothwell indicated that he had paid some 37 personal "visits" to Berlin, Emden and other German cities.

A robust and red-headed young man of 22 years, Lt. Rothwell is a veteran of more than two years of combat flying, and wears the Distinguished Service Cross. He was in training with the RAF six months before the outbreak of war, and began flying in combat shortly after the start of hostilities.

He took part in the desperate and heroic efforts to fight off German planes during the "miracle of Dunkirk." He attributed much of the success of the evacuation to the British fighter command and to the bomber command which smashed the advancing German columns and relieved pressure on the hard-pressed rear-guard at Dunkirk.

He described many changes in his country. Most of the golf links have now been converted into patches of cabbages and carrots, he declared.

The young officer told of seeing women and children killed and maimed in bombing raids over England. He also related one instance of where a comrade, forced to bail out of his burning plane in the glare of a searchlight and his body riddled with bullets.

He paid a tribute to the stamina of the American planes which are being used. Once he flew in after a raid and, after landing at his airdrome, found a hole three feet in diameter in one of the wings of the plane.

He has been in America only three weeks. His one impression of the country, he said, may be summed up in the word "colossal." He remarked on the many wooded areas which may be found in all sections of the country where he has visited.

H. G. Turner, president of the Fellowship Club, presided at the meeting.

Left: An interview in a newspaper in America.

Below: This 1942 picture shows Geoff, far right, in Billy Rose's Deadwood Horseshoe Night Club in New York.

1942, Birmingham, Alabama: Geoff with H. G. Turner and Jack Gatiss.

Geoff, left, and a fighter pilot, Johnny Freeborn, right, stand on either side of the film star Tyrone Power who was in naval uniform on the set of *Crash Dive* in 1942. Geoff didn't get to see this film until 1988.

Above: 1942. One-armed
Archie MacLachlan, whom
Geoff met while Archie was
doing a familiarisation flight.
Archie, who lost his arm
during the defence of Malta,
used his knees to hold the
stick and was able to fly
'hands free' most of the time.

Left: Jacky Drawbridge,
RNZAF, was Geoff's
navigator. They met at the
end of January 1943, at
RAF Stradishall during a
course on Stirlings.

Mac McGredy, flight
engineer, left, and Ian
Entwhistle (Whistle),
wireless operator, right,
were also part of the crew
that were formed in 1943.

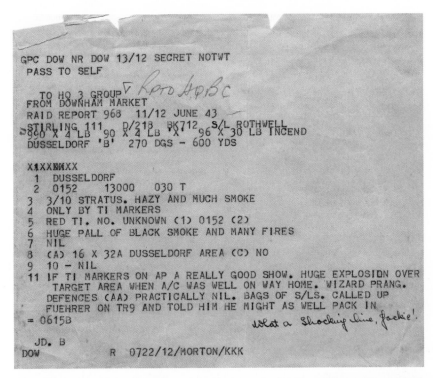

```
GPC DOW NR DOW 13/12 SECRET NOTWT
PASS TO SELF
                     V Rpto A@BC
    TO HQ 3 GROUP
FROM DOWNHAM MARKET
RAID REPORT 968  11/12 JUNE 43
STIRLING 111   D/218  BK712   S/L ROTHWELL
800 X 4 LB  90 X 4 LB  X   96 X 30 LB INCEND
DUSSELDORF 'B'  270 DGS - 600 YDS

XXXXXXX
  1  DUSSELDORF
  2  0152    13000    030 T
  3  3/10 STRATUS. HAZY AND MUCH SMOKE
  4  ONLY BY TI MARKERS
  5  RED TI. NO. UNKNOWN (1) 0152 (2)
  6  HUGE PALL OF BLACK SMOKE AND MANY FIRES
  7  NIL
  8  (A) 16 X 32A DUSSELDORF AREA (C) NO
  9  10 - NIL
 11  IF TI MARKERS ON AP A REALLY GOOD SHOW. HUGE EXPLOSION OVER
     TARGET AREA WHEN A/C WAS WELL ON WAY HOME. WIZARD PRANG.
     DEFENCES (AA) PRACTICALLY NIL. BAGS OF S/LS. CALLED UP
     FUEHRER ON TR9 AND TOLD HIM HE MIGHT AS WELL PACK IN
 = 0615B
                            What a Shocking line, Jackie!
    JD. B
DOW          R  0722/12/MORTON/KKK
```

This 1943 report from Downham Market is on the Stirling raid over Dusseldorf, including Geoff's comment to Jacky Drawbridge.

Wing Commander Wilf Burnett, centre, with 138 Squadron officers in 1944.

1944: The above image shows Geoff's crashed Stirling on the Dutch island of Texel.

The two images on the left show Geoff's Stirling after a mission to Stuttgart while he was stationed at Downham Market in 218 Squadron. They were taken as evidence of the damage that was caused after what Geoff believed was contact with a high-tension pylon and how the aircraft looked as if it had been cut open with a can opener. *The Daily Telegraph* reported the damage to the aircraft.

This picture shows the scene of the crash on Texel and the remains of Geoff's Stirling a few months after it happened.

Geoff on his way to Udine, Italy, in 1946.

RAF Station Udine, Italy. Geoff is on the far right of this picture, taken in the officer's mess.

Geoff, second from right, in Udine in 1948, with the Archbishop of Canterbury.

Geoff commentating on a cricket match in Italy in 1948.

Above left: Pat Harrison (Sweet Pea).

Above right: Geoff in a new clearing with Hussein, the head man, and Leehman Singh, escort, in Malaya in 1953.

Below: Geoff and Judy socialising in the 1950s in Malaya.

The Rothwell family:
Maurice, Judy, Pat,
Geoff, Simon and Ethel,
in Norwich, 1962.

Left: The manager's
bungalow at Sungei
Kahang Estate.

Below left: Geoff with
William Holden during
filming of *The 7th Dawn*.
Geoff had a small role
in this movie, which was
released in 1964.

Below right: Geoff with
Simon and his sister Pat
in Malaya.

2001: Geoff, right, with his rigger Stan Hurd at Downham Market beside the memorial to Flight Sergeant Louis Aaron, VC.

Geoff with secret agent Bram de Vos at the reception field in Holland, in 2001.

Geoff looks at the graves in the War Cemetery in Texel in 2002.

Above: Fiona Hilton, Geoff's granddaughter, Zelie Hilton, Geoff's daughter, and Simon Rothwell, Geoff's son.

Left: Gabrielle and Geoff at the book launch of *The Man with Nine Lives* in 2005.

Two days later he was escorted across a courtyard and into an office with the name *Feldwebel* Bauer-Schlictergroll on the door. The occupant was none other than the German with the Oxford accent who had come to his cell. Bauer-Schlictergroll sat behind a desk, busily writing. After a moment or two he looked up with a charming smile.

'Sit down, old boy,' he said. 'Good to see you again.'

Geoff glanced around the room, noticing the filing cabinet, cupboard and other office furniture, a hatch into a secretary's office, and the window looking over the compound. Then he rubbed his eyes in disbelief, thinking he was dreaming. On Bauer's desk was a feast fit for a king. A large plate of cocktail snacks, consisting of several types of biscuits, some with fat sardines, others with different types of cheese and Spam, floated like a dream in front of his eyes.

Scarcely taking his eyes off this feast, he hardly heard what Bauer was saying. 'I can understand your predicament, old man, being an Air Force man myself – I flew as a gunner in Focke Wulf Condors on Atlantic patrols.' Geoff took this with a grain of salt and then Bauer continued, all the while seemingly oblivious to Geoff's obsession with the food, telling him more about his time with the *Luftwaffe*. It was obvious he was trying to establish a friendly relationship with him, *but... that food!*

After chatting for a few minutes Bauer spoke on the telephone and Geoff picked up the words *'neun und neunzig'*. Now, it doesn't take a professor of languages to translate that into 'ninety-nine' and Geoff guessed Bauer's conversation must have something to do with his first tour squadron. Sure enough, a girl brought in a file with the title covered by a slip of paper. I'll get you now, you bastard, Geoff thought.

'This is really unnecessary,' he said to Bauer, 'as I know the file is on 99 Squadron.'

'Good God,' said an alarmed Bauer. 'Can you speak German?'

A pig's ass, I can! he thought to himself, but to Bauer he merely grinned and said nothing. Rather sheepishly Bauer tore off the paper and exposed the title which was, of course, 99 Squadron.

There was an uneasy pause and suddenly, Bauer clasped his brow.

'Good God, man,' he said. 'What have I been thinking of? I'm terribly sorry for my deplorable lapse in manners! Can I offer you some refreshment?'

Refreshment? *Refreshment?* Could he be hearing correctly? Within two minutes Geoff had demolished the lot, making no apology for his greed and pointing out he had been half-starved for the last two weeks. He was to find out later that the food had come from Red Cross parcels to which every POW was entitled. Then to Geoff's amazement and consternation Bauer read from the 99 Squadron file, giving a summary of his service with the unit, including the citation for his decoration. Finishing with a charming smile, he said, 'So you see old boy, we know quite a lot about you. In fact, you could say we were expecting you. What was the name of your CO in 1940. No, don't bother to tell me, here it is, Group Captain Evans-Evans, nickname "Good 'eavens-Evans!" Hah! Hah! Hah! What a sense of humour you English have.'

Geoff could not help laughing as he had never heard this nickname before. He could not even recall such an officer having been stationed at Mildenhall during his time because the CO during his tenure was Group Captain Joe Fogarty. Bauer might have had the wrong information about Evans-Evans. Actually there *was* a Group Captain Evans-Evans, but he wasn't known as Good 'eavens-Evans. (Coningsby RAF Station Commanding Officer Group Captain Evans-Evans, DFC, was killed in 1944.)

Bauer then mentioned names such as Charles Pickard, Bob Gordon, Hank Lynes, and a few others with whom Geoff had served. 'We have, shall we say, a little bird who works in your SOE. Hah! Hah! You didn't know that, did you?'

A chill ran through Geoff's blood. There was definitely something sinister about the way Bauer spoke about SOE. It *might* just be a ploy to gain information but he had an eerie feeling that something was not quite right. There *could* be a mole in SOE as the Germans certainly knew a lot. If only he could get a message back to Wilf in 138 Squadron. How on earth had they found out so much about him? Nothing more was said and later, back in his cell, Geoff pondered on his conversation with Bauer. There must be some way to get a message back to England.

It is difficult to determine the reason for Bauer's statements to Geoff. Professor Michael Foot, the most authoritative historian on SOE, makes several references to security in the Special Operations Executive. Perhaps the most illuminating is his chapter on 'Security and Penetration' in *SoE – The Special Operations Executive 1940–46.*

> Considering how leaky SOE's own agents could be, in spite of all that they had been taught at Beaulieu about the need to keep their mouths shut when in enemy hands, it is not surprising that captured sub and sub-sub-agents often said a great deal more than they might have done, and helped the enemy's security forces in their task of unravelling what SOE was up to.

And in *SOE in the Low Countries* he states:

> ...in both the War Office and the Air Ministry about forty busybodies in each had arranged, by the end of 1940, to see, in clear, a copy of every message that entered the building. Most of them belonged to the same service clubs, where over a late whisky they liked to exchange news of the day...

Despite this, in *The Special Operations Executive 1940–46* he points out that:

> None of the Axis powers succeeded in planting an agent at any SOE headquarters or training school (so far, it must be added, as is known)... Similarly, some of SOE's enemies have supposed that there must have been a traitor in Baker Street, but have never been able to produce one... However, there is no getting away from the fact that the Germans did manage three important break-ins to SOE operations through what they called Funkspiele, wireless games ... they

had to fall on the ploy of running enemy circuits through captured codes, captured sets and prisoners who changed sides.

Two days later Geoff's cell door opened to reveal Bauer in all his glory with the insignia of a *Feldwebel*, but no aircrew badge. So, I was correct, thought Geoff elatedly. The man had bluffed when he claimed to have flown in Condors. He felt he had scored a minor victory.

'It's such a glorious day, old boy,' said Bauer. 'I thought you'd enjoy a walk in the forest.'

Geoff was so amazed that for a moment he was speechless. It *was* a beautiful autumn day and as he felt the need for fresh air and exercise he eagerly accepted the invitation. When they passed the office, Bauer produced a parole form and asked Geoff to sign it. He debated whether or not to do so, but decided his physical well-being was important, so he signed with a scrawled signature which anyone who was familiar with his normal one would detect as being false. The camp surroundings were picturesque and beautiful, with wooded hillsides and glimpses of small villages and churches through the trees lining the path. It was an odd feeling that in the midst of all the beauty of his surroundings he was actually in the enemy camp, *on the other side*. I'm actually talking to the enemy, the dreaded 'Hun', he thought, and really, they are just like us. In many ways the man Bauer was charming, but he knew he must never forget he was a prisoner of war, and he must be careful what he told Bauer. Mac later told Geoff his interrogator had produced a letter signed by Geoff authorising any members of the squadron coming through Oberursel to answer any questions put to them in order to verify their credentials. Mac said Geoff's signature was perfect so it must have been obtained from some source other than the parole form.

After a while Geoff's ribs began to hurt and he had to stop to take a breath. Bauer led the way to a seat and then began a session of intense interrogation. All pretence of charm disappeared.

'We know what you were doing in 138 Squadron' he said, 'and we regard men like you with contempt. While you were in 99 and 218 Squadrons your career had been honourable. We lost you there for a while between your first and second tours, old chap. What happened to you?'

That would have been when Geoff was in the United States. So they did not know everything about him. But they knew a lot. It was extraordinary.

Bauer went on, 'I liken Special Duties to that of a bank robber who asks someone to drive the car to and from the bank. You, old boy, are a thug just as much as those you supply with weapons. Now you must be prepared to accept the same treatment. Reconsider, old boy. Co-operate with us and life will be easier. Let's face it, I could, shall we say, make life more agreeable for you. I can arrange for you to go into the town, go to the cinema, have a meal, in fact I can even arrange some female company for you. On the other hand, you have acted like a thug and you should be treated like one. I could hand you over to the Gestapo.'

The situation was definitely heating up and Geoff asked Bauer to take him back to his cell. He had turned out to be a nasty bit of work and he was not going to talk any longer with a bastard like him.

'I've no wish to listen to abuse from the likes of you,' he said.

So ended the interview. He was never to see Bauer again. (After the war Bauer received eighteen months' imprisonment from a War Crimes Tribunal for the ill treatment of prisoners.)

During the evening of 26 September, eighteen days after crashing and after fourteen days in Cell 8B, the door opened and Geoff was taken to a hut filled with RAF officers. It was bedlam inside as crews were reunited, men slapped each other on the back and tongues were loosened.

If the Germans had bugged the hut they would have gained more information from listening to the men talking about their operations and squadrons than from any interrogation.

It is unlikely any of the POWs gave this a thought. Having steadfastly refused to give any information, now the floodgates just opened up. For Geoff it was wonderful to be out of solitary confinement and in the company of other RAF personnel again.

Suddenly he noticed the stockily built man with the long Roman nose – his neighbour from 10B. He was a Polish pilot named Bohdan Arct, known as Dan, and they immediately struck up a conversation. When Geoff told him he had thought he was a German 'plant' due to his absence of a flying badge, Dan laughed, his eyes crinkling up at the corners and disappearing almost completely. The simple explanation was that Dan had been wearing the metal emblem of the Polish Air Force to denote his flying status and not RAF wings. The two men were to become best friends. Dan had been wearing best blue on his last operation. It turned out that he was due to go on leave as soon as he returned from the operation and to save precious time he had already changed into his leave dress before take-off. Geoff dubbed him 'the best-dressed *kriegie*' – that was until they received their prison clothes, which consisted of British and American airmen's uniforms. (The word '*kriegie*', a popular name for POWs, is derived from the German word for that sorry condition. As with many German words it is a composite one, 'war's prisoner', '*kriegsgefangener*'.)

Bohdan was born in Poland on 27 May 1914. His father was a Warsaw publisher and his mother a writer of books for children and young people. In 1932 he went to flying school which he finished in 1934 with the rank of Flying Officer. In 1935 he was a student at the Warsaw Academy of Art. On 1 September 1939 he was mobilised as liaison officer in the Polish Air Force. In 1940 after being trained in France he arrived in England. In 1944, Arct, by now a Squadron Leader in 316 Squadron and on a mission to Holland, was forced to bale out when his plane caught fire. He was captured and spent the rest of the war in Stalag Luft 1. It was during the seven months as a prisoner of war that he wrote his log book. After the war *Prisoner of War: My Secret Journal* was to become a best-seller. Describing his first meeting with Geoff, Dan writes:

I noticed my neighbour in 8B. He was a tall, red headed squadron leader in a dirty R.A.F. battle dress, his face adorned by an enormous flowing moustache. Whenever tea or coffee was issued, he produced a large wine bottle, which the Germans always had difficulty in filling. This was Geoff Rothwell, who was later to become my companion and best friend – in my prison life.

In a group of eighty or so RAF personnel, Geoff and Dan left Oberursel the next day. They assembled outside the barracks before entraining for the transit camp Dulag Luft at Wetzlar.

'Behave like the officers and NCOs that you are and like the gentlemen which you are supposed to be,' said one of the officers on the staff of the interrogation centre. They had to promise not to escape during the journey, otherwise they would be deprived of their shoes, belts and braces and put under a double guard.

The journey was long and uneventful, with no food. One or two of the men had cigarettes and they were watched enviously by those less fortunate. Late in the afternoon they arrived at Wetzlar station, left the train and marched through the little town and out into the country towards the Dulag Luft transit camp. Part of the camp was surrounded by a double row of high barbed wire fencing with watch towers on the four corners, guarded by German sentries with machine guns. The other part of the camp, where they were taken for documentation, was occupied by German offices and quarters. They were then taken to the barbed wire compound, which was to be their home for the next week. There they were issued with kit bags containing soap, razor, vest, pants, cigarettes, razor blades, sewing kit and other odds and ends which were invaluable in prison life and provided through the Red Cross.

It was in this camp that Geoff was first aware of Red Cross food. There was a communal mess hall and the food was placed at the end of one of the tables by British and American NCOs. Their first meal consisted of salmon and potatoes, cheese and biscuits, sheer luxury for the half-starved men. Things were looking up. Geoff and Dan quickly chummed up with Harry de Belleroche, 'Woody' Woodhatch and Charles de Moulin, all squadron leaders. A little bizarrely and much to their amusement, they were called 'the five sad sack squadron leaders' by an American colonel in charge of the prisoners in the camp. They never did find out the meaning of this rather odd expression.

During their time at Wetzlar there were numerous air raids, when the men were hurried into overcrowded shelters. They stood around, cheering loudly as they watched the large formations of Flying Fortresses accompanied by Thunderbolts flying overhead. This was always a boost to their morale.

A week passed and it was time for them to move to their permanent camp – Stalag Luft 1 at Barth. They duly assembled then set off in a long column to the station, surrounded by swarms of armed soldiers and watched by curious crowds. They arrived in the town of Wetzlar to see two railway coaches with heavily barred windows waiting for them in the goods yard.

The journey from Dulag Luft to their future prison camp turned out to be the worst any of them had experienced, taking four days and four nights. There were ten men to a compartment, one lavatory to a coach, no water for washing or shaving, no hot food, except for an occasional cup of ersatz coffee, and only half a Red Cross parcel each for the whole journey. Consequently many of the men developed stomach ailments, the problem compounded by having to queue a long time for the only toilet. Harry de Belleroche, one of the five 'sad sack squadron leaders', had developed dysentery and seemed to be in perpetual motion between the lavatory and the compartment. He was a fearful sight as his naturally protruding eyes were set in pools of blood, owing to his aircraft having been hit by flak and his bomb, a 4,000-pounder, exploding. The aircraft disintegrated, and when he regained consciousness, he was on the ground with the collapsed parachute beside him. It was a miraculous escape, one of many Geoff was to hear about from fellow POWs.

At night they suffered from severe cold, shivering and dreaming about overcoats and blankets. The train travelled on, right across Germany, stopping at many stations and waiting often for several hours in open fields. They approached Berlin, passing through its leafy green suburbs. Some trees were already shedding their leaves. Geoff could see many ruined houses and factories. An air raid siren sounded and the vulnerable men prayed.

The train continued north, and on the fourth day in the afternoon they finally arrived at the small, desolate railway station of Barth in Pomerania. The guards unlocked the doors of the carriages. Geoff and Dan jumped down, dazed, hungry and exhausted. A cold wind was blowing in from the north and Geoff pulled the collar of his jacket up around his neck. A wave of depression swept over him. Burly German guards, heavily armed and with fearsome-looking Alsatian dogs, stood on the platform. This was it – their final destination.

13

THE END IS NIGH

If you can wait, and not be tired by waiting...

– Kipling

Europe, 4 October 1944

There are signs that morale among the Allied armies in
north-west Europe is not what it was a few weeks ago.
A month ago it looked as though final victory was but a few
weeks away. Since then there has been the failure at Arnhem,
and desperate fighting continues around Aachen and Metz.
The German armies have largely recovered from the disasters
of the summer and have signalled their intention of fighting
every inch of the Allied way forward.

– *Daily Telegraph*

The POWs set off from the railway station on foot and in half an
hour passed through the heavily barbed-wired gates of Stalag Luft
1. The camp was well guarded, with double barbed-wire fences and
numerous watch towers, all equipped with machine guns. What
hope of escape? They were shown to a wooden barrack, where
they were segregated, stripped and searched. Their identity was
checked and then they were taken to a small brick building, where
they were deloused and examined by a doctor, after which they
were able to enjoy a hot and much-needed shower. They were given

British or American clothing – shirts, trousers, boots and jackets, plus blankets and mattress covers and a choice of a greatcoat or extra blanket. Geoff chose the blanket as the greatcoats were too small for him. Finally a British officer allocated blocks and rooms – Geoff was in Room 2 Block 11 with Dan Arct and Woody Woodhatch. Later, as accommodation became scarce, they were joined by Fraser Stooks, Jan Penz and Charles de Moulin.

> Block 11 was not a very luxurious place – I would rather say it was awful. Cold, overcrowded and with no indoor conveniences, it had to accommodate sixteen people in one room the size of a medium bedroom. We had double bunks instead of beds and wooden boards instead of springs. Fortunately, three of us, Geoff, 'Woody' and I, all squadron leaders, were accommodated in a tiny room by the end of the barrack, and though we had very little space, we had some privacy, which in prison camp is a precious thing.
>
> Bohdan Arct, *Prisoner of War: My Secret Journal*

Stalag Luft I, situated on the Pomeranian coast at the most northerly point in Germany, looked across the Baltic Sea towards neutral Sweden. It was always cold, with a bitter wind blowing. The camp, surrounded by fir trees and built on sandy soil, contained roughly nine thousand prisoners and was divided into several compounds, known as 'lagers', in which there were fourteen overcrowded barracks. A huge barrack for kitchen, church and theatre, the latter built entirely by prisoners, stood at one end of the compound.

At the other end was a parade ground where roll call, or *Appel*, took place, and where in their spare time the prisoners would play soccer, rugger, softball or other games. Ten yards or so inside the double barbed-wire fence surrounding the camp was a trip wire known as the 'warning wire'. There was no second chance for a prisoner who crossed that wire – the guards were instructed to fire immediately without any warning, and in fact an American Lieutenant Wyman was shot and killed by a trigger-happy guard.

The prisoners referred to the guards as 'goons' and Geoff and Dan soon became avid goon-baiters. Desperate for exercise,

Geoff and Dan took walks around the compound in the lukewarm autumn sun wherever possible, greeting the guards smilingly, 'Good morning you square-headed bastards!' they would say. Other times Dan would change this to: '*Guten* ferkin *Morgen!*'

'*Guten Morgen,*' the guards would reply.

It was a wonder they got away with it.

Shortly before Geoff and Dan arrived in Barth, a communiqué had been circulated throughout Stalag Luft I. It was addressed to the senior American and British officers in all the compounds.

Kriegsgefangenenlager Nr. 1, d. Lw. Barth den 2 7.44 Gruppe II
To: The Senior American Officer North Compound
     The Senior American Officer Main Compound
     The Senior British Officer Main Compound

Re : Use of the word 'Goon'

The use of the word 'goon' was granted to the PoW by the Kommandant under the condition that this word would not have any dubious meaning.

It has however, been reported to me that PoW have been using the 'focking goon up' the meaning of which is beyond any doubt.

Consequently the use of the word 'goon up' or 'goon' is prohibited, severest punishment being in future inflicted for any disobedience against this order.

Schroder
Major u. Gruppenleiter

The guards were everywhere. They patrolled inside and outside the camp, in the towers, they milled around the barracks, and were at every gate of the camp. They paid unexpected visits to the rooms, searching for anything which would aid an escape, or any weapon they deemed dangerous. A pocket knife, an iron bar, even a piece of wood if found would be confiscated immediately. Diaries, notebooks, and drawings were also forbidden and had to be hidden in a safe place.

Often the men would return from roll call to find their barracks locked and a crowd of ugly-looking Germans searching inside and underneath. These searches could last several hours; they would always be unexpected and nobody knew what would be confiscated. Everybody talked about escape, it was uppermost in their minds, and as soon as Geoff and Dan settled into the camp they started to make plans.

Derek Shaw, Geoff's flight engineer, arrived at Stalag Luft 1 some six weeks after Geoff. Apart from a deep scar on his forehead he did not seem the worse for wear. 'What's the griff (RAF slang for information)?' he asked Geoff as they greeted each other enthusiastically. Geoff told him all that had happened and was saddened to hear that Roger Court, Wally Walton and John Hulme had not survived the crash.

To the *Kriegies* news from the outside world was important, especially the war news. Officially they were allowed to listen to the German wireless, which was broadcast to all the barracks. German propaganda newspapers written in English were distributed and these were hilarious, as Hitler was depicted as an angel and the Germans harmless sheep who had been betrayed and forced into war by other bloodthirsty nations. Such reports were regularly translated and pasted on to a blackboard outside Block 5, where the senior British officer lived. In the same barracks was a large wall map marked with eastern and western fronts, and as the war situation changed, the lines on the map were moved accordingly.

But the most eagerly awaited news was from the BBC. It was the highlight of the prisoners' day. Access to a wireless set, cleverly hidden (reputedly in a broom handle) in one of the barracks, was allowed to only a few people. Later a BBC communiqué handwritten on toilet paper and rolled up to form a tiny cylinder was delivered to special 'news officers' and circulated to the senior officers. The Germans knew about the secret radio and continually searched for it. They would go mad with rage, scream and stamp their feet, but they were never able to trace it. They would search for hours and turn the barracks upside down, all in vain. Occasionally, a duty guard would be bribed to turn on the BBC over the public address system at night.

To avoid being caught out by the Germans, a duty 'goon guard' stood by the entrance to each barrack, and as soon as any German approached, the guard would shout 'Goon up!' ignoring the prohibition on the word. On hearing the call, all illegal activity would cease, and the news sheet would be hidden smartly in somebody's pocket. The Germans never found out.

It was not long before Geoff settled into POW life. He had no choice but to make the best of his situation and looked forward to taking long walks with Dan each morning in the watery winter sunshine. The air was fresh, and they would meet other *Kriegies*, all deep in thought or talking with their friends and room-mates. It felt like freedom. They would talk about their lives, their experiences during the war, their friends on their squadron, their families and the loved ones they had left behind. For a moment they could forget their present life in captivity, and it was only when they glanced up and saw the menacing grey figures of the guards with mounted machine-guns above them in the tower that the bitter wind would blow in from the north and the reality of their situation would be driven home to them.

Back in Essex, Geoff's family had no idea he was missing. Although Bomber Command knew that his aircraft had not returned they did not know if he had been killed or if he had been captured. Some three weeks after Geoff had gone missing, a telegram sent by Air Ministry arrived at 'Watersplash'.

MUCH REGRET TO INFORM YOU THAT YOUR SON, 42726, SQUADRON LEADER G M ROTHWELL HAS BEEN REPORTED MISSING. THE PRIME MINISTER DESIRES ME TO CONVEY TO YOU ON BEHALF OF THE GOVERNMENT HIS SYMPATHY WITH YOU IN YOUR ANXIETY

MINISTER OF DEFENCE

Ethel Rothwell had always known that something like this could happen. She had lived with this continual fear, which was like a tight knot in the pit of her stomach, and for months now she had not been sleeping. It wasn't only the noise of the doodle

bugs and the deep rumble of the bombers passing overhead on their way to Germany every night that kept her awake. As soon as she saw the postman walking up to the front door that morning with a telegram in his hand she knew something dreadful had happened.

After she had read the telegram she put on her old shoes and gardening jacket and went out into the garden. She didn't seem to notice the cold wind blowing or the dark clouds gathering. She didn't even look at the mounds of golden-red leaves at the foot of the trees or the vegetables in the kitchen garden, green and ready to eat. She didn't see anything at all. For a long time she just sat on the seat beneath the oak tree, feeling nothing but a terrible fear and loneliness.

At the time when Geoff's family received the telegram Maurice Rothwell was battling a minor outbreak of dermatitis, but the sudden shock of receiving this stressful news accelerated the skin disease all over his body. He was unable to shave or bathe with water for weeks. Pat Rothwell had been away during the school holidays and when she arrived home she found it difficult to recognise her father. She had never seen him with either a moustache or beard and now he had both. One afternoon she was in the school cloakroom getting ready to go home when she was approached by one of her teachers, Sister Evangeline, who knew that Pat's brother was in the Air Force. How was he getting on?

'I was very frightened that I would never see Geoff again,' she says. 'I remember breaking down in tears in front of Sister Evangeline and telling her Geoff was missing, and we didn't know if he was alive or dead. She was most sympathetic and told me she would immediately say a rosary for Geoff and also get the other nuns to pray for him.'

In London Pat Adams was also concerned over the lack of communication from Geoff. They had corresponded fairly regularly. After several weeks had gone by without any news she thought it was out of character, but put it down to the fact he was probably busy with his war work. She knew he was involved in something dangerous and secret, but never asked him what it was.

'I didn't think too much about it at first, because I was horrendously busy with my ambulance work. There were still many people being injured through air raids and the deadly German rockets. But I still wondered.'

Pat is on her way home from school when a friend stops her in the road. 'Have you heard the news?' she says. 'Your brother is a prisoner-of-war! Your mum and dad have had a telegram.'

She feels light-headed and jumps on her bike and pedals as hard as she can for home. At last she is there and she throws down her bike on to the wet green grass. Ethel meets her at the door and they hug each other. They weep and the world stands still.

The air letter was addressed to Miss Patricia Rothwell, Bracken Bank, Hutton, Essex, England. The sender's name was a S/L G.M. Rothwell, Gefangenennummer: 5865, Stammlager Luft 1 via Stammlager Luft 3, Deutschland.

With shaking hands, Pat ripped it open.

Pat darling
I hope you have received news that I am safe as a POW by now. There are six of us living together and sharing parcels. We take it in turns in cooking. The other day I served porridge for breakfast. Fried bully beef, potatoes, cabbage and carrot salad covered with cheese sauce for lunch, prunes and custard for sweet. For dinner we had a stew. We have made a chess set out of bread and had considerable fun out of it. Parcels can be sent to Stalag Luft 1, Barth, Pommerania, but mail has to go via Stalag Luft 3. The weather has been quite good since I came down but we have winter underwear in case it turns cold. I am trying to improve my French and have also taken up German twice a week. We have a very good library so we are not so badly off. How are you getting on with your riding lessons? I hope you have not had too many falls yet. We have plenty of cigarettes which are the only recognised article

of money which we possess, but there is very little tobacco. I have met one or two people I know here, but not as many as I had expected. It is quite healthy here being near the sea. I have been down five weeks now so I expect you will have had word about me. I hope you won't worry about me 'cos I am quite well and looking forward to seeing you all again soon. Hope Mother and Dad and Granny are well. Lots of love always, Geoff.

The days at Stalag Luft 1 passed slowly. It was important to keep up morale despite the shortages of food and the absence of any freedom, as boredom and depression could descend on the men however philosophical they might be. One of the secrets to combating the gloom was to keep themselves occupied. As Geoff wrote in his letter to Pat, he and Dan had devised an ingenious way of doing this; they had made a set of chessman. They moulded the black goon bread into shapes and coloured them with blue ink and toothpaste. Then they drew a chessboard on the end of the table and spent hours playing the game, but as good as he was, Geoff was never able to beat Dan.

There were other ways of relieving the monotony of prison life. In the early days when Red Cross parcels were plentiful they would have a 'brew up' in the middle of the night. One of them would wake and call the others to have a party. They would indulge for an hour or so and then go back to bed. People would say that Dan and Geoff were 'barbed-wire happy'.

One night they attended a seance after lights out. The organiser was a huge, burly, tough paratrooper named Conchie (pronounced 'Conky' for obvious reasons). After they had settled down around the table and there was quiet, Conchie called out: 'Are you there, O Spirit?' This was too much for Geoff and Dan and although they tried to suppress their mirth, they burst into raucous laughter. Conchie was furious and announced, 'There are unbelievers here. Please leave.'

But they were not to be done out of their entertainment and after apologising and promising to behave they were allowed to remain. 'If you are there, O Spirit, give us a sign,' Conchie asked.

After a while Geoff felt the table rise slightly, and he thought, 'Oh yeah.' Sliding his hand along the underside, he felt Dan's knee with the table resting on it. He did the same and between them they managed to create a sort of rocking movement. This caused great excitement.

'Then we started to piss ourselves with laughter. We just collapsed, and old Conchie became suspicious of us and chucked us out.'

They were never invited again, having been classed as disruptive influences. However, they could hear through the walls, and whenever a seance was in progress and Conchie asked: 'Are you there O spirit?' Geoff and Dan would bang like mad on the walls, much to the annoyance of the non-sceptics.

Some of the *Kriegies* moulded the black bread into shapes resembling turds for the goons to find when they searched the barracks. They also poured boiling water through the floor boards when the goons were below, searching for tunnels. The infuriated Germans fired shots through the floorboards and it was a wonder nobody was hurt.

Two types of trading went on in the camp. The prisoners traded amongst themselves, mostly for food, cigarettes and chocolate and having no money they created a currency – cigarettes. For example, a bar of chocolate would be valued at a certain number of cigarettes, and a tin of margarine would equal half a tin of bully beef. The other kind of trading was an exchange of goods with the Germans, who were desperate for cigarettes and coffee – the *Kriegies* had both when there was a plentiful supply of Red Cross parcels. The Germans, of course, were strictly prohibited from trading with the prisoners so they would have to do so in secret.

One day, Jan Pentz, a Polish flight lieutenant and a room-mate of Geoff and Dan's, made a delicious cake out of some of the ingredients from the Red Cross parcels. 'It's a marvellous cake, Jan,' they said, suitably impressed.

'It is sh-e-e-e-t cake!' replied Jan, being a perfectionist.

One of the German officers at Stalag Luft 1 was an Austrian aristocrat, Hauptman von Beck. He took a fancy to the occupants of Room 2 and often visited them in the evenings, bringing a loaf of crisp, white French bread, sheer luxury to the *Kriegies*, who were used to the harsh and unappetising black goon bread. At that stage the prisoners were still receiving Red Cross parcels and Geoff and Dan would turn on a brew-up of coffee and biscuits when von Beck arrived. He would entertain them with various stories of his time in England. On one occasion, when staying at a country house, he had disgraced himself by shooting a fox.

They felt sad for von Beck when they heard that his home on the outskirts of Vienna had been overrun by the Russian Army. It was obvious he preferred the company in Room 2 to that of his mess, where, he told them, he was unpopular, being not only an Austrian but in the supposedly invincible *Luftwaffe*.

Thoughts of escape began to diminish as time went on. At night they had to remain inside the barracks with the door and windows locked, as prisoners would be shot if they attempted to get out. Through the holes in the walls they could see the empty camp, strong lamps illuminating the barbed wire and the searchlight beams moving slowly to and fro. Guards with dogs wandered inside the compounds, and several patrols circulated outside. There was no chance of slipping through that net. Later, they were instructed via the secret wireless that they were not to attempt escaping as the Allies wanted all POWs to be together in one place to assist in repatriation. Also, Hitler had announced that escaped prisoners would be treated as *francs tireurs* (guerrillas). Besides they all knew the war was coming to an end – it couldn't be far away, surely?

The weeks dragged by and the days grew steadily colder. The severity of the climate in that part of Germany meant the POWs were perpetually cold. In addition, the barracks proved to be very draughty, and the small issue of coal entirely insufficient. Although the men put on every item of available clothing, they stayed in their tiny room, shivering around the iron stove. When they went to bed they would dress instead of undressing and still they would wake in the morning stiff with cold.

Christmas 1944 arrived and with it the promise of extra food in the Red Cross parcels. An American POW, certain the war would be over by Christmas, had made a bet: 'If this is not so,

I'll be eating my dinner in the shithouse!' he told everybody. It was cold and frosty with snow lying thick on the ground when a table laden with food was taken into the draughty lavatory. The over-optimistic *Kriegie* took up his position on one of the seats and went steadily through the menu before an amused audience.

A fellow American had also made a bet.

'If the war's not over by eleven o'clock on Christmas Day, I will kiss my friend's bare ass in the middle of the parade ground,' he told all and sundry. Consequently at 10.45 a bugle sounded and a stage was erected, around which a large crowd formed a circle. The trousers belonging to the man's colleague were lowered, and another man carefully washed and powdered the part which was to receive this gesture of affection. With due ceremony the friend, delivered the kiss while icy winds swept across the sports field. The crowd were uncertain as to who exactly won the bet!

The New Year dawned and Geoff and Dan were transferred to No. 5 barrack, which was more solidly built and warmer. Their spirits lifted. BBC news on the hidden radio was positive. The Red Army had crossed the German frontier and infiltrated deep into Pomerania, capturing Dresden, 95 miles from Berlin. In Britain Churchill warned the Germans that giving in now would be easier than enduring what the Allies had in store for them.

The supply of Red Cross parcels, the prisoners' main food supply, was dwindling and by the beginning of February they had ceased to arrive altogether, causing them to live entirely on German rations. Their daily diet now consisted of four thin slices of black bread, one or two potatoes or kohlrabi, a type of turnip (the latter, being cattle fodder, was so tasteless, according to Dan Arct, that a respectable cow would refuse to consume it), a little margarine and three or four cups of the evil-tasting German coffee. Every morsel of food was more precious than gold. The strain of living in this 'starvation period' showed up, especially when one of the six room-mates cut the black bread as five other half-starved men watched.

Geoff devised a system which satisfied everybody. Firstly, six playing cards were dealt face down on the table, and an identical six from a second pack were dealt to the room occupants. A ruler was used to mark the width of the slices, extreme care being taken to cut the bread exactly according to the marks. The slices, and any other food they were fortunate enough to have, were then placed in bowls beside each card on the table, the cards turned face up, and each man would take the food according to the card he had been dealt. This method avoided any arguments and complaints.

As the days passed, the men became thinner and thinner, their reserves of fat disappearing rapidly. This was apparent in the showers when they found the fatty parts of their bodies, such as thighs, upper arms and stomach, had shrunk and hollows had formed. They had, literally, been living off the fat of their bodies. They were so weak they had to hold on to the sides of their bunks when they got up as they had a tendency to black out. There was a continual feeling of hunger, pain and intense cold. Even little pleasures such as reading exacerbated the feeling of hunger as it seemed each book contained descriptions of food. Geoff was reading Dickens at the time and the accounts of Mr Pickwick and friends dining on roast venison and huge breakfasts of bacon and eggs was too much for a starving *Kriegie* and he had to abandon it. *An Innkeepers Diary* by Fothergill was almost as bad, and the starving men came to the conclusion that whatever they read would be sheer torture, with descriptions of food consumed in unlimited quantities. Consequently, much time was spent dreaming up elaborate menus which they would consume ... one day.

Now they were forced to cut down their walking, and activities such as playing games had to be abandoned. A few of the more hardy took short walks and occasionally played games like volleyball. There was a court just outside one of the barracks and they would play until exhaustion or hunger forced them to discontinue. Afterwards they would have to lie down for hours to regain some strength. On the odd occasion when they played a game, the men would refuse to give up and, although exhausted after the first five minutes of the game, would crawl about the field.

There were rumours – people talked about thousands of Red Cross parcels which were on their way, or someone would say that trucks loaded with food had actually been seen arriving in the camp – but they were always unfounded.

Living in extraordinary circumstances can cause human beings to react in strange ways. This was evident one day when the Germans suddenly produced quantities of ripe, creamy and smelly Camembert from an unknown source. Despite the fact the Americans were starving, they turned up their noses at the cheese, enabling men like Geoff, who were connoisseurs of European food, to take advantage of the extra rations.

Spring arrived, and with it an inkling of hope, the days becoming warmer and the first leaves on the trees turning green. For days the sky was a deep shade of blue, somehow symbolising the end of the long war and the beginning of a new life.

The one bright spot in the camp which didn't require any effort was the entertainment, usually in the form of the camp theatre and orchestra. Some of the prisoners had been professional artists, managers and decorators in Civvy Street, and the plays were excellent. Some dressed as female impersonators, bringing wolf whistles from the audience.

The orchestra consisted of forty versatile musicians who played Chopin, Grieg, Tchaikovsky and Beethoven on instruments sent by the International Red Cross. For a while the men could relax and forget their hunger, but after the show came to an end they would stagger back to their rooms to the same old problem. As a special treat they would prepare an extra 'brew', a cup of watered-down coffee without sugar. In March they were deprived of even that as the Germans ran out of *ersatz* coffee and produced more *'Tee'*.

As March drew to an end, another rumour circulated that thirty thousand Red Cross parcels had arrived in the camp. Many refused to believe it, thinking it was just another false alarm. Some pessimists even said that someone had misunderstood the news and that thirty thousand razor blades had arrived. This time, however, the rumour turned out to be true. Large trucks bringing hundreds of parcels arrived in the camp but only a limited number were distributed. The Germans pierced tins in the parcels to stop the prisoners hoarding them, but they were either preserved in the cold weather or the contents used immediately.

With the advent of more food, people went mad arranging 'glutton parties', and one American baked himself a rich cake, announcing that he was going to eat it at one sitting. He did – and died, his body unable to cope with the large quantity of food after so long on starvation rations.

Easter was celebrated with a wonderful meal. The menu consisted of Easter greeting eggs, *tartines a' l'Arct*, *salade polonaise*, *crème de fromage*, grilled Spam, roast potatoes, *Kriegie* pudding, *gâteau à la Penz*, coffee, biscuits and cheese, and lastly cigarettes. They spent almost three hours consuming it, and by the end of the meal they felt satisfied, if a little sick.

'Anyone can see that one good, strong heave all together will bring the war in Europe to an end,' said Churchill to his troops on the Western Front on 5 March 1945.

April dawned, and with it a wave of optimism and tension in the camp. Everybody, including the German population, knew the Allies had thrust deep into the heart of Germany. Now it was a race between Montgomery's army spearheads and the Russians, and some of the more enthusiastic *Kriegies* started to pack their belongings into their kitbags, expecting to leave at any time. Each day a large crowd of prisoners gathered around the news board, hungry for any information. The Germans who could understand English also gazed at the board, commenting grimly on the German High Command communiqués which could no longer hide the reality of the situation.

The weather continued to improve and much of the time was spent sunbathing, talking about the date of the end of the war. Some *Kriegies* took bets on when this would be. Rumours were rife, often spread by the Germans, who knew the end was coming. They would ask for protection from the Russians whom they feared more than anybody else.

Some of the guards were posted to the front lines to defend their collapsing Third Reich, but they went reluctantly, showing no fighting spirit. They were replaced by the *Volkssturm*, at this stage a bunch of old men who could hardly walk and who had probably been dragged out of retirement. These men were thoroughly fed up with Hitler but still had to obey orders and guard the POWs. There were still air raids over Germany, with bombers as well as fighters sweeping low on their way to Berlin and harassing the German rear and their lines of communication. It was a most encouraging sight to the prisoners and their spirits rose when a Mosquito buzzed the camp one day.

The climax came at the end of April. British troops crossed the River Elbe and gunfire was heard frequently. When night fell and silence prevailed after lights out, an American in one of the blocks encouraged the Russians with a cry to Josef Stalin, 'Come on, Joe,' he yelled at the top of his voice – it could be heard all over the camp. He repeated this three times. Panic reigned in the V*orlager*, where the German administration was more interested in saving their own skins than guarding their prisoners. Files, papers, confidential reports and copies of *Mein Kampf* swelled the flames in the incinerators. Somehow the prisoners' identification cards were rescued to be kept as souvenirs.

Each morning Geoff and Dan looked through the window at the nearest watch tower to see whether the guards had done a runner in the night. They could hear the gunfire getting closer and closer, sounding much like thunder. Finally, late in the afternoon of 30 April 1945, the senior British and senior American officers, Group Captain 'Ginger' Weir and Colonel Hubert Zemke, were summoned to the German Administration block for a conference with the Kommandant, Oberst Warnstedt. Orders had been received to move the camp westward.

'We are unwilling to move,' said the officers. 'What is the German response to a refusal?'

'I will not tolerate bloodshed in the camp,' said the Oberst, 'and if the prisoners refuse to move I will evacuate my men and leave sole possession in the hands of the captives.'

During *Appel* late that afternoon Geoff noticed the Germans were strangely excited and guessed they were drunk. That proved to be the last roll call. Later they were seen packing their belongings outside their barracks. They did not lock the gates to the camp and the barracks seemed strangely silent after dusk had fallen. The men, well prepared for this eventuality, were now in charge of the camp. Orders were issued, and a large white flag was erected outside the Kommandant's office.

On 1 May they awoke to the eerie scene of deserted sentry towers and not a solitary German in sight. The senior camp officials warned them through the public address system to remain in the confines of the camp until contact had been made with the Russians who were rumoured to be in the vicinity. Life would be extremely dangerous, it was emphasised, if they roamed around outside the camp as the Russians were known to be trigger-happy and liable to shoot anyone in uniform. However, at 8 p.m. two Stalag scouts, Major Braithwaite and Sergeant Korson, raced out to a crossroads five miles south of Barth, with the order to 'find Uncle Joe'. They searched southward, defying a rumoured Russian curfew that stated anyone seen moving would be shot on sight. Braithwaite and Korson returned in the early evening. There was still no sign of the Russian Army, but they were coming! They had seen thousands of people on their travels, some sitting down and waiting for orders.

Geoff found it strange to be able to wander around the camp unrestricted, meeting men from other compounds. It was as though they had been living in a small village and had been transported overnight to another town. Unfamiliar faces appeared in his compound, looking for comrades, and when they found them they enjoyed a happy reunion. The officer in charge of Red Cross parcels went on a foraging expedition and found a store full of food parcels. These were distributed and lasted until repatriation took place.

Geoff and Dan had heard that some Polish forced labourers were kept in atrocious conditions, and one day, in the company of other Polish prisoners, they commandeered a vehicle and drove to a camp not far from Barth village. However, the prisoners were not Poles but mixed nationalities, mostly Russian. It was to be a most distressing trip. At first sight there appeared to be no inmates. In the corner of a small compound lay a heap of kohlrabi, which they discovered later were the sole rations. They entered the barrack-like block. A filthy tiled floor with an open drain ran down the centre of the hut, and living skeletons lay or sat on the bunks which lined both sides of the wall, their pitifully thin matchstick legs dangling over the sides. Geoff's gaze went to one of these bunks covered by a dirty, crumpled prison blanket and, to his astonishment, saw it move. Slowly emerging from the folds appeared a gaunt skeleton. 'I would not have believed it possible for a human body to be concealed under that blanket.'

Another man sat on a bunk with a bowl in his lap, a stupid grin on his emaciated face and a strange light in his eyes. Geoff looked in the bowl and saw a raw egg. 'The poor chap was unable to take his eyes off this luxury item, let alone eat it.' They tried to comfort the men as best as possible, telling them they were going to be liberated, then, sick at heart and in a sober and distressed state, went back to their camp.

Late one evening, a few days after this visit, the camp erupted with shouting and cheering. 'Come on, Geoff, let's see what's going on,' shouted Dan, and they joined the others running to the main entrance to the camp. An astonishing sight met their eyes. Outside the gate was a drunken Russian officer on a white horse waving a bottle of schnapps over his head and firing a weapon into the air. The prisoners surrounded him, jostling to shake his hand. It was obvious to some of the Polish and Czech prisoners who could understand Russian that their knight in shining armour wanted to tear down the compound fence and have the prisoners embark on a night of revelry in the local town. Fortunately, he was subdued with a supply of American cigarettes and copious quantities of Nescafe.

The camp newspaper, *Barth Hard Times*, reported:

...the barracks jiggled with cheering and back-pounding. Toasts were drunk: 'To the destruction of Germany – she will never rise again.' As the first explosions from the flak school reverberated under the sullen Baltic sky, the new order toppled on down like a house of cards. Red flags and white sheets began to appear in the windows of the ginger bread houses. Flight was futile and the old stood querulously on their door steps, wringing gnarled hands and weeping. Pictures of Hitler were torn down and scattered like confetti.

Barth, like the whole of Deutschland-über-alles Germany, was on its knees in terror. But mayhem did not materialize. Wine, not blood, flowed through the streets. We got drunk.

Some of the senior officers went into the local village to discuss repatriation, at the invitation of the Russian commander. They were filled with schnapps, and as they had been unused to alcohol for a long time, they returned to the camp in a state of intoxication, having achieved precisely nothing.

There was so much noise and so much excitement around Geoff he could not really take it all in. *Peace has come, peace has come at last.* He knew that the war was over and yet his mind could not accept it. Part of him felt euphoric and yet there was a strange numbness as though he was seeing everything from a distance. It was as if he was watching a film with the sound off, looking at the characters as they danced and swayed amidst a huge throng of people, including the soldier on horseback. It was an odd feeling.

Liberation. What was it going to mean for him? And how was he going to fit into normal life again? Six long years of war, of regimented life, eating, drinking and living it all, knowing what he was going to do, day in and day out. His years on the Active List were over, finally over.

And so the days passed by. Geoff listened to the BBC, now broadcast though the public address system into all the barracks, he read, and after the long period on starvation rations, built up his emaciated body with ample food supplied by the Russians. As they had had no fresh meat since capture, pigs and cattle were herded into the compound. One of the Americans was a butcher and soon they were sitting down to roast pork and very tough steaks, at the expense of the local farmers whose animals had been filched by the victors.

One afternoon they were invited to a concert party by a group of Russians. A makeshift stage had been constructed in one of the compounds and a piano 'liberated' from a local household. The pianist sat with a Thompson sub-machine gun strapped across his back.

More rumours flew thick and fast, one being they were going to be evacuated through the Russian port of Vladivostok. By now the POWs were fast becoming tetchy as there was no news regarding their repatriation. A week went by and finally they heard that Germany had surrendered at midnight on the night of

8/9 May. After the events of the previous week, this news was an anti-climax.

The days dragged on interminably until the morning of 12 May. Geoff was playing deck tennis with some of the others outside the barrack block when the BBC programme broadcast over the public address system was suddenly interrupted by an announcement from the adjutant.

'You are to be prepared for evacuation at thirty minutes' notice. You're to be airlifted from a local airfield and will march there in an orderly manner, wearing the best uniforms you can muster block by block.'

The transformation among the prisoners was incredible. Everybody whistled and joked and patted each other on the back. They laughed and sang as they packed their few belongings, ramming them into kitbags, and within two minutes they were all ready and prepared to march.

The next two hours seemed like a lifetime. As they stood inside the camp gates a formation of Flying Fortress B17s flew over to land at the local airfield, and then, at long last, it was their turn to march through the gates.

They were free at last. Weak, thin, and many of them ill, but holding their heads high, the ex-POWs proudly marched to attention through the village of Barth, swinging their arms as they walked. The people of Barth watched with sullen faces.

Geoff, was given charge of a flight of seventeen mostly American prisoners and allocated to Flying Fortress 31338755. The captain, 1st Lieutenant Naylor of the US Air Force, invited him to the cockpit, where he was asked to map read. The flight from Barth to Cambrai on the Belgium/French border was fascinating as he was able to see Germany in daylight for the first time. It looked clean and green and peaceful, somehow untouched by six long years of war. It was an incongruous sight. Where was the evidence of destruction and slaughter?

The journey took three and a half hours, then it was on to an airfield at Roye near Amiens, where seven of the POWs were dropped and everyone was given a meal at a field kitchen. They had to wait until daylight making a quick flight across the Channel.

Then the first sight of the white cliffs of Dover glistening in the early morning sunshine, on to Ford in Buckinghamshire and home!

> I have loved England, dearly and deeply,
> The white cliffs of Dover I saw rising steeply
> Out of the sea that once made her secure
> Alice Duer Miller, *The White Cliffs of Dover*

13 May 1945

After an absence of nearly nine months Geoff landed back on English soil again. As mentioned earlier, out of all the people he could meet who should be amongst the many RAF Bomber Command personnel at Ford but his old foe, Stevens, who was still the CO of nearby RAF Station Westcott. He did not appear to have seen Geoff, who quickly got out of his way. He joined the many men who were sprayed with DDT delousing powder. They were handed cigarettes and treated to a good meal provided by the Red Cross. Then on to a reception camp where they were given a Red Cross parcel containing shaving gear etc., then a bed for a few hours before being driven to London. *London*, Piccadilly Circus. Leicester Square, Westminster Bridge and Pall Mall. How strange it was to be back. To be on the crowded streets, alive with uniformed figures, all celebrating the end of the war.

At Watersplash in Hutton, Essex the telephone rings. A fifteen-year-old girl with strawberry blonde hair rushes to answer it. In another room Ethel Rothwell hears here daughter's scream of excitement. 'It's Geoff, mother!' she yells. 'He's in London and he is coming home!'

Thank God! Thank God! She says a silent prayer of thanks. It is all finally over, and he's safe. She looks out of the window to a beautiful day. The birds are singing and the sun is shining, even brighter than before.

But they have to wait for the reunion as all ex-prisoners have to be medically examined, debriefed and identified officially before given travel warrants, identification documents and ration cards at a special unit at RAF Station Cosford.

They leave home to meet him, walking quickly, she and Pat, all the time talking excitedly and making plans, plans for meals, plans for the future when they will all be together again. And he is on a train, the sound of voices all around him. He doesn't have the strength to listen to what they are saying. The green fields flash by. Not long now. Finally he is there and he alights from the train. He feels strange, light-headed. It is if he is in a dream; everything seems unreal. There is the village post office, the newsagent, people he knows. It's funny but everything looks just the same. He starts to walk up the hill and just as he comes to Hutton Mount he sees them. And at the same time they see him too. This tall slim Air Force officer, Ethel's dearly beloved son and Pat's hero brother. He breaks into a run and as he does so they do the same, and suddenly they are laughing and crying together, all three of them, their arms around each other.

14

ENGLAND AND RHODESIA
1945–1950 – A NEW LIFE

Home is the sailor, home from the sea,
and the hunter home from the hill.
                    – Robert Louis Stevenson, *Requiem*

Britain, 18 June 1945

Mass demobilisation begins today for servicemen in Britain's armed forces, even though the war continues in the Far East. Government officials predict that initially 30,000 men will return to 'civvy street' each week, but this figure is expected to rise to around 60,000 a week by August.

                    – *Daily Telegraph*

It was a jubilant homecoming for Geoff. He delighted in being back with his family and in doing old familiar things again. Ethel was allowed extra rations for this very occasion. He was very thin and felt perpetually hungry and took great pleasure in savouring his mother's delicious meals, although he was able to eat only minuscule quantities as his stomach had shrunk. He would have strange cravings for certain types of food, like Nestle's condensed milk, and at times like these she would look at him with a mixture of fierce pride and pain, pain that her son had suffered deprivation and grief, and pride so acute that at times she thought she would burst.

Sometimes he would still have a gnawing in the pit of his stomach not long after a meal and he would say, 'Mother, can I make a beetroot sandwich?' and she would look at his thin, tired face, telling him he could have anything he wanted. 'You don't have to ask, Geoff,' she would say, 'Just help yourself.'

The weather in England was glorious that spring/summer of 1945 and he spent much time sunbathing in the garden. It looked its best, with daffodils, crocuses and bluebells still in bloom. Lying in the deckchair warming his emaciated body in the sun, he would spend hours listening to the birds and reading the newspapers. He had been starved of news and he wanted to catch up on all that had happened in the lead-up to the end of the war.

Ethel encouraged him to visit his friends and relations, but all he wanted was to stay at home – he had little energy and no desire at all to see anyone other than his family, not even Pat Adams. He was emotionally drained, unable to take up the threads of life again. He had fought in a war which had made him old before his time. He had laughed, loved and drunk to try to cover up emotional distress. Now he had nothing left to give – he had given it all and just wanted to be left in peace.

His family wanted him to talk about his life in POW camp, thinking it would ease the burden, and he would tell them a little, then say he was tired and needed to rest. Fifteen-year-old Pat spent as much time as possible with her hero brother, and would bombard him with the inevitable questions, but Ethel, always patient and loving, would gently chide her to leave him alone.

'All in good time, Pat,' she would say, 'Geoffrey will tell us when he's ready.'

> When you come home, we shall not talk of war,
>   Nor worry what the future holds in store,
>   We'll shut our door upon a world of strife,
>   And think of all the lovely things in life.

Now he had time on his hands to think over all that had happened and slowly began to realise how lucky he had been to have survived – he was one of the fortunate ones. He thought of his friends, like the irrepressible Mick Brogan, who was buried in Denmark. He grieved for him, his crew and all his friends who had been killed or were still missing. Why had he survived and not them? He read about the mass shooting by the Germans of prisoners of war in *The Great Escape* and thanked his lucky stars he had not been in Stalag Luft III, as he, too, might have been involved in that escape.

There were the inevitable questions about his crash. What had happened? Had they hit a balloon cable which had broken free from the convoy in Den Helder harbour, or could they have been shot down? The latter was unlikely as surely a German night fighter, flying at 300 feet, would find it difficult to mount an attack or for radar to track the Stirling. And could a fighter cause damage such as shearing off an engine propeller? The Germans had been just as mystified because they had no fighters airborne and no flak batteries in the area.

As the days grew warmer and he became fitter he walked along the sea front at Bournemouth with his father, delighting in the sunshine, the sea breeze gently stroking his face. When he felt it was time to go back he turned to Maurice and said, 'We should turn back now, Dad. It's prohibited to walk on the beach where there are concrete anti-tank obstructions.'

Maurice looked at his son, telling him gently that the war was over. 'You can walk wherever you like, my boy,' he said. And with that Geoff realised it would be some time before he would adjust to peacetime living again.

Eventually when he felt stronger there were trips to various watering holes in the company of friends like Jack Parker and Slim Ormerod. There was also a delightful reunion with his old POW mate Dan Arct, who was living in North London with his wife Beryl and new daughter Katherine. Dan had been unaware of Katherine's existence until he was liberated. When Geoff stayed at their flat, much time was spent talking and laughing about their experiences in camp and life in general. When the time came to leave, the two old friends hugged each other, not knowing when they would see each other again because Dan thought he might return to live in Poland with his family. 'We will keep in touch, old friend,' he said. Some time later Geoff received a sad letter which spoke of his disenchantment with England. 'They don't seem to want us, Geoff,' he read, 'and I'm going back to Poland. I suppose you can get used to the Communists in time.' Sadly, although they did keep in touch, albeit sporadically, that was the last time they were to see each other. A talented and sensitive man, Dan spent the rest of his life in the country of his birth, where he wrote more than forty books and died at the age of fifty-nine of heart failure.

Geoff and those friends of his who had been POWs tried to return to normal life, but the problem was they had no clear vision of what was normal after five and a half years of being entirely wrapped up in the war. Although it was delightful to meet up with old friends again and most of all to be free, this period after the war was a most unhappy one for Geoff. Perhaps the secret was to drown his sorrows in a pint or two – or three? He no longer shared a close relationship with Pat Adams as they had not seen each other for over a year, a fact which unsettled him even more. All the time he had been at Tempsford he had been totally immersed with his SOE work to the exclusion of everything else. Then he had become a POW, with all the anxieties that entailed, and when he was released there was the inevitable 'low' period following the 'high' of the war's end, culminating in the urge to stay close to his family. And now with the war finished, Pat was embarking on a new career as one of Britain's first air hostesses.

In the company of Jack Parker, Geoff returned to Tempsford for a reunion, and it was here that he met Valentine Anderson. Tall, with auburn hair, she was vivacious and attractive. Val was in the FANYs (First Aid Nursing Yeomanry) at Buckden and was attached to Station 61 at Gaynes Hall, the country house which had been used as a holding unit for SOE's agents. The personnel at Station 61 and Tempsford often socialised together and it was not until one of the Tempsford staff had mentioned casually to Geoff that 'the redhead over there quite fancies you' that he took another look at Val and liked what he saw. They had struck up a conversation and Val told him a little about herself. She had been at St Albans High School when war broke out but after staying on for another year, she had worked as a driver for the de Havilland Aircraft Company. At the age of seventeen she had driven all over England in the dark without maps, her only companion being her fourteen-year-old sister, Coral. Later Val joined the FANYs and in the beginning spent a great deal of time greasing cars. Nicknamed 'Panda' by her workmates because of the amount of black grease and oil she managed to rub on her face, her principal duty was to drive the agents to and from the airfields. Many years later she told her daughter, Zelie, about those days.

'She would tell me about the people she met as she sat in the dark waiting for planes, learning songs in Norwegian or Polish,' says Zelie. 'One of them was Claus Helberg, one of the saboteurs who blew up the heavy water plant in Norway – they later made a film about it starring Kirk Douglas.'

At his parents' home some time later, Geoff was surprised to receive a letter from a Major Leslie Prout: 'Val is eating her heart out for you, and please don't take any notice of the fact that she is known as the CO's girlfriend.' It was gratifying to hear that Val was interested in him, and as he was no longer involved with Pat he arranged to see Val again. After the period of loneliness he had experienced as a POW, it was not surprising that he was bowled over by Val – 'the first friendly, good-looking woman I saw'. He associated Val with his 'glamorous' life in SOE – 'the exciting period in my life'. She had been part of that glamour and she had some understanding of what his life had been like at that stage. That was something he had been unable to share with Pat.

'I think I must have gone through a period of emotional instability after the war. I found it difficult to concentrate on anything serious but I was free, and I was flattered when I heard that Val was interested in me.'

It was not long before Geoff fell in love with Val and a wedding was arranged for early July, with a special licence. There was some urgency because by now he had been posted to Egypt and it was uncertain when he would return to England, as the war in the Pacific was still being fought.

At the end of the war there was a headlong rush into marriage. People had not only married at a younger age during the war and just after, but the marriage rate jumped by nearly 50 per cent in 1946 and remained over 20 per cent above pre-war levels throughout the decade.

On 5 July 1945 Geoff and Val were married in Bournemouth and the happy couple honeymooned in the New Forest. Two weeks later Geoff said farewell to his new wife and left for Egypt to join Transport Command in the Middle East. He had been granted an Extended Service Commission in the Royal Air Force and he hoped this posting would enable him to gain experience in route-flying and passenger-carrying, which would stand him in good stead in civilian life. At a later date he was granted a Permanent Commission.

He was posted as Officer Commanding, first to a Ferry Unit at Heliopolis in Cairo and later at Cairo West airfield on the road to Alexandria. The day's duty would start at dawn and finish in the early afternoon. From its tree-lined suburbs with sumptuous European-style homes and white buildings shimmering beneath the oppressive blistering heat to its dirty streets and beggars – '*You give baksheesh, efiendi! Ana mishkin. Mush qwoise, George?*' – Geoff found Cairo a fascinating city. The pyramids of Giza stood out amidst the desert haze, rather like a huge gateway to the limitless desert beyond. Endless sand and barren land stretched as far as the eye could see. At night, after the intense heat of the day, the desert would be bitterly cold, and on some of these clear, beautiful, starry nights, in the company of some of the other pilots, he would go out into the desert looking for gazelles.

His unit ferried Hellcats, Corsairs and Dakotas from Takoradi on the west coast of Africa to Burma and India until the war in the Pacific ended. Then there were more ferry trips in Liberators from Italy to England, from Karachi to Cairo. The transporting of aircraft to the Far East was under the terms of American Lend-Lease, and when the Japanese war ended this aid stopped and went into reverse, and aircraft were ferried back to Britain.

One day he was asked to ferry an aged Wellington from an airfield near Cairo to Rabat/Sale near Casablanca in French Morocco. All went well until they were approaching Benghazi, when the revs on one engine suddenly dropped and the aircraft pulled to one side.

'The starboard engine's cut,' he said to Mackenzie, his second pilot. 'Operate the manual fuel pump.' He applied full rudder to keep the aircraft on a straight course and after a minute or two the engine stuttered into life again. Nothing further happened and the Wellington flew on to French Morocco. They landed at Castel Benito, the RAF staging post at Benghazi, and he was filling in the flight plan when he looked at the date: 8 September – the date he had crashed on Texel exactly one year before! It was a strange coincidence. He could find no reason for what had happened other than the fact that the Wellington had stood for some months in the hot desert sun and may have suffered condensation in the fuel tanks.

On a trip to England some months later, Geoff packed some parachute silk into his luggage, a gift from his CO. He knew Val and his mother and sister had been starved of such luxuries for a long time and would welcome the precious silk and make good use of it. He landed at Lyneham and was just about to shut down the engines when he noticed two Customs & Excise officers standing at the edge of the tarmac, probably waiting to catch people like himself smuggling in goods with duty owed. He pulled out the parachute silk, which was lying on top of his bag, undid his tunic and quickly stuffed the silk down his trousers. As he was wearing a flying jacket the bulge was not too obvious, but as he started to walk from the plane the slippery silk began to filter down his trouser legs. There was nothing for it but to hold his hands over his stomach and walk with his thighs close together. The Customs officers immediately started to search the luggage and presented him with a list of dutiable goods, of which 'silk goods' was one. After they searched his bag he was told he was free to go.

Hardly able to believe his luck he walked out of the customs shed to where the rest of his crew were waiting. When he arrived at his accommodation he released the cascade of beautiful white silk and was just packing it into his bag when he heard a knock at the door. Who should be standing there but the officer from the

Customs! Knowing the game was up, he prepared to hold out his wrists to be handcuffed.

'Just came to give you these, sir,' said the Customs officer with a friendly smile as he handed Geoff his silk flying gloves. 'You left them in the shed. Very nice silk they are, too,' he added appreciatively.

In September came another posting – this time to Italy, where Geoff took command of another Ferry Unit. It was to be a romantic and blissful posting. In Italy wives were allowed to join their husbands and Val travelled out by boat. The unit in Naples was situated on an airfield at the foot of Mount Vesuvius and they were accommodated in a villa high above the city in the suburb of Vomero. The bedroom had a breathtaking view across the Bay of Naples to the Isle of Capri. Geoff immediately fell in love with Italy as it was everything he had ever imagined: the warm-hearted people with their Latin temperament, the poetic language, which he quickly learned to speak, the colourful and picturesque scenery and idyllic climate.

Geoff's headquarters were in Bari on the other side of the peninsula and it was from there that he received a visit one day from Barker, the chief accountant, nicknamed 'Bacchus'. When Geoff told him he was taking a Liberator to a Care & Maintenance Unit at Melton Mowbray the following day, Bacchus immediately showed great interest, telling him an interesting story. Radmilovic Reistich, a Yugoslav Partisan leader and a cousin of King Peter, had escaped from the country to Italy when Tito called upon all resistance movements to swear allegiance to him. Ever since then Reistich had been hunted by the Yugoslav secret police, and several assassination attempts had been made on the partisan's life. Efforts were now being made to get Reistich out of Italy to Britain, in the hope that the leader would provide valuable information to the Foreign Office.

Geoff was intrigued by this interesting tale and convinced it was genuine – he never gave a thought as to how an accountant had become involved. If it was possible to get this partisan down to Naples by early morning, he would take him on the Liberator to England. Then the bombshell dropped – Radmilovic Reistich was not a 'him' but a 'her'! This was getting more interesting by the minute. Then things moved fast.

Bacchus barked some orders down the telephone and told Geoff the British Embassy would provide a fast car, driver and escort for Reistich. They would rendezvous just outside Naples on the road to Caserta. This seemed to confirm the authenticity of Barker's story and Geoff was eager to put the plan into operation.

His mind raced, thinking of all that was necessary for the success of the operation. For a moment he was transported back to his days with SOE. This, too, was a cloak-and-dagger operation, but how he wished he had Charles Tice or 'Bunny' Warren, the Station 61 Conducting Officers at Buckden, to arrange everything. But this operation was far more complicated, despite the fact that Barker said all he had to do was get the girl to England and she would know what to do after that.

The time had now come to take others into his confidence and he started with Pilot Officer Browne, the flight engineer, who was greatly excited as it sounded an adventurous undertaking. After finding some flying kit for Radmilovic – flying helmet, battle dress top and a pair of overalls – they were ready to go. Bacchus, Browne and Geoff piled into a Morris van and set off for the rendezvous on the Rome road. There it was — an official car parked on the side of the road. Radmilovic stepped out of the car and Barker made the introductions. Geoff and Browne stared at her. This was no tough partisan leader. Instead they saw a beautiful woman with shoulder-length blonde hair, about twenty-five years of age, who spoke excellent English. Geoff shook her hand and told her she would have to remain on the aircraft when they landed for refuelling and clearance.

'And on no account are you to remove your flying helmet,' he added. Radmilovic nodded in agreement, tucking her long hair into the helmet. After saying farewell to her companions they were off.

When they arrived at the airfield, Geoff drove direct to the Liberator, where he did his best to divert the attention of the ground crew while Browne and Radmilovic clambered aboard. All went well. The navigator and wireless operator were told there was a passenger on board whose identity was a secret – and it had to stay that way. This was accepted without question. All went well until they were over Le Havre, when they learnt that conditions at Melton Mowbray were 500 yards visibility and 300 feet cloud base. There were no radio or radar aids at Melton Mowbray, so they were diverted to St Mawgan on the north coast of Cornwall.

Little did Geoff know of the trouble ahead. One reason he had taken on this mission was its apparent safety – the airfield at Melton Mowbray was run with only a 'corporal and a dog' in charge, as the saying went – in other words, it was more or less defunct, except as a repository for old aircraft. Landing at an airfield such as this and depositing Radmilovic should have been accomplished with ease and no questions asked. Now the situation was different, at a busy Transport Command station, and he began to feel apprehensive.

However, there was nothing he could do and eventually they sighted the airfield at St Mawgan. After landing, Geoff busied himself with running down the engines until he spotted the aircrew bus arriving to take them to the officer's and sergeant's messes. As they got into the bus he breathed a sigh of relief. Mission just about completed.

At nearby Newquay he booked Radmilovic into a hotel, inviting her for a drink. Later, when they were all sitting in the bar, he noticed a squadron leader and a police constable enter. 'Don't worry,' he said to Radmilovic. 'You're in no danger, he's a British policeman.'

Famous last words.

It was at that very moment that the policeman came over to their table.

'Could I have a few words with you, sir? Would you be Squadron Leader Rothwell? I have reason to believe you have introduced into this country an unauthorised alien in the person of a female, sir.'

The game was clearly up, so he answered simply, 'Yes.'

This honesty floored the man, who did not know what to say as he had obviously expected Geoff to deny the whole thing. Stuttering and stammering, he eventually said they would all have to accompany him to the police station.

'Could we finish our drinks first?' enquired Geoff.

He learned later what had happened. When they had boarded the crew bus at St Mawgan, the driver had looked through the window behind him to see whether the rear doors were closed, and it was at this exact moment that Radmilovic had taken off her helmet and let her golden hair cascade down. In the Passenger & Freight section later, he remarked, 'That bint wot come in the Lib was a bit of aw right.' By a stroke of misfortune the squadron leader in charge overheard this juicy piece of information. He investigated further and questioned Geoff's faithful flight lieutenant, who had ferried a second Liberator. 'Oh no, sir, Squadron Leader Rothwell would never do anything like that! You've made a mistake!'

'What loyal personnel I had and what misplaced loyalty,' thought Geoff.

The upshot was that Radmilovic was taken into custody and Geoff was put under open arrest until he saw the station commander the following morning. By then he had worked himself into a state of extreme agitation and his nervousness was not eased by the fearsome attack from the group captain.

'Who the bloody hell do you think you are – the Scarlet Pimpernel? Or are you a white slave trader smuggling bloody Jug popsies into the country?' Geoff recalled:

There was much more in a similar vein until he was interrupted by a phone call. I was able to piece together the conversation by what the CO told me afterwards. The call was from the Chief Immigration Officer in the district wanting Riestich to be returned to Italy in the aircraft in which she had arrived. He said this is what would have happened had she travelled by sea. The Group Captain exploded and told the officer he had no authority to direct aircraft around the world and suggested that as they were both minor pawns in the game they should await instructions from higher up the ladder.

During the course of the day the CO became quite friendly, insisting on buying Geoff a drink in the mess. 'I thought you were a bloody nuisance at first,' he said, shaking Geoff's hand, 'but now it's all over, it was actually quite a lot of fun.'

But was it? Later in the morning Geoff was told a sleeper had been booked for him on a train leaving Newquay in the evening and that he would have to report the next day to the Senior Air Staff Officer at Transport Command Headquarters at Bushey Park. As he boarded the train at Newquay he saw Radmilovic in the distance, being escorted by a civilian, but had no chance to speak to her. (Reistich was on her way to a Rehabilitation Centre for processing.) He reported to the Senior Air Staff Officer, Group Captain Graham, at Bushey Park.

'How many hours have you flown on Liberators?' asked Graham.

'Oh, about fifty, I think, sir.'

'Well, that's sufficient to carry passengers. That's all.'

And that was all there was to it – a question which could have been answered by a telephone call. What a strange business it had been. He had expected a rocket, possibly even a court martial, for smuggling an unauthorised person into the country, but all he had got was an enquiry regarding flying hours. Group Captain Graham would, three and a half years later, become Geoff's CO in Rhodesia.

The Ferry Unit was in the process of disbanding, and while HQ arranged his next assignment, Geoff attended a six-week flying instructors' refresher course at Lulsgate Bottom in Somerset before returning to Italy.

It was at Lulsgate Bottom that he met the New Zealander and Victoria Cross winner Len Trent, who had been in Stalag Luft III of *Great Escape* fame. From the moment they met, Geoff and Len developed a rapport, and Len became Geoff's greatest friend. In their leisure time they would walk for miles over the Mendip Hills, enjoying afternoon tea in such places as Cheddar, of Gorge and cheese fame, Axbridge, Wookey Hole and other delightful English villages, and return by way of numerous old pubs where they drank pints of the local ale, or scrumpy. The two men had much in common, including both having survived terrifying experiences which had resulted in them becoming PoWs – Len by parachute when his aircraft exploded, and Geoff in a crash out of control. As a result they shared similar outlooks on life.

Geoff was right in thinking the Reistich affair was not over. In the middle of a lecture one day he was taken for an interview with the Special Investigation Branch. 'We want to know all about the alien who has been brought into the country,' they said.

Here we go again, thought Geoff, and this time he revealed everything he knew, including all the high-ranking names Bacchus had told him were involved.

When he returned to Italy he was immediately summoned for an interview with Gilbert Howie, his Wing CO. Howie, hearty, bluff and good-humoured, was universally liked.

'What on earth has been going on?' he asked Geoff. 'I've been told not to allow you out of the Central Mediterranean Forces area.'

Geoff told him the whole story and Howie gave a good chuckle. 'You've been a silly bugger, but you're lucky you got away with it.'

Some time later, after Geoff had been posted to RAF Station Pomigliano, near Naples, he received a visit from Howie, who told him that 'the Reistich Affair', as it was known, had gone as far as Ernest Bevin, the Foreign Minister, who had given instructions for the whole matter to be dropped. Obviously Radmilovic had, as Bacchus had surmised, valuable information to give to the British Government. Geoff never saw or heard of Reistich again.

The months passed in Italy, with Geoff engaged in administration and serving as a senior member of a war crimes tribunal in Naples, and also attending the war crimes tribunal trying Field Marshal Kesselring. During this period Geoff was an acting squadron leader, but when he was posted back to England to complete six-month flying instructors' course at the Central Flying School at Little Rissington, he reverted to his war substantive rank of flight lieutenant. This was to be another unhappy period. His marriage to Val was proving to be unsuccessful and they were drifting apart. From different backgrounds, they had different expectations, and in 1947 there seemed to be no option but to separate. It was a sad time for them both, particularly as Val was expecting a child.

'In retrospect, Val and I should never have got married,' says Geoff. 'We had little in common and the longer we lived together, the more unhappy we became.' But he had no wish to give up on his marriage and pressed Val for them to try again, but she made it clear she wanted an end to it and he had no choice but to accept the situation.

On 25 February 1948, their daughter Zelie, so named after the opera singer Zelie de Lussan, was born. In the company of his sister Pat, Geoff went to London to see the child. Sadly, it was to be the only time he saw Zelie. A posting had come through to Southern Rhodesia (now Zimbabwe), and in view of the fact he had no idea how long he would be there, or even if he would be returning to England, he made a heart-rending decision not to develop a relationship which would split Zelie's loyalties in the future. There was also the possibility that Val would marry again, so it seemed to be the only course of action in the circumstances. He instigated divorce proceedings on the grounds of desertion and was eventually granted a decree absolute.

Southern Rhodesia proved to be an enjoyable posting. Geoff was made a flight commander, first instructing student pilots on Harvards at No. 4 Flying Training School at Heany, near Bulawayo, then in 1949, student navigators at No. 3 Air Navigation School, Thornhill, Gwelo (now Gweru). After his wartime activities this could have been an unexciting and somewhat tedious role, but he tackled it with remarkable energy and enthusiasm, giving much encouragement and advice to the young pilots and navigators. He was also made the instrument rating testing officer, an occupation which took up much of his time.

It was while he was in Southern Rhodesia that he met Jerry Jarvis, who was to become a lifelong friend. Jerry was a flight lieutenant navigator who had also been posted to Thornhill as an instructor.

'By sheer force of personality and by creating excellent relations with his pilots, Geoff's flight worked at peak efficiency, with very high morale. With Geoff's exuberant spirit there was rarely a dull moment,' says Jerry.

While he was in Rhodesia Geoff was able to make full use of his acting talent. He and Jerry joined the Thornhill Players, a local repertory company, Jerry doubling as stage manager and actor while Geoff, being tall and handsome, played the male romantic lead, which he did extremely well. They acted in mainly light comedies, such as *George & Margaret, French Without Tears, Worm's Eye View* and *The Man Who Came To Dinner.* All performances were well received and the plays were taken to Bulawayo, Salisbury (now Harare) and other smaller towns. Whilst they were on tour, most afternoons were spent drinking at various hostelries and then sleeping it off on the set.

However, as much as he was enjoying instructing in Rhodesia, Geoff was becoming disillusioned with the RAF, which he had served with devotion for over twelve years. To achieve the rank of squadron leader, which he had held for so long during the war, he was now required to pass promotion examinations. Although he was annoyed, he buckled down to study, finding it difficult as he had lost the art. He sat his first exam and passed all subjects with the exception of Imperial Geography, in which he achieved 72 per cent, the pass mark being 75 per cent. He discussed this with Wing Commander Gilbert Howie, his friend from Italy, who was now in Air Ministry.

'It's a shame, Geoff,' said Howie. 'The authorities are worried that the active service wartime officers with proven leadership abilities like yourself are failing exams, and those who are passing are the younger ones with no experience. They've decided to lower the pass rate to 70 per cent to help get the officers they want.'

When Geoff pointed out he had passed under those rules, Howie said he was desperately sorry, but they couldn't award passes in retrospect and that he would have to pass again in all the subjects.

'Like bloody hell I will,' said an infuriated Geoff. 'As far as I'm concerned, the Air Ministry can stuff their promotion exams. I'll soldier on as a flight lieutenant until I'm the most senior flight lieutenant in the Air Force, because I have no intention of sitting any more exams.'

Apart from the promotion problem, Geoff had detected a gradual change in the camaraderie amongst the officers as many were married and lived off the station. No longer was the mess life as attractive as it had been in wartime. He felt there was a lack of purpose in flying as there were no longer operational sorties.

However, it was a huge decision to quit the service he had grown to love and he gave it much thought. But there seemed no other way, and finally he submitted his application to resign his commission. The CO liked and respected Geoff, and recognising that he had become disillusioned with the RAF, strongly recommended his application. Group Headquarters also strongly recommended it but the Air Ministry turned it down. Their reasoning was that Geoff was a highly qualified pilot, instructor and instrument rating testing officer. Having a green card, he was unrestricted by weather conditions, which gave him added value as a pilot. In retrospect it was not unnatural for the authorities to want to keep him. In cases such as this the applicant resubmits the application with a request that it goes to the next highest authority, in this case the Air Council. In due course they also turned it down on the grounds that it would set a precedent. Again, the reason given was that he was a highly experienced instructor and they could not afford to lose him. So the next step was to resubmit to the highest authority – namely the king. This he did.

Geoff had been in touch with his parents' MP in Britain, who was lobbying on his behalf, but he knew there was little chance of His Majesty turning around a decision by the Air Council. He pondered what he should do next. Being an Aries, he would not acknowledge that the brick wall was there to stop him; it had to be bulldozed. He could think of only one way. *Right, I'll desert, and then they'll have to sack me.*

He was due for a month's leave, which he spent on a tobacco farm. At the end of it he flew to Nyasaland (now Malawi) for three weeks' fishing, thinking this would establish desertion. On his return to Salisbury he was promptly arrested and thrown into a cell. Trying to sleep on a wooden bed, his head swam. It was all reminiscent of POW camp. Bugger it, he thought, they can't treat an officer in the Royal Air Force like this, so he hammered on the door, demanding to see the inspector. Fortunately the inspector was a reasonable man who was impressed with Geoff's war record, and he allowed him to return to camp, in the company of a senior RAF officer, where he was placed under open arrest.

Eventually he received a visit from a Squadron Leader Bass, who had been one of his instructors at Grantham in 1939. The charge was not going to be desertion as Geoff had expected, but absent without leave, the penalty for which was likely to be a loss of seniority. Geoff was devastated.

'Look, if you promise to plead guilty, I'll try to get the charge changed to desertion,' said Bass. 'The Wingco leaves a lot of this sort of work to me, so I think I can manage it.'

He was as good as his word and the court martial passed a sentence that he be cashiered, but this meant disgrace and the inability to serve in any public office. (This was abandoned in 1970.)

He flew back to England, where he was put under open arrest until the final sentence was promulgated. Eventually a letter arrived from Air Ministry telling him: 'King George VI has graciously seen fit to remit the sentence of the Court Martial to one of dismissal.'

In hindsight, after all he had gone through, all he had to do was say he was going to stand for Parliament in a by-election and he would have been allowed to resign.

It was time to move on and now Geoff put all his energies into looking for an agricultural job, preferably in Rhodesia, where he knew there was a job waiting for him if he wanted it. He applied for a visa to Southern Rhodesia but it was turned down. 'I learnt from an MP friend that the bastards at Air Ministry had blocked it because they didn't want this used as a precedent by others who were wanting to leave the Air Force.'

In the meantime he had to earn a living and a job with Airwork Limited as a flying instructor filled the gap. One day he saw an advertisement for a rubber planter in Malaya which sounded interesting. He wrote straight away to the rubber company and, while waiting for a reply, decided to go and see Chris Harrison, Pat Adams' father, who had been a planter in Malaya. After listening to Geoff, Harrison advised him to go for it. 'You know there's a Communist uprising in Malaya, don't you?' said Harrison. 'But I've heard the situation is not nearly as bad as reports indicate. And if you don't get into rubber, get into tin. The important thing is to get to Malaya. A fine life is yours for the asking.'

Then Geoff asked about Pat. Where was she now and what was she doing? He learned she was living in London, and that she had married again, this time to an Army officer, James Cooke, and they had a son, Andrew. He asked for her telephone number and they arranged to meet.

Geoff found Pat unchanged, the same sweet girl he had fallen in love with ten years ago. *Ten years.* Could it really be that long? They had much to catch up on and they pledged to keep in touch. Although it was unspoken, he knew he was still in love with her and would never forget her. And then he had to go.

When he returned home a letter awaited him from the rubber company asking him to go to London for an interview. Rubber Estates Agency was a reputable and established concern and he was immediately offered the position of assistant manager.

On a beautiful bright day in August 1951 he stood outside Normanhurst with his family as he waited for the taxi to take him to London Docks to board the *Ben Vorlich*. They were all there, Pat with tears in her eyes, Maurice shaking his hand and wishing him the best of luck, Ethel determined to be brave, and Wimpy looking forlorn, knowing that Geoff was going away. He hugged them all and then it was time for him to leave. He was off on another adventure to start a new life in a new country, a country still at war.

15

MALAYA 1951 – *LE DESTIN EST DRÔLE*

Suddenly a puff of wind, a puff faint and tepid and laden
with strange odours and blossoms, of aromatic wood, comes
out of the still night – the first sigh of the East on my face.
That I can never forget. It was impalpable and enslaving,
like a charm, like a whispered promise of mysterious delight.
                                        – Joseph Conrad, *Youth*

Shortly before 8.00 a.m. on 16 June 1948, three young Chinese
Communists erupted into the office of a large, remote rubber
plantation, greeted Arthur Walker, its veteran British manager,
with the usual salutation – 'Tabek, tuan' – then shot him, and
calmly rode off into the jungle on their bicycles.

Thus, only three short years after the end of the Japanese
occupation, war came again to Malaya... The British Government
delicately referred to this bloody and costly struggle as the
'Malayan Emergency'.

Malaya, with a population of approximately 40 per cent Malay,
35 per cent Chinese, 20 per cent Indian and the remainder European
and Eurasian, was a predominantly Islamic country. The reasons
for the Emergency, which lasted twelve years and cost thousands of
lives, among them those of many women and children, date back
to the occupation of the country by the Japanese in World War
II. The horrors of the war and the occupation were still fresh in

people's minds; they did not want to be ruled by the Communists as they felt that if they were in power it would make government in Malaya impossible. Essentially, they wanted independence from Britain – most Malayans and Singaporeans dreamt of independence from their colonial masters. The Communists had played on this way of thinking by terrorising the Europeans in the hope they would abandon the country. Malaya, they cried, had been a simple, happy, self-sufficient country until the white man arrived and robbed the people of their country's riches – until the Japanese had come along. Why should the running dogs, as the Chinese Communists called the Europeans, be allowed back into a country they had been unable to hold?

The Communist terrorists were skilled in jungle warfare; many of them had served in the Malayan People's Anti-Japanese Army, which had fought a guerrilla war with Force 136 after the country had been captured by the Japanese. They calculated that if they spread enough terror amongst the planters and tin miners to cause a large-scale exodus, this would damage the economy to such a degree they would be able to achieve their objective and take over the country. But they did not count on the fortitude and stubbornness of the Europeans, many of whom were middle-aged and had been prisoners of the Japanese, or had escaped to fight with the Allied Forces.

The Japanese had let the rubber and tin plantations become run-down. However, by the time Geoff arrived in 1951 the industry was almost back on its feet again. The planters, who were bearing the brunt of the civilian casualties lived on isolated estates with only a small police escort. They still had to go about their business on the estates and on dangerous roads. For Geoff, who was putting his head in the lion's mouth again, it was a dangerous situation to be in, but then he had always thrived on danger. Before going to Malaya he had asked his friend Fraser Stooks from Stalag Luft 1, who was now a planter, about the bandit situation and he had replied: 'Well, as far as I know there's not a bandit behind every bush, but there could be.'

Arriving in Singapore's Keppel Harbour, Geoff leaned over the rail of the *Ben Vorlich* thinking of what Stooks had told him.

What *had* he let himself in for? Although it sounded like a big adventure, too good to miss, was he tempting fate and would the good fortune which had so helped him in the past help him again?

They had anchored on a beautiful, gleaming August morning, everything shimmering in the intense, almost liquid haze that was Singapore, a land less than a hundred miles from the equator, and ten thousand miles from England. Tiny islands, some no bigger than rocks, were dotted all around the harbour, which was clogged with hundreds of ships, both big and small, a cluster of masts and cranes and hundreds of sampans. These were alive with small figures constantly moving, working in the blinding heat. Away in the distance he could see coconut palms and buildings, all silhouetted against a deep blue sky. When they docked he was hit by the exotic smell peculiar to the East – a strange mixture of sweet spices, dried fish and frangipani. It drifted up to him in waves, to be ingrained in his memory forever, bringing to mind all he had ever read about the East.

The quayside was like a beehive, swarming with hawkers, Chinese and Tamils with their bullock carts, while piled up along the quay were stacks of ingots of tin waiting a to be shipped out, as well as canvas bales of rubber and copra. There were more smells, the sweet nutty smell of drying coconut mingling with the pungent odour of fish drying in the sun, the stench of the monsoon drains and the spiciness of cloves and pepper.

Geoff had been booked on the morning train to Gemas on the northern border of Johore and Negri Sembilan State, and was collected by an agent and taken to Singapore railway station in a comfortable saloon car. There was so much to take in – exotic vegetation, the bright colours of bougainvillea and hibiscus, people of all nationalities, Chinese, Malay, Tamils, Sikhs selling their wares, slight Asian figures, their shirts saturated with sweat, pedalling trishaws carrying fat European *Mems,* and European businessmen in spotless white shirts and trousers carrying briefcases. The city was so alive, so colourful – it was different from anything he had ever seen.

His shirt was already soaked through. 'Does it get cooler in the rainy season?' he asked the agent, who laughed, saying the temperature hardly varied from one month to the next.

'As Malaya is so near the equator,' he said, 'there are practically no seasons and the sun rises and sets at about the same time all the year round. At night there is a welcome drop in temperature.'

The train to Gemas crossed the causeway which joined Singapore Island with the State of Johore in the Federated Malay States, and travelled through paddy fields, jungle, rubber and oil palm plantations. On arrival at Gemas Geoff was met by Paul Rooth, whom he was due to replace as assistant manager on Gemas Estate. Rooth, a tall, sun-tanned man with deep blue eyes, gripped Geoff's hand warmly with a 'Welcome to Malaya.' He carried a Sten gun and wore a belt with two pouches containing hand grenades and was accompanied by a bodyguard of Malay special constables wearing tropical uniform – khaki shirts and shorts.

As the train had been air-conditioned Geoff was immediately hit by the intense heat and was soon bathed in sweat even though he was wearing a lightweight tropical suit. They set off in a massive armour-plated estate car, a Marmon-Harrington with a Ford V8 chassis – 'a real bastard to drive on the narrow estate roads as the colossal weight of the armour plate made steering shaky,' says Geoff. 'We frequently ended in a ditch and had to be pulled out by a tractor.'

The roads were well-maintained and lined with tall rubber trees. Beyond stretched the rich, green jungle. The sky seemed to be higher, more grandiose and more flamboyant than any he had ever seen. It was an odd colour, not deep blue like the skies he had seen in Italy or Egypt, but more opaque. He was reminded of Somerset Maugham's description of the Malayan sky, 'a blue sky, not pale with the languor of great heat, nor violent like the skies of Italy, but as though Prussian blue were mixed with milk.'

The huge vehicle swung into the driveway of Gemas Estate and the planter's bungalow came into view. Standing well back from the drive, it was built on a hill, surrounded by barbed-wire fencing reminiscent of Stalag Luft I, a hedge of bougainvillea and a cluster of coconut palms, and fringed on either side by casuarinas, brilliant red flame trees, banana plants with shining green leaves and frangipani bushes. The enormous garden contained yellow, orange and red canna lilies, bougainvillea and many other flowering shrubs.

A large open verandah furnished with cane chairs ran the full length of the house. Geoff alighted from the car to the unceasing noise of a million cicadas.

Two Army units, the Green Howards operating from Seremban in the north and the Cameronians from Segamat in the south, were fighting the Communist terrorists, or CTs as they were known. For some unknown reason the soldiers stopped their operations short of the Gemas river, the boundary between the two states, thus creating a buffer zone. Consequently, the terrorists were able to use the Gemas district as a sort of safe haven. All the compounds at Gemas were surrounded by barbed-wire fences, which were constantly patrolled by armed guards during the day and illuminated by powerful floodlights at night.

'You'd be pretty secure with all this protection, wouldn't you, Paul?' asked Geoff.

'You might think that,' Rooth replied, 'but there's hardly a night when I have a good night's sleep.'

He soon found out Paul was right.

That first night at Gemas, tired from the journey, Geoff fell asleep beneath the confines of a thick mosquito net to the croak of bullfrogs and the strange sound of a night bird singing just a note or two. But in the early hours of the morning he was awakened by the *crack-crack-crack* of automatic firing. The noise was so close it seemed to be coming from inside the bungalow.

He went to Paul's room and woke him asking what all the noise was. 'It's probably just the bandits,' said Paul, seemingly unconcerned, but they went to investigate and discovered it was, in fact, the special constables firing on the terrorists. It was a commonplace occurrence, said Paul. Geoff came to realise that this was to be the pattern every night.

He was enrolled in the Auxiliary Police and supplied with a Sten gun, later replaced by a lighter and more accurate carbine and hand grenades. At first he was too busy becoming acquainted with the Malayan way of life and learning the business of rubber planting to be apprehensive about the terrorist situation, but after hearing news on the radio every day of planters being murdered, he realised that the bandit situation in North Johore was even more serious than he had imagined, with daily raids on the rubber estates. About ten days after his arrival Rooth went on leave, and Geoff found that apart from a cook, amah and the special constable escorts, he was on his own. Paul had drummed into him the importance of changing his routine each time he went on his rounds of inspection of the estate. This was a precaution against being ambushed by the bandits.

Not long after Paul had left, Geoff set off in the company of his special constable escorts, plus Nair, a new Indian conductor, and the two dogs which always went with them. The early light of dawn filtered through the canopy of the rubber trees before the day's heat, which would soon be beating down upon them. The soft Malayan air was sweet and moist, and the dew, still glistening on the lallang (a type of coarse grass), made everything look newly washed and clean. The jungle, huge and dense with bright green foliage, seemed to open its arms in welcome. Brightly coloured birds called to each other as they flitted from tree to tree.

Geoff parked the armoured car at the side of the estate road where a track led through the rubber to a nursery of young trees he wished to inspect. The party walked down the path, a guard leading about twenty yards ahead of Geoff, Nair and another guard. The third escort brought up the rear – a 'tail-end Charlie'. The dogs ran ahead, sniffing the night smells on the tracks and roaming just a little in front of the men as they approached the nursery. After the inspection, when preparing to head back to the armoured car Geoff remembered what Paul had told him – *never, never, under any circumstances use the same route on more than two successive days, or return the same way if avoidable.* When reaching the gate to the nursery he turned to the right rather than the left, which was the way they had come. They had gone only a short distance when a fusillade of shots rang out.

Geoff's escort roughly pushed him into some bushes. '*Tinggal sini.*' (Stay here.) Nair took off at a run, scared out of his wits. The firing stopped and the Gurkha guards shouted to each other. The guard with Geoff took off his jungle hat and stuck it on the end of his rifle, shaking the branches of the shrub and raising the weapon above his head. Immediately there was more automatic weapon fire but where was it coming from? They were in a valley between two *bukit* (hills) and the sound echoed all around, mingling with the screeches of the monkeys. Geoff knew the fire was coming from somewhere on the hillside so he hid behind a tree. Without pausing to consider the danger he was in, he ran from tree to tree and as he did so more shots ran out.

Then he realised the firing was coming from the direction of the path they had taken to the nursery. He kept dodging from tree to tree, keeping the trunks between himself and the enemy. He *had* to get back to the safety of the bungalow somehow. He ran like mad, sweat running down his face, nearly blinding him. He knew he must be visible to the bandits as bullets whizzed past him, some nearly winging him. The CTs were well-trained ... that was too close for comfort. The special constables were trying to track down the bandits but he knew deep down they would not find them – they were too clever, too experienced in the ways of trekking in the jungle. His breath was now coming in great gasps and the trees seemed to be crowding in on him. The fusillade started up again, ripping into the ground beside him, only just missing him as he sprinted for cover. He ran towards a massive tree, tripped over a vine and sprawled flat on his face.

It was as he lay there exhausted that he noticed them. Leeches. Ugly, black creatures on his arm and starting to move up his body. He had read that the human neck was a favourite place – a path to the warm hidden crevices of the body. They were already beginning to swell as they sucked his blood. He felt like vomiting but somehow had the presence of mind to remember something else Rooth had told him, '*If any of the buggers grip on to your body, burn them off with a match or the tip of a cigarette.*'

He lit a match and then another, putting them on each creature until the last one had writhed and dropped off his arms, leaving a couple of spots of drying blood where they had been sucking. Then he stumbled to his feet, not noticing the pain in his knees or the dirt in his mouth and staggered to the bank at the side of the road. He was nearly there now, he could afford to slow down – the firing had stopped and there was no sign of the terrorists – but he had to be careful. The compound came within sight twenty yards, fifteen yards, ten yards ... He had done it! Scratched, bleeding, exhausted, he had taken over an hour to get home.

Once back at the bungalow, he telephoned the local police and told them of the incident. Later an Iban tracker attached to the unit found some cartridge cases on the ground and five ambush positions on the hillside overlooking the track which Geoff and his party had used to visit the nursery. Nair was eventually found in a Gemas coffee shop, where he had downed several brandies to steady his nerves. He had decided Gemas Estate was not the healthiest of workplaces and left the following day.

> In the early morning the colours are brilliant, yet tender, and then as the day wears on they grow tired and pale.
> – Somerset Maugham

Geoff soon settled into the life and ways of the country. 'This is Malaya,' Paul Rooth told him. 'Occasionally things get done but more often they don't.'

The pace of life was slow, laid back, but after the constraints of England and his previous life he felt fresh and alive. He couldn't believe his luck in finding a job he loved so much, for which he was well paid, and for the first time in his life he was his own boss, which gave him a sense of well-being.

There was the constant danger of terrorism but he knew without a doubt he had made the right decision to come to this country, which held an irresistible attraction for him. At first he found it difficult adjusting to the climate as the heat, so different from Egypt and the Mediterranean, took some getting used to. He sweated profusely and his legs felt heavy, almost rubbery, until his body began to adapt.

Each morning he woke full of energy and excitement. A typical day would start around 5.30 a.m. when he would breakfast on cold fresh lime juice, coffee and a mixture of fruit such as bananas, papaya and pineapples. Then in the company of his armed guards he would inspect the estate before returning to the bungalow in the late morning for substantial *makan* (food) such as *ikan* (fish) or bacon and eggs. The walks on the estate always yielded something new. After brunch he would supervise the collection of the thick, creamy latex yielded by the trees. After the rubber had been collected at the weighing stations which were dotted around the estate, Geoff and Paul would go back to the house for a 'lie-off' – the period in the day when the planters had a rest in the drowsy heat of the afternoons, usually between the hours of 1.30 and 3 p.m. The air was always heavy, stifling. Covered by a mosquito net, he would lie on his bed, sleep not far away, and listen to the droning of the mosquitoes, the buzzing of the flies, and the *whir-whir* of the ceiling fan. Then after sandwiches, tea and fruit at 3 o'clock there would be office work, which would take an hour or so.

In the cool of the evening, just before dusk, when the air was soft, the trees seemed to part and withdraw from the rest of the jungle, as if they were trying to hold on to the last slow ebbing hour of daylight. It was this time of day, apart from very early in the morning, that he loved the most.

After a shower he would change into long trousers and a long-sleeved shirt to protect himself from the mosquitoes. He would sit on the verandah, now cool after the heat of the day, sip ice-cold Anchor beers and talk over the day's activities with Paul while listening to classical records playing softly in the background. Then suddenly it was dark, which always came as a surprise to those unaccustomed to the tropics. The night was lit up and filled with fireflies like tiny, moving candles, and the limpid air turned warm and balmy once more.

To be a successful rubber planter meant Geoff having to learn the business from scratch, how the rubber trees grew, how to maintain the vegetation in the fields and the production of the latex from the field through to the factory, and lastly, and probably most importantly, he learnt about the administration of the estate and the labour force. The Tamils had an expression – 'You are my mother and my father, sah' – and that was precisely how they viewed the estate manager to whom they brought all their problems. He was the judge and jury in disputes and his decision was always respected.

There were often humorous moments, like the day when he was in the office looking over some accounts and noticed a discrepancy.

'I think there's a mistake here,' he said to the Indian chief clerk, Periera.

Periera slapped his forehead and said, 'Tchk! Tchk! Daily I am breaking my head to find this mistake and you are finding it at once!'

Geoff had been in Malaya only a short time when he received a sad letter from home. His beloved Wimpy, the little dog he had bought in the pub in the early days of the war and taken back to the mess in the folds of his greatcoat, had been knocked over by a car and severely injured. Ethel and Pat had rushed him to the local vet, but unfortunately there was no choice but for him to be put down. It was a tragic and painful loss to them all.

It was on a visit to Segamat, the nearest town, that Geoff experienced the taste of the infamous durian fruit for the first time, a huge fruit the size of a football and covered in spines. The durian, which has a creamy consistency and a frightful, pungent smell, has been described as 'like sitting on the lavatory eating custard'. However, Malays believe the fruit is a powerful aphrodisiac and have a saying, '*Bila durian durz'an jatoh sarong naik*' (When the durian falls sarongs rise). Geoff loved it and endeavoured to eat it whenever he could. He also became addicted to the taste of curry the first time he tried it, so much so that he engaged an Indian cook by the name of Velu whose curries were legendary in Malaya. At least six feet tall, Velu was an imposing figure and spoke very good English. He was to stay with Geoff for over sixteen years.

Geoff's first experience of tropical weather came over the Christmas period of 1951–52 when the monsoon season started. The rivers flooded and for days there was heavy continuous rain. North Johore was completely cut off and food had to be dropped by helicopter to the workers on some of the estates. It was all hands on deck as everybody, chest-deep in water, carried sacks of rice on their heads as they waded across the swollen streams, often in the company of snakes desperately swimming for dear life.

In those days of the Emergency the rubber company, realising that its employees were under severe stress from constant terrorist attacks, granted all their European staff four days' leave with expenses paid once a month. Leaves were spent mostly in Singapore, which Geoff grew to love, or in the cool air of the hill stations of Cameron Highlands and Frasers Hill where the rubber company had a bungalow fully staffed with an amah and cook.

Although he learnt the business of rubber planting quickly, Geoff had no idea whether his work was satisfactory, as Jack Longmore, manager of Gemas Estate, was an unfriendly and reticent man who refused to give any opinion on his work. Geoff had met all types in the Air Force but had never come across a character like Longmore before. 'I thought I'd done reasonably well, but Longmore was a real hard nut to crack. In the end I thought, Bugger it! I'll apply for a posting.'

He knew Paul Rooth's tenure as acting manager was coming to an end, and rather than continue under Longmore when he returned from leave in the UK, he decided to ask Hedley Facer, the chairman, for a transfer.

'Why do you want a posting, Geoff?' asked Hedley.

'Because I'm finding it difficult to get on with Longmore.'

Facer was a wise old bird and knowing the two men fairly well went on to say: 'I can see that sometimes there's a clash between two men of strong character. I'm going to send you to Sungei Kahang in Johore to Soldier Densham, with whom *everyone* gets along.'

Facer was right. Geoff and Soldier hit it off straight away, their friendship lasting for many years. Christened Frederick, but nicknamed 'Soldier' because of his time spent as a POW in both world wars, sixty-three-year-old Soldier was a short, stocky man who looked like the actor Leo McKern of *Rumpole* fame. He drank like a fish, had a wonderful sense of humour, was tremendously generous, and was loved by everybody. He was idyllically happy with his *keep* or Malay housekeeper, Kechil. They had two adopted daughters, Ruby and Rosie, one Chinese and the other Malay. Ruby had been the daughter of the local Chinese ferryman, who had a large family to feed. Soldier had first met Ruby on a trip into the local town on the ferry. The little girl held on to Soldier's finger, looking up at him with grave dark eyes. 'Well,' said Soldier, who adored children, 'What could you do, Geoff?' Soldier ended up buying her from the ferryman, who was only too happy for the child to go to a man who would so obviously look after and care for her.

Geoff blossomed under Soldier's guidance. He learned much about the rubber planting business and almost straightaway Soldier made him a divisional manager with his own labour force. Although Geoff's bungalow was reputed to be haunted by a Chinese *towkay* (merchant) who had hanged himself many years ago, he was quite unconcerned but hoped the *hantu* (spirit) was friendly.

Life on Sungei Kahang centred on the club in the town of Kluang, about twenty-five miles from the estate, Kluang, situated in the centre of Johore State, had been built on either side of the main trunk line of Malayan Railways. This ran north from Singapore across the causeway which spanned the Straits of Johore, through Kuala Lumpur to Butterworth, opposite the island of Penang, and ended at the Siamese border at Alor Star. The land was flat in the vicinity of Kluang, with just the odd *bukit* rising from the jungle floor.

Essentially a loner, Geoff settled in to life on the estate as if he had been born to it. Every Sunday he and Soldier would go into town and head for the Kluang Club where, having stacked their carbines, Stens and any other weapons behind the bar, they would knock back cool Anchor or Tiger beers along with planters from the other neighbourhood estates. Then they would head for home, eagerly anticipating the delicious curry prepared by Velu before going for a lie-off in the heat of the balmy afternoon. Afterwards they would relax on the verandah for a couple of hours drinking stengahs, the very weak whisky and soda or water, more of a thirst-quencher than an alcoholic drink. On days like these England seemed far away.

Correspondence arrived regularly from England, from his family, his friends and Sweet Pea, and he opened these eagerly. At first Pat's letters were enthusiastic about their meeting again, her life and her son Andrew. She wanted to know about his life in Malaya. *What a wonderful life you must be having out there, darling, but I'm worried about you. I hear much about the Communist uprising … It sounds dangerous … Please be careful.*

And then gradually the letters took on an unhappy note. She wrote that her marriage was unhappy as James, her husband, was schizophrenic, frequently hallucinating and leaving her for long periods. She had been warned he should not be left alone with their young son.

Geoff was saddened to think of his lovely Sweet Pea, so tender and kind, being unhappy. But there was little he could do, except to support her and offer encouragement.

Early one morning several months after his arrival at Sungei Kahang, Geoff set out to inspect a particular field of newly planted rubber trees. As there had been few terrorist incidents for some months it was felt unnecessary to use more than one Malay special constable as escort. The bandits who had been active in the area, being deprived of food and medical supplies, had moved away to other districts where it was easier to obtain the supplies essential for their survival. Geoff's dogs, Sandy and Ben, accompanied them, having proved to be extremely useful in sensing danger. Many a planter's life had been saved by his dogs.

Geoff's journey involved crossing a wooden bridge across a deep, wide ravine. It was a route he had undertaken many times before and, apart from proceeding rather gingerly when negotiating the narrow bridge, it involved no special precautions. However, what he did not know was that a party of Communist terrorists had escorted a committee member for an important meeting in the Labis district and were returning to their base at Kota Tinggi in the south of the state. It was highly dangerous for the bandits to travel near the main trunk road as military patrols were in operation and there had been numerous battles in which the Communists had suffered severe losses, but by keeping to jungle paths and staying in remote kampongs they were comparatively safe.

The CTs were within sight of the jungle on the south side of the Kluang–Mersing road when they heard Geoff's Jeep approaching. They plunged into the thick undergrowth at the edge of the road and waited until the vehicle had passed and was out of sight. Knowing he had to return by the same route, they decided the opportunity was too good to miss and they set up an ambush, with two bandits positioning themselves behind trees on either side of the road and facing the bridge, whilst the third stationed himself in the roadside ditch behind a small jungle shrub. They did not have long to wait for their prey to return.

The Jeep approached the bridge and had to slow down as it ran at right angles to the road. Geoff and his Malay escort were barely a third of the way across when the first fusillade of bullets was fired from one of the bandits' Sten guns. He was still in third gear when he heard the firing. There was no time to feel fear, no time to feel anything other than his old instinct of self-preservation, which had got him out of many emergencies in the past, and that told him to get out of there like a bat out of hell. With the dogs barking excitedly in the back, he slammed his foot down on the accelerator and the Jeep leaped forward as a spray of bullets ripped into the lower half of the vehicle.

With his heart pounding and sweat pouring off his face, he reached the end of the bridge just in time to see a khaki-clad figure with a distinctive three-pointed cap with a red star run across the road from one side to the other.

Throwing the wheel over to the left, he tried to run the figure down, but narrowly missed him. It was all over in half a minute or less, and when he looked over at his Malay escort in the passenger seat he saw the poor fellow had fainted.

Geoff drove flat out with the radiator erupting like a geyser until he reached the twenty-second mile, where Soldier was waiting for him. The Malay Constable had come round by now, and the two dogs who were none the worse for their experience, jumped into Soldier's Land Rover. At Soldier's bungalow Geoff explained what had happened.

A party from the Gurkha Rifles was dispatched to search the area but failed to find the terrorists. However, there was ample evidence of the ambush, and no fewer than twenty-two cartridge cases were found. An inspection of the Jeep showed it had suffered eight hits which punctured the radiator, shattered the windscreen and damaged a rear spring. How such a full head-on assault had failed to wound or kill the occupants of the vehicle remains a mystery.

The Communist terrorists were not the only dangers in the jungles of Malaya. One early morning not long after the bridge episode Geoff was walking along a jungle path with his special constable. As he walked he listened to the sound of the jungle, and for a moment he stood transfixed by two bulbuls hungrily sucking the nectar from some tree orchids, their bright red, green and yellow bodies a vivid contrast to the pale flowers. He was brought up with a start by his special constable saying softly: '*Jaga baik, Tuan*. There is a snake, just there!'

For a moment Geoff's heart stood still and he felt the colour drain from his face. Only a few feet away and curled almost lazily around the trunk of a tree was a huge black cobra, its hood expanded and its tongue flicking in and out. His heart hammered in his chest and his legs felt light and shaky. He stood very still, scarcely daring to breathe. Very slowly he reached for his carbine. He only had one chance. He pulled back the safety catch and aimed the gun at the snake then squeezed the trigger. The shot rang out sharply in the still jungle air as the snake fought for its life for a brief second or two and then lay twitching.

'You did well, *Tuan*,' said the special constable, 'but next time you see snake throw a stick at him and he will go away.'

It was a lesson he took to heart as he hated killing any of God's creatures – except mosquitoes and leeches.

It was Christmas 1954 and Geoff was staying at the Gap Rest House on the way to Frasers Hill with Pat Cooke's brother, Chris Harrison, who had come to Malaya as an assistant manager. Both keen ornithologists, they decided to do some bird-watching, and as Geoff brought his binoculars to his eyes to focus on a kingfisher, its colour flashing like a brilliant jewel in the bright sunlight, he said, 'You feel cold, Chris?'

'No, I'm hot.'

Geoff grew colder and colder, then he started to shiver. 'Hate to say it, but I don't feel too well. I'll have to go back to the Rest House.'

Once there, he went straight to bed, piling all the blankets he could find on top of him, and even then he was still shaking and shivering. He grabbed all the mats off the floor but was still freezing cold. His body was soon soaked with sweat, then he became delirious. All night long he lay there, at times sinking into unconsciousness, unaware of Chris hovering anxiously over him, bathing his forehead with a cold damp cloth.

The following morning, although very weak, he felt a little better and was able to get up and go back to the estate. However, on the way home the symptoms started again and by the time they reached the estate he was feeling wretched. He went straight to bed, but his temperature soared. Velu brought him a bowl of Chinese soup, hot and steaming, with shreds of chicken. Geoff took one sip and immediately started to retch. Velu was very worried. 'I think Master very sick. I will get dresser,' he said. (Dressers, usually Indian, are hospital or medical assistants.)

Williams, the Anglo-Indian dresser, took Geoff's temperature.

'Oh sir, you have very high temperature,' he said. 'I think you have malaria.'

He took a sample of blood and when it was analysed, it revealed that he did, indeed, have malaria – one of the most dangerous types, Benign Tertiary, which attacks the brain. For the next few days Geoff's life hung in the balance. He lay in bed dangerously ill, with his teeth chattering, every bone in his body aching and a racking headache. His temperature soared to over 104 degrees.

Alternately shivering and sweating with each bout of rigors, he had no idea how long he lay there or what time of day it was – the only clue was the light filtering through the blinds in his bedroom and the sounds of the birds somewhere in the jungle. As he lay there, hovering between consciousness and unconsciousness, he was vaguely aware of a shadowy figure standing at the foot of his bed. Sweet Pea, he murmured.

As the figure came closer to him, he put out his hand to touch her. Then he pulled her gently towards him. She smiled and he took her hand and led her outside, where he felt the heat of the day and smelt the summer flowers. They lay under a tree and he watched the clouds go slowly by and felt the cool breeze brushing softly against his face.

Then they were dancing to the lilting strains of Moonlight Serenade and she was looking up at him with the look she reserved only for him. He held her closely and they slowly moved and swayed to the music, then it started to go faster and faster, the figures on the dance floor swirling round and round like horses on a merry-go-round. They merged and swayed with them until he felt himself getting hotter and hotter. It was so hot he couldn't breathe.

He was fighting to get out, get out ... He was in the aircraft and it was on fire, and he couldn't undo the straps. He was stuck, he could feel the flames all around him. He pulled and pulled and suddenly he was free and he was floating down through the clouds and the air was cool and fresh on his face. Sweet Pea ...

'Master, Master, you will be better now.'

Velu sponged his head with a cold damp cloth. Williams had given him chloroquin, the fast-acting drug that was the standard treatment for malaria. This had brought his temperature down. By the end of the week he was up and about but on light duties.

Geoff was in the middle of his meal one evening when the lights flickered and petered out. The electric power was supplied from a generator driven by a reliable Lister engine and housed in a shed at the foot of the hill on which the bungalow was situated. For some unaccountable reason, the shed had been left outside the barbed-wire fence. Two of the guards were sent to investigate.

The compound gate was unlocked and one of the guards, shining his torch, approached the engine shed some twenty to thirty yards away. He was about to open the door when he heard a soft voice calling from the high bank on his left. He flashed his torch towards where the sound had come from, but saw nothing. Rushing back to the gate, he told his mate, '*Lekas, tutup pintu. Ada orang jahat dalam belukar.*' (Quick, lock the gate, there's a bandit in the bush.) As they watched from the safety of the compound, they saw lights flickering in the vicinity of the shed, but, undecided as to whether they were caused by fireflies or torches, they withheld their fire.

The following morning they discovered the belt driving the generator had been pushed off the pulley. Geoff gave instructions that the engine shed door was to be secured by a padlock every night and there was no further trouble.

On another occasion, information was received that there was a terrorist courier visiting relatives in the labourers' huts and he would be leaving the following morning. To avoid a skirmish which might involve innocent workers, Geoff formulated a plan. An ambush would be set up on a jungle path used by the CTs with the Ghurka Sergeant Dalbahardur Shastri, who had served in Force 136 during the war, plus a Malay special constable, a police lieutenant and Geoff.

On reaching the ambush area the patrol carefully took up their positions on the jungle path. The police lieutenant positioned himself in the fork of a tree where he would have a clear view of the track and a branch on which to rest the barrel of his carbine. He was to drop a leaf from his notebook to signal the approach of their quarry. Geoff stationed himself behind a large tree at the edge of the path with Shastri, who had turned down the Sten gun as the weapon of choice in favour of his traditional *kukri* (curved knife) a few feet away. The Malay constable stationed himself further down the path.

In the early light of dawn the police lieutenant saw a khaki-clad figure carrying an evil-looking *parang* (knife) approach stealthily a few yards from the tree sheltering Geoff. The terrorist must have moved quickly, because the next moment Geoff looked up to see the raised arm with the parang ready to strike. But Shastri leapt like a panther at the terrorist with an athleticism belying his forty-three years. The razor-sharp *kukri* flashed in the pale dawn light and bit deeply into the terrorist's neck. Blood spurted from the jugular as he fell and within three minutes voracious *changkiak,* or large black biting ants, were feeding on their prey.

Geoff was due for six month's leave and looked forward to returning to England, where he could be with his family – and Sweet Pea, as she was now separated from James Cooke and living with nine-year-old Andrew in London. Geoff was supportive and sympathetic to her situation, and his understanding of her predicament at this unhappy time helped her immensely.

'I don't know how I would have got through without his positivity and moral support,' says Pat. 'It bucked me up so much.'

Geoff's family were still living in Hutton, and Pat had kept in touch with them, often visiting with Andrew. Geoff made arrangements for her to collect an MG Magnette from the factory near Oxford and drive to Genoa, where he would meet her after disembarking from the *Asia*. The reunion was everything he had dreamed of and more. He looked at her. She had not changed except she was a little thinner; the deep dark eyes were just the same.

Pat had travelled to Italy with a friend, who went with them as far as Florence. After touring Italy they returned to England on a grey, rain-lashed day in May 1955. Geoff had almost forgotten about the weather in England after living in the shimmering heat of Malaya for four years.

There was much excitement in the Rothwell house that day. Ethel had waited so long to see her son and she and Pat, now a beautiful young woman, had cooked and cleaned for days in the lead-up to Geoffrey's return.

He had phoned from Winchester and told them what time to expect him and he would be here any minute. She could feel her heart beating with the anticipation of seeing him again. Would he have changed? And would he be happy coming back to England again, after so long away?

She heard a sound behind her and there he was, the same tall figure with the smiling blue eyes, set in a sunburnt face – her good-looking Geoffrey. He had filled out slightly and his hair was bleached the colour of ripe corn. 'Mother!' he said, and he held out his arms to her.

Geoff and Pat spent an idyllic six months together. Andrew was at school, so they made the most of their time together. They holidayed again in Italy, where they had been so happy, and time stood still. Days were spent sight-seeing and swimming in the warm Mediterranean, and sitting on the balcony of their *pensione* at dusk, eating *prosciutto con melone* as they looked down on a velvet black sea, the lights of the town in the distance. In the

MG they drove all over Italy, Germany and Austria, Holland and Liechtenstein.

'Never have I been so happy,' says Geoff, 'and I vowed I would never let her go again.'

They eagerly made plans for their future. Sweet Pea would come out to Malaya with Andrew as soon as she could and they would marry when her divorce from James was finalised. Andrew would attend the planters' school in Malaya with the other English children. James would just have to agree and Sweet Pea could see no difficulties.

All too soon Geoff's leave was up and it was time to return to Malaya. This time there was no sadness. His family knew he loved his life in the country where the sun shone almost every day. Besides, the Emergency would be coming to an end soon. Nothing would ever happen to Geoffrey – he was as strong as an ox, indestructible. And as for Sweet Pea, she would be seeing him before too long.

The letter, when it came, hit him like a bolt from the blue. For a long time after he read it, he felt numb. Surely it was a cruel joke? Then slowly it sank in. He read it again, the words running together, blurring in front of his eyes. It was true. Sweet Pea was not coming to Malaya. James had gone to court to stop her taking Andrew out of the country and an order was now in place. She could leave England but not Andrew.

> I am so sorry, my darling. There is no answer. I have no choice
> in the matter – you know how precious Andrew is to me, and
> I can't leave him as James is not to be trusted with him ... We
> could never be happy knowing Andrew was in danger ...

Just when they had found each other again, he had lost her once more. *C'est la vie!* They were star-crossed lovers, doomed, never destined to be together.

For the first time in his life Geoff gave himself up to grief. For a long time he lived in a dream, angry and depressed and unable to concentrate on anything. He lost all enthusiasm for the work which he had loved. Now nothing seemed to matter. One day his good friend Soldier took him aside.

'Bloody women, they're the curse of mankind! Trouble is, we need 'em! One day you'll find someone else, my boy, but now what you need is work.' And he piled more responsibility on him.

Gradually Geoff felt better. He knew he could not leave Malaya, at least not for a long time. He loved everything about the country, from its spicy smells and early misty mornings before the day's steaming heat, to its strange and colourful tropical birds, like the racquet-tailed drongo that would dive-bomb him each morning when he left the bungalow. Apart from the fact he had lost the love of his life he never ceased to realise he was a lucky man.

When Soldier was hospitalised with an ulcer Geoff managed the estate in his absence, and when Soldier returned he wrote a letter to the agents recommending Geoff for promotion.

> In my absence in hospital Mr Rothwell managed the estate in a most capable manner, and it was obvious the estate was run in exactly the same manner as if I had been there myself. I feel Mr Rothwell is wasted as the Senior Assistant on this estate and I therefore recommend that he be given a management position ...

In 1956 Geoff was given the management of Sabai, a 4,000-acre estate in Pahang State, east of Kuala Lumpur. Sabai was a hilly estate with panoramic views over neighbouring rubber estates and the thick green jungle.

He loved working on Sabai. There was little interference from the board or their agents and he was his own boss. His two dogs, Sandy and Ben, had the run of the estate and went everywhere with him. Ben was so enamoured of Geoff that if he went away for a few days, he would remain by the gate at the entrance to the estate until his master returned home.

He had been in Malaya now for six years, inspecting vast acreages of rubber. Although it was a profitable business, sometimes it could be demoralising as elephants could destroy large areas of a plantation in a night. One would always know when they were about as they would be heard all over the jungle, their mighty trumpeting sound starting on a shrill note and finishing in a deep reverberating growl. They would charge through a clearing of young trees, uproot them, chew the roots like radishes then throw them away.

One weekend Geoff and his Danish neighbour Andy Andersen went to a party in Raub. That weekend was to change both their lives forever. It was here that Geoff met Judy Walters and Andy met Valerie Johnson, whom he married soon after. Judy had been married to Hugh Walters, the local visiting doctor at Raub, but was now separated and was returning to England shortly. The four struck up an immediate friendship. Judy, a tiny, vivacious woman with honey-coloured brown hair, had a young son, Simon. She and Geoff had much in common. Like him, she had been attached to the Special Operations Executive. She had been posted to Burma, working in the Codes and Cyphers section.

Time passed and Geoff saw much of Judy. She made him feel happy again. She was full of life and it was impossible not to be captivated by her. He was also developing a strong relationship with her four-year-old Simon, whom he had grown to love. The little boy, whose hair was the same colour as his own, loved accompanying him when he was bird-watching.

'Simon was such a dear little boy,' says Geoff. 'I always remember him looking up at me and saying: "Will you be my Daddy, Geoff?"'

A letter arrived from England one day from Pat Cooke. She was going to marry a teacher, Owain Trevaldwyn, whose brother was one of the planters in the same agency as Geoff. Referring to Owain as 'the interloper', she wrote: 'He's a good man, darling, and he will make me happy. I hope you understand and I want you to be happy too ... we were star-crossed lovers, you and I ...'

Not long after this he received a telegram from Judy, who by this time had returned to England. Hugh Walters had died suddenly and Geoff, who was due for leave, decided to return to England instead of going to New Zealand to renew wartime friendships as he had planned. By this time Judy had met Geoff's family and shortly after his return he and Judy decided to get married. Simon was thrilled with this arrangement as he already looked on Geoff as his father. They married on 19 March 1959, and when they returned to Malaya on the *Oranje,* Geoff's sister Pat went with them.

Geoff experienced a recurrence of malaria before their leave ended. He was admitted to Norwich Isolation Hospital and given the standard treatment of one chloroquin tablet. 'That's not enough,' he told the medical staff, 'I want three.' The flustered staff must have complained because, shortly after this incident, Geoff was visited by another doctor who had been a RAF medical officer during the war. They chatted for a few minutes and then the doctor said: 'I believe you've been giving my staff some trouble over the treatment. I realise you treat malaria more radically in Malaya so I've given instructions that they can increase the dose if you don't improve.' Fortunately, Geoff reacted quickly to the treatment and, although weak from the attack, he was discharged after five days.

Shortly after his return to Sabai, Geoff was posted back to Sungei Kahang, where he was the *Tuan Besar* as Soldier had now retired. The Emergency was at long last on the wane and he and Judy settled happily into married life. Simon attended the planters' school in Penang. It was a wonderful life for a young boy, playing with the dogs, swimming in the pool or roaming the grounds in the company of the gardener, or *tukang kebun.*

Towards the end of the Emergency 'White Areas' were declared where bandit activity had been negligible and it was considered safe to relax restrictions.

The labour forces could once again take food out into the fields and for the first time in eight years Geoff was able to roam freely over the estate, no longer having to worry about ambushes. At last they were back to peacetime. The Communists had been beaten by a combination of aggressive jungle warfare, cutting off supplies and the establishment of multi-racial co-operation between the respective race-based parties in Malaya. Tunku Abdul Rahman became Malaya's first Prime Minister and in 1960 declared the Emergency over. Significantly, Malaya achieved its independence in 1957 on British, not on Chinese or Communist terms. But it was an uneasy peace as independence meant little to the Communists. To their way of thinking the capitalists would still get up to their old tricks. In one or two states the slayings went on, with attacks redoubled on villages and ambushes on motorists. The Malayan Emergency had tested the planters and miners to the limit. Most refused to submit to terrorist threats, but it had torn the country apart; nearly 2,000 members of the security forces had been killed, more than 2,500 civilians murdered and another 800 or so were missing.

There were other, even more deadly dangers living in the Malayan jungle. One Sunday morning Geoff and Simon were driving on one of the estate roads in the van when he became aware of a presence keeping pace with them. It was on Simon's side and at that same instant a *hamadryad*, or king cobra, one of the most deadly snakes in the world, reared up to the level of the window, its forked tongue darting out of its mouth.

'Close your window!' he yelled to Simon, as he slammed his foot on the accelerator – only just in time, as the venom splashed on the window protecting Simon's eyes. The van leaped forward, sending up a cloud of dust, and eventually left the snake behind. It had been a narrow escape.

In 1963 Geoff became a part-time visiting agent, or planting adviser, and was given Wardieburn, a small estate of 1,500 acres, to manage. He had now reached the top of his profession and in six months was appointed a full-time VA. *The Seventh Dawn*, based on the book *The Durian Tree* about the Malayan Emergency, and starring William Holden, Capucine and Susannah York, was filmed on the estate and caused great excitement among the locals. Geoff was asked to advise on sites, and one day while he was watching the filming a good-looking man with an American accent and wearing a shoulder holster with a gun asked him a question on tapping the trees. Geoff took him over to a tree and found a tapper to show him how to tap the rubber. Later he pointed the man out to Judy.

'You silly idiot,' she giggled. 'That's William Holden!'

Geoff was offered the part of an estate manager in the opening scene of the film. The part called for him to be shot whilst paying the labour force and he had to fall each time the scene was shot. The crew provided a mattress for him to fall on, but as the scene was shot over and over again, by the time it was perfect his hips and thighs were black and blue.

In 1968, after a leave spent in Australia and New Zealand, Judy and Geoff returned to Malaya to find the country in the grip of race riots. Once again a state of emergency was declared, with looting, raping and killing causing panic and terror. Tension between the Malays and the Chinese had been on the rise since the Emergency of 1951, with issues of Chinese involvement in business and commerce and Malay special rights leading to greater dissatisfaction between the races. The Chinese controlled most of the wealth and this had generated jealousy amongst the Malays.

'I could feel the undercurrent of deep feeling,' says Geoff. 'It was like living with a time bomb. The writing was on the wall as far as Malaya, or Malaysia as it had now become, was concerned. The national disturbance made us feel continually uneasy and because of this we decided the time had come for us to pack up and start a new life. We did not want to return to England and New Zealand seemed to be a good, safe country in which to live.'

Events were brought to a head when Judy's Chinese friend returned to her house after the rioting ceased and found her amah had been beheaded by a parang-wielding terrorist who deposited the head in the icebox. The Rothwells learned that their amah had also been threatened and it was only a matter of time before their own lives would be in danger. Sadly it was time for them to leave.

For planters like Geoff who had spent almost twenty years in a country which had been at war for almost all of that time, the golden days of Malaya were over, perhaps forever. The country might never be at peace. In the years Geoff had lived there he had dodged bullets and assassination attempts, he had survived a deadly strain of malaria, encounters with snakes, had fallen in love again, married and was now a father to Simon. Not only had he developed business skills, learning about investments and money management, but he had learnt about race relations and he had developed a love of nature which he would carry with him for the rest of his life. It had been a remarkable twenty years.

Now on this last day the soft sigh of a warm gentle wind reminded him he was finally leaving a land he loved deeply, a land that had been good to him. His love for this country was like a sickness; it had seduced him from the first moment he had set foot on its hot soil, when he had smelt its strange aromatic smells and been captivated by its beauty and culture. It was a sickness which he would always be prone to and one for which there was no cure, no getting away from, only acceptance.

It was destiny which had brought him here and it was destiny which was taking him away to a strange new country. And as he stood there the brilliant orange-red of the flame trees outlined against the blood-red of the sun merged into the hills in the background, and the sun and the hills and the flame trees suddenly became one as his eyes were dazzled.

EPILOGUE

All precious things, discover 'd late,
To those that seek them issue forth,
For Love in sequel works with Fate,
And draws the veil from hidden worth.
                    – Alfred, Lord Tennyson

There is silence in the room except for the patter patter of rain falling softly outside and drowning out the sounds of the night. As if in answer to my thoughts he says: 'That will be good for the garden. We've had a drought this year.'

I have been sitting there for a long time listening to his remarkable story, looking at photographs and through his log book, an impeccable record of his service career over the years, and reading letters and documents. It is an amazing story of a larger-than-life man – a man who has always been able to see the funny side of life, who could be thoughtful and intelligent, a lover of animals and birds, who could be obstinate but who would always be prepared to listen to another's point of view. A man with an intense dislike of humbug and one who valued honour and fair play over anything else. It has been a rich life and one to be proud of.

But I needed answers to many questions – there were gaps to be filled in. 'Did you ever find out the reason why you crashed on Texel?' I ask him.

'This has always been a mystery to me,' he said. 'Over the years I have gone over it a thousand times, and I have come to the conclusion that the aircraft must have struck a barrage balloon cable, which may have come adrift from the convoy of coastal ships I saw in Den Helder harbour the day following my crash. Remember, there had been a furious storm the previous night and it's possible that a balloon could have been wrenched from its mooring. But there are still one or two questions in my mind which need answering. There were other Special Duties aircraft which crashed in unexplained circumstances, one of which, flown by my old mate Mick Brogan, came down in Denmark. I have tried unsuccessfully over the years to find out just what could be the probable explanation now that SOE has released certain of its records to the public, but I have been blocked each time.'

What do you mean, blocked?

'I wrote letters to various personnel at SOE and people I spoke to – people in high places – all fobbed me off, some with cock-and-bull stories saying the crashes would have been pilot error. Pilot error, my foot! These were experienced, highly skilled pilots with good crews – if they hadn't been they wouldn't have been flying on SOE operations.'

What else could it have been then? Sabotage?

'That thought has crossed my mind many times but there is no proof. When Mac and I were taken to the Luftwaffe interrogation centre at Oberursel, the Germans told us there had been no flak and no aircraft flying the night we crashed, You know, the Dutch salvaged pieces of my aircraft some years ago. They are diligent and devoted to their work in resurrecting crashed Allied aircraft. They sent me the ignition switches and the brake for the trailing aerial – they're over there.' He pointed to where they sat on a beautifully carved camphor wood chest in a corner of the lounge.

Then there is the mystery of *Feldwebel* Bauer. Bauer, the interrogator who spoke perfect English with an Oxford accent, who held a thick dossier on Geoff. What was it he had said? 'We were expecting you, old boy. What took you so long?'

'Ah, Bauer. We'll probably never know the answer to that one.'

I had heard there was a recent book written by a German historian which stated that Geoff's Stirling LK200 was shot down by a German fighter.

'Poppycock!' says Geoff. 'We would have seen him in the brilliant moonlight. In any case, a fighter couldn't have caused all the damage done to my aircraft, and it is most unlikely that it could have picked us up at three hundred feet, which is below the level of radar coverage.'

'Did you ever hear what happened to Biallosterski and de Vos, the agents you dropped on your last mission?'

'Oh, yes. Draughts, Biallosterski, was killed but Back gammon, Pieter de Vos, tracked me down through a Dutch historian several years ago and we are in constant contact. We have become close friends and correspond regularly. We met for the second time in 2001 when I went to Holland. He believes this was the first occasion when a Dutch agent and pilot met up after the war. I visited the island of Texel where I crashed and saw the graves of my crew who were killed – the first time I had done this.'

'An emotional trip, surely?'

'Very.'

For a moment his voice breaks. There is a pause and I look away, not wishing to embarrass him or pry into such a personal experience. Fifty-six years ago, and still there is the emotion, the sadness, evident in his eyes.

'Did your parents and sister stay in England all their lives?' I ask him as a way of changing the subject.

'Pat married Tom Burns and they emigrated to Perth, Western Australia. They have two sons, Roger and Alistair, now grown up, and we have spent many happy holidays together, both in New Zealand and in Australia. My parents sold up in England and also emigrated to Australia and both are buried in Perth.'

His friends were getting fewer as each year passed. Len Trent, VC, passed away in 1986 at the age of seventy-one. It was because of Len's glowing reports of New Zealand that Geoff and Judy settled in that country.

Some years before he received a call from Danish television. They had found he was one of two still living who had served in 99 Squadron at Newmarket in 1940. An episode of *This is Your Life* on Morrie Hansen, a Danish rear-gunner and a colourful character who had served in the squadron at the same time as Geoff, was being shown that night. The producer had tried to contact Geoff without luck. They would have flown him to Copenhagen for the show, but Geoff had to be content with leaving a verbal message for Morrie, who, at eighty, was still driving a taxi in Copenhagen.

'What happened after you left Malaya for New Zealand?' I ask him. 'You must have found it difficult to settle in, initially?'

'I had found during the war that I got on well with New Zealanders. They were always telling me New Zealand was a wonderful country, so we decided to see for ourselves. On first sight it was one of the loveliest countries I had ever seen and now, some thirty-four years later, I still feel the same. It was clean and green and safe, under-populated and unpolluted, and the people were friendly – it was heaven. Judy and I knew at once how lucky we were to have found it and we have never regretted for one moment moving here.'

When Geoff arrived in Kerikeri he went into business with Dick Broadbent, his mate from Air Force days who had taken over his flight in 75 Squadron at Newmarket. Dick owned the Central motel, the only motel at that stage in Kerikeri, and together they opened a wine shop and bought the local bookshop, which today is Kerikeri Paper Plus. In addition Geoff joined the Forest and Bird Society, somehow finding time to serve on the committee of the Kerikeri Stone Store Preservation Society, and also be a church warden and recorder in the little Anglican church of St James, which is perched high on the hill above the Old Stone Store, the oldest building in New Zealand.

During the 1970s and 80s he took a keen interest in politics and, always a mover and a shaker with abundant energy, spent many hours writing letters to politicians in an attempt to right some wrong. Perhaps one of his greatest pleasures in living in the Bay of Islands was sailing. He was a natural and likened the sport to flying. Many happy times were spent with family and friends fishing, picnicking on the beaches in the beautiful bays and eating oysters off the rocks washed down with the local white wine.

I had heard that Hollywood wanted to make a film about his life. What was the story behind that?

'I was on leave in London not long after *The Seventh Dawn* was made on Wardieburn Estate and I was introduced to an American producer. Maybe William Holden had told him something about me because he tried to persuade me to go to Hollywood to talk to some people about a possible film about my life. I declined, of course,' he said.

'Of course?'

'I didn't want any fuss, and as far as I was concerned I hadn't done anything out of the ordinary. Anyway, I didn't pursue it.'

'What happened to your first wife? I ask him. Did you ever meet her again?'

'I never actually met up with her after our divorce but we kept in touch over the years, mainly because of our daughter Zelie. Val died in London in 1998.'

Ah – the daughter. 'Did you ever meet up with her again?'

His face lit up as he showed me a photograph of himself with his arm around a tall, fair girl. On the back was an inscription: *Richmond, London 2001*. The resemblance to Geoff was remarkable.

'This is the most extraordinary event and one of the happiest of my life. For fifty-three years I wondered about her. In 1968 when Zelie became engaged to a Mark Hilton, Val sent me a copy of the engagement notice in *The Times* and I wrote to Zelie offering her my congratulations. I asked her to come and see me if she ever came to New Zealand but I never heard from her so I thought well, that's the end of that and I couldn't blame her. And then last year a very dear friend of mine had the energy and wisdom to search for her. She had no idea where to look – I had lost touch with Val and she was unable to find her. There was only the old cutting from *The Times*. After a long search she eventually found Zelie living in London. She had indeed married Mark and one of the most amazing coincidences was that she was living not two miles away from my son Simon. Another extraordinary thing was that she, too, had been trying to find me and had actually telephoned a friend in New Zealand the previous night to ask her to help in finding me. We talked and talked for days and weeks on the telephone, and then I flew to England to meet her for the most memorable reunion of my life. She, Simon and his wife Jo have a wonderful relationship and there is the added bonus that not only do I now have a wonderful new daughter, but I have a lovely and talented twenty-six-year-old granddaughter. I am truly blessed.'

He took up a new challenge – writing – which gave him immense pleasure and in which he achieved success, having written two books – one a cookery book – and many articles for magazines and periodicals. At the age of eighty he decided he would learn about computers and completed several courses.

He was often asked to talk at a variety of meetings – Anzac Day, at which he was a regular parade attendee, although the days of attending the Dawn Service were long gone – the local schools, Probus, Rotary, church services and book launches. He was a strong, clear speaker, forsaking a microphone.

His dear Judy died in late spring 2000 after a long illness and he felt her passing keenly. For a while, lonely and sad, he floundered, looking for some meaning to life. Eventually, he just got on with it and his natural resilience, positivity and effervescence returned again.

There was just one more thing I needed to know. What happened to Sweet Pea?

'Over the years we wrote to each other and then somehow or other the correspondence just petered out. She had another son, Julian, by Owain Trevaldwyn, but tragically, her first son Andrew died from an asthma attack. And then a couple of years ago she wrote to tell me Trevaldwyn had died. Our correspondence started up again and last year when I was in England I saw her again.'

'It must have been wonderful to see her again after such a long time,' I say. 'It would have been a serendipitous reunion.'

'Oh yes, it most certainly was.'

I was dying to ask the question. Now, surely, after all these years, would they get together?

He seemed to guess what I was thinking, for there was a twinkle in the deep blue eyes. 'You'd like that, wouldn't you? You must be a romantic. But my life is in New Zealand and hers is in England where her family live.'

Amongst the memories he most treasured were the deeds of his comrades of long ago, of the exploits they and not he performed. He was insistent that the medals he received should have gone to the team as a whole.

I have always felt embarrassed that they were given to me – I was just the guy flying the damned aircraft. It was a joint effort and those men were the bravest of the brave.

While writing this book there were times when I caught him with a faraway look in his eyes. Was he thinking about the time he first joined the Air Force and the difficulties that entailed, or the first time he went solo on a Tiger Moth, or the time he was bombed on Newmarket Racecourse? Or his many hazardous bombing operations – dodging the flak and enemy fighters, running out of fuel, his aircraft shot up and icing up, landing on Newmarket Heath, the wheel passing over a gun emplacement pit? Or drinking in the local pubs with his mates, knocking down WAAF officers and raiding the group captain's asparagus beds, beating up football matches, Sweet Pea? Or his Stirling crashing into a pylon, his Special Duties Operations, culminating in his crash on Texel and his months as a POW?

Or meeting Val and the birth of his daughter, his years in Malaya – assassination attempts, snakes and bouts of malaria, Judy and Simon – and last of all his years in New Zealand? Or was he thinking about his old mates who did not return? Men like Freddy Harrold and little Joe Ready, who coached him on engines in 1939; John Allen, the Battle of Battle Spitfire pilot; Mick Brogan, the debonair Irishman who bought it in Denmark; Don Saville, the gallant Australian with the pencil moustache who died on a raid over Hamburg; Canadian Bud Keller, whom he witnessed being shot down over Kiel; and his faithful crew who flew with him on many missions, Roger Court, Wally Walton and

John Hulme, who lost their lives in that fateful last mission from Tempsford.

*

The writing of *Last Man Standing* has not been an easy task as one would expect from someone going through grief and grappling with loss and it has taken some time to get my thoughts in a coherent order. I hope I have been able to capture all I love about my husband. When we first met up in Kerikeri straight away I liked what I saw ... very much. Later he told me he felt the same way. He was tall with very blue eyes and red hair, sprinkled with grey. As soon as I laid eyes on him I knew he was special – he had an aura about him and a big smile which lit up his whole face. I was immediately attracted to this good-looking man who loved the simple life. We became very good friends first, which I think is always the best way to start a love affair. It was inevitable that we would fall in love ... but that came a long time later.

In 2001 we went to England where Geoff took me to the airfields he had flown from all those years ago ... Newmarket, Downham Market and Tempsford. And I met for the first time Geoff's other great love, Pat Trevaldwyn, in Winchester where she was living. They had not seen each other for fifty years. Immediately I could see why Geoff had fallen in love with her all those years ago ... she was still lovely with a wistfulness, a vulnerability, a sweetness.

We married in January 2002 looking out over the beautiful Bay of Islands sparkling in the summer sun. We were so close that we could read each other's thoughts.

Geoff passed away in November 2017, one day after the last but one SOE woman agent, Yvonne Baseden. It was the end of an era. Right up to the end throughout his long illness Geoff showed his steadfastness, his great strength of character which had always got him through. He had dodged so many bullets that his passing took me by surprise.

I look back on our wonderful years together. I miss him more than words can say. And now what will I do without him?

APPENDIX A

EXTRACT FROM *LONDON GAZETTE*
DATED 17 JANUARY 1941

The King has been graciously pleased to approve the following award in recognition of gallantry and devotion to duty in the execution of air operations:

Distinguished Flying Cross

Pilot Officer Geoffrey Maurice ROTHWELL (42726)
Royal Air Force No 99 Squadron

Pilot Officer ROTHWELL was detailed as Captain of Aircraft to take part in a raid on MUNICH on the night of 8/9th November 1940. On approaching the target the aircraft ran into an AA barrage at ULM. There was a bright moon at the time and the Captain decided to circle the town in view of the intensity of the AA fire. He noticed a large factory which in his opinion merited an attack. He made two attacks descending to 5000 and 4000 feet respectively, releasing one bomb on each occasion. Each bomb was seen to burst on the factory and fires broke out.

Pilot Officer ROTHWELL then proceeded to his primary objective which was satisfactorily attacked, one of the bombs being of 1000 lbs calibre. On the return journey two low level machine gun attacks were carried out on aerodromes at ULM and LEIPHEIM in the course of which the pilot descended to 1500 feet. The factory previously attacked at ULM was blazing fiercely.

Since 19 May 1940, this officer has taken part in 33 major bombing attacks over BELGIUM, FRANCE, and GERMANY, involving 169 flying hours.

At all times he has displayed conspicuous determination in pressing home his attacks in the face of heavy enemy opposition. By his persistent determination and outstanding skill this officer at all times sets an example of the highest order.

EXTRACT FROM *LONDON GAZETTE*
DATED 10 SEPTEMBER 1943

The King has been graciously pleased to approve the following award in recognition of gallantry and devotion to duty in the execution of air operations:

Bar to Distinguished Flying Cross

Acting Squadron Leader Geoffrey Maurice
ROTHWELL DFC Royal Air Force
No 218 Squadron

Throughout many attacks on enemy targets, Squadron Leader Rothwell has consistently displayed courage and determination of a very high order which has had an influence on the results obtained by the whole squadron. He is now on his third tour of operational duty, which has consisted mainly of attacks on major targets in Germany.

EXTRACT FROM *LONDON GAZETTE*
DATED 27 JUNE 1947

The KING has granted unrestricted permission for the wearing of the undermentioned decorations conferred upon the personnel indicated in recognition of valuable services rendered in connection with the liberation of Belgium.

Conferred by HIS ROYAL HIGHNESS
THE PRINCE REGENT OF BELGIUM

Order of Leopold II with Palme and Croix de Guerre 1940 with Palme

CHEVALIER

Acting Squadron Leader Geoffrey M Rothwell DFC (42726) 138 Squadron

Squadron Leader Rothwell has completed three tours of operational sorties and throughout has shown the greatest determination to attack, often in the face of intense enemy opposition and adverse weather. He is a most skilful pilot and an excellent Flight Commander and his unswerving devotion to duty, both in the air and on the ground, have been an inspiration to his Squadron.

APPENDIX B

75 (New Zealand) Squadron had an interesting history starting in 1939 when a Flight of New Zealanders was formed to ferry Vickers Wellington aircraft to New Zealand. Shortly after the outbreak of war the New Zealand Government presented the squadron for service with Bomber Command for the duration of hostilities, and it commenced operating from RAF Station Feltwell. It was from this base that Sergeant Jimmy Ward won the Victoria Cross in July 1941. By the end of the war members of the squadron had, in addition to the VC, been awarded:

6 Distinguished Service Orders
4 Bars to the Distinguished Flying Cross
2 Conspicuous Gallantry Medals
88 Distinguished Flying Crosses
16 Distinguished Flying Medals

A meritorious achievement by any standards.

INDEX

Also available from Amberley Publishing

FEATURED IN THE *NEW YORK POST*
AND *THE DAILY TELEGRAPH*

HER FINEST HOUR

THE HEROIC LIFE OF DIANA ROWDEN,
WARTIME SECRET AGENT

GABRIELLE McDONALD-ROTHWELL

Available from all good bookshops or to order direct
Please call **01453-847-800**
www.amberley-books.com